PLACE PERIPHERAL

PLACE PERIPHERAL

Place-Based Development in Rural, Island, and Remote Regions

Edited by
**Kelly Vodden, Ryan Gibson,
and Godfrey Baldacchino**

ISER

**Institute of Social and
Economic Research**

Library and Archives Canada Cataloguing in Publication
    Place peripheral : place-based development in rural, island, and remote regions / edited by Kelly Vodden, Ryan Gibson, and Godfrey Baldacchino.

(Social and economic papers ; no. 33)

Includes bibliographical references and index.
ISBN 978-1-894725-25-5 (paperback)

    1. Rural development--Case studies--Congresses. 2. Community development--Case studies--Congresses. 3. Sustainable development--Case studies--Congresses. 4. Culture--Economic aspects--Case studies--Congresses. I. Vodden, Kelly, 1970-, author, editor II. Gibson, Ryan, 1981-, author, editor III. Baldacchino, Godfrey, author, editor IV. Culture, Place and Identity at the Heart of Regional Development (Conference) (2011 : St. John's, N.L.) V. Series: Social and economic papers ; no. 33

HN49.C6P63 2015   307.1'412   C2015-905270-X

Cover photograph: © Anja Sajovic
Design and typesetting: Alison Carr
Copy editing: Richard Tallman

Published by ISER Books — Faculty of Arts Publications
Institute of Social and Economic Research
Memorial University of Newfoundland
297 Mount Scio Road
St. John's, NL A1C 5S7
www.arts.mun.ca/iserbooks/

Printed and bound in Canada

CONTENTS

Godfrey Baldacchino Professor of Sociology, University of Malta, Malta; Island Studies Teaching Fellow, University of Prince Edward Island, Canada; President, International Small Islands Studies Association (ISISA); Chair, Scientific Board, RETI (Research Network of Island Universities). *godfrey.baldacchino@um.edu.mt*

Sarah-Patricia Breen PhD candidate, School of Resource and Environmental Management, Simon Fraser University, Canada. *swbreen@sfu.ca*

Laurie Brinklow Co-ordinator, Institute of Island Studies, University of Prince Edward Island, Canada. *brinklow@upei.ca*

Jennifer Burns MER graduate, School of Graduate Studies, Memorial University of Newfoundland, Canada. *jenniferkburns@gmail.com*

Michael Clair Leslie Harris Centre of Regional Policy and Development, Memorial University of Newfoundland, Canada. *mclair@mun.ca*

Gordon B. Cooke Associate Professor, Faculty of Business Administration, Memorial University of Newfoundland, Canada. *gcooke@mun.ca*

Jennifer Daniels Research Assistant, Department of Geography, Memorial University of Newfoundland, Canada. *jenniferkdaniels@gmail.com*

David J.A. Douglas Professor Emeritus, Rural Planning and Development, University of Guelph, Canada; Past President, Canadian Rural Revitalization Foundation. *djdougla@uoguelph.ca*

Françoise Enguehard Writer, business owner, Past President of the Société Nationale de l'Acadie.

Christopher Fullerton Associate Professor, Department of Geography, Brock University, Canada. *chris.fullerton@brocku.ca*

Bojan Fürst Leslie Harris Centre of Regional Policy and Development, Memorial University of Newfoundland, Canada. *bfurst@mun.ca*

Ryan Gibson Assistant Professor, Department of Geography and Environmental Studies, Saint Mary's University, Canada; Past-President of the Canadian Rural Revitalization Foundation. *ryan.gibson@smu.ca*

Andrew Jennings Lecturer, Centre for Nordic Studies, University of the Highlands and Islands, Shetland, Scotland, UK. *andrew.jennings@uhi.ac.uk*

Sarah Mann Associate Professor, Department of Management, College of Business and Economics, University of Guelph, Canada. *smann@uoguelph.ca*

Sean Markey Associate Professor, School of Resource and Environmental Management, Simon Fraser University, Canada. *spmarkey@sfu.ca*

Irene Novaczek Marine ecologist, Basin Head Marine Protected Area, Fisheries and Oceans Canada; Adjunct Professor and Research Associate, Institute of Island Studies, University of Prince Edward Island, Canada. *inovaczek@upei.ca*

Brendan O'Keeffe Lecturer, Department of Geography, Mary Immaculate College, University of Limerick, Ireland. *Brendan.OKeeffe@mic.ul.ie*

Kelly Vodden Associate Professor (Research), Environmental Studies, Memorial University of Newfoundland, Grenfell Campus, Canada. *kvodden@mun.ca*

Deatra Walsh Postdoctoral Research Fellow, Centre for Women and Gender Research, UiT The Arctic University of the North; Adjunct Professor, Yukon College. *Deatra.walsh@uit.no*

Gary N. Wilson Professor, Department of Political Science, University of Northern British Columbia; Honorary Research Fellow, Centre for Manx Studies, University of Liverpool, Isle of Man. *wilsong@unbc.ca*

ACKNOWLEDGEMENTS

This volume came about as a result of the 2011 conference "Culture, Place and Identity at the Heart of Regional Development" held in St. John's, Newfoundland and Labrador, Canada, in October 2011. The conference was a partnership of the North Atlantic Forum (NAF); the Canadian Rural Revitalization Foundation (CRRF); the Small Island Cultures Research Initiative (SICRI); and Memorial University's Leslie Harris Centre of Regional Policy and Development. The editors thank each of these organizations and the individual organizers of this event both for inspiring and for providing the space for this compilation and each of its individual contributions. In particular we are grateful to the conference co-chairs and steering committee, the conference coordinator and artistic director, and the entire staff of the Leslie Harris Centre of Regional Policy and Development for their hard work, vision, and dedication in ensuring the success of this timely and important international event.

We also extend our gratitude to the Social Sciences and Humanities Research Council (SSHRC) for its financial support of the conference and this publication. The Federation for the Humanities and Social Sciences Awards to Scholarly Publications Program; the Environmental Policy Institute, Grenfell Campus, Memorial University; St. Mary's University; and Island Studies Resources at University of Prince Edward Island provided additional financial support.

Thanks are also due to each of the contributors to the volume for their intellectual inputs and their patience as we worked collectively through the steps involved in creating this publication. The quality of our work has been enhanced by the generosity of time and valuable feedback of the peer reviewers. We also acknowledge the contributions of cartographer Charlie Conway and Sarah Minnes, who assisted in preparing the index for this volume. Finally, we extend our sincere thanks to ISER Books Academic Editor Sharon Roseman, Managing Editor Alison Carr, and the Faculty of Arts, Memorial University, for their work and support in bringing this volume to fruition and thereby helping to share the stories of struggle, hope, and resilience that follow within these pages.

Kelly Vodden
Godfrey Baldacchino
Ryan Gibson
May 2015

This volume explores the unique and valued features of rural, remote, and peripheral places that shape the identities of individuals and their communities. One of these key features — or indeed an amalgam of them — is culture. Culture is a ubiquitous and integral part of regional development. Yet, it can be easily ignored, sidelined, or forgotten.

The freedom of action available to the regional development practitioner, the tools available to him/her, will vary considerably in different areas of the globe: not just because of public policy and the operations of government departments, but because of the very cultural fabric underlying these societies. The authors in this volume deal with culture as consisting of those tangible and intangible characteristics that can be used to differentiate one society — and often one place — from another. These characteristics have arisen organically over time and include architecture, interactive cultural–natural landscapes, artifacts, works of art, traditional occupations, language, oral traditions, humour, culinary traditions, music, and clothing. Culture, in this context, consists of an inherited component (such as cultural heritage) and a creative component (such as the contemporary arts).

This book explores how culture can help create a "sustainable region," understood as one where the quality of life is attractive to residents and potential immigrants, and whose economy competes successfully in its chosen markets. Culture — as cultural heritage and contemporary arts — can indeed play an important role in sustainable regional development. Cultural tourism is one of the fastest-growing segments of the tourism industry; people travel all over the world to visit museums and historic sites, to sample food and music, and to discover how other people live their daily lives. Tourism is an important export activity in many regions, resulting in new money being injected by visitors from outside the region.

The cultural industries are also important contributors to many regions' economies. These include those commercial activities that depend on a cultural core feature, such as the film and video scene, recorded music, theatre, publishing, art galleries, and video gaming. These are all exportable products or activities that bring new revenue to a region.

Other initiatives also depend on cultural heritage and/or the arts, which are often not at the top of the agenda with regional development practitioners: architecture, advertising, and design are some notable examples. These knowledge-economy activities can create high-paying jobs that can be located anywhere, not just in urban settings.

This book is an outcome of the conference "Culture, Place and Identity at the Heart of Regional Development" held over three days in St. John's, Newfoundland and Labrador, Canada, in October 2011. The conference had as its objective the critical exploration of the harnessing of culture for economic gain, but without compromising the integrity of that culture. The conference drew over 200 registrants representing governments, academia, non-governmental organizations, regional development practitioners, artists, tradition bearers, and others. Participants primarily came from eastern Canada, but also from the rest of Canada and the North Atlantic Rim (Greenland, Iceland, the Faroe Islands, Norway, Denmark, and Germany), and from as far away as the Indian Ocean, Australia, Nepal, Nigeria, and Argentina. Over 60 papers were presented. Most of these have been preserved on the conference website at www.naf2011.com.

The conference was a partnership of three organizations: the North Atlantic Forum (NAF) is a "collegial assembly" focused on the islands in the North Atlantic, which shares the results of research and best practices in regional development and governance, and which supports community, industry, and government exchanges for mutual benefit; the Canadian Rural Revitalization Foundation (CRRF) achieves its mission through education and research for rural leaders in the community, the private sector, and in government; and the Small Island Cultures Research Initiative (SICRI) brings together scholars and local activists involved in the development and preservation of cultural heritage and in its interrelationship with tourism and socio-economic development on island locations.

As conference co-chairs, we wish to thank the members of the program committee for their advice and guidance during the planning of this conference. We also thank all the presenters who shared their knowledge and expertise with the registrants of the conference. We also gratefully acknowledge the generous financial assistance of Memorial University of Newfoundland, the government of Canada, and the provincial government of Newfoundland and Labrador, as well as the many other funders who saw value in the conference. The event was made all the more interesting thanks to the active participation of all the registrants.

Finally, we are indebted to Dr. Larry Felt, former Director of Memorial University of Newfoundland's Institute for Social and Economic Research (ISER), for his interest in the conference and his invitation to submit a volume of selected papers from the conference. A special thanks is also extended to Dr. Kelly Vodden of Memorial's Environmental Policy Institute, Grenfell Campus, for her unstinting help as a member of the organizing and program committees, and for editing this volume together with co-editors Dr. Godfrey Baldacchino and Dr. Ryan Gibson, both of whom also played important roles leading up to and during the event.

Appreciating a region's cultural heritage and harnessing its creative energy are important for ensuring a region's sustainability. Understanding the past, reinventing it for contemporary audiences, using it to define a region's identity, to enhance its quality of life, and to tap it to inspire innovations . . . these are all initiatives that today's regional development practitioner ignores at her or his peril. Culture is not just the frozen legacy of a historic past, but a vibrant present and possibly the key to a future for many so-defined "peripheral communities." We are confident that this timely volume contributes to this ongoing discourse and will encourage new ideas and activities in successful regional development.

Françoise Enguehard
Michael Clair

Places evolve as systemic dimensions of our lives, and they engender their own meanings. In our discursive conversations with place, and in the contested flux that makes up others' agendas for our places, a dialogic dynamic nurtures both the reproduction of place itself and our own co-construction as situated persons. And these persons function as members within the cultural matrices of various communities, which themselves function interactively in, across, and, notably, *with* various places.

This complex, mysterious aggregation that we call "place" resists the clinical reductionism towards which we are spurred by our heavy epistemological baggage. We have almost retrieved the concept and the reality of place from the extended hegemony of economics, but at times we uncritically swoon in adulation of the notion, with its elusive definition and its metaphoric allure. We are somewhat perplexed in the current age of globalization to witness the time–space compression, which at once appears to threaten the relevance of our places while facilitating something of a resurgence of our awareness of place, and perhaps its revaluation.

Among the enormous diversity of spaces that we have come to know as places in our lives and stories, smaller rural, insular, and remote places are of particular interest; and it is such locales that are showcased in this timely volume. Here we find vivid expressions of what is called *place-based development*: a conscious and deliberate approach to identifying and harnessing local assets (people, culture, environment) for the benefit of durable, integrated, community-based development. In addition, the role and relevance of the arts and culture in this process of purposeful development is a central theme throughout this book.

Place Peripheral neatly addresses the challenges of creative, innovative, and strategic global positioning of rural communities, islands, and regions in our rapidly changing world. The received fixity of core–periphery relationships is addressed. The rich record of community-based, endogenous, or bottom-up energies, resources, and achievements is augmented through a variety of case studies. The pivotal role of organizational development, as an appropriate technology in itself, is aptly highlighted in these pages. The highly contested concepts of culture, the instrumental stratagem of "branding," the risks of commodification, and other topics are expertly addressed. The complexity of the interrelationships between such concepts as sense of place, quality of life, quality of place, identity, governance, and "new regionalism" are critically acknowledged.

The conceptual and practical specifications for place-based development and the instrumental roles of arts, culture, and place-based identities can be either onerous or permissive. As an example, *community* economic development (CED) contrasts with the more externally sourced and "expert"-driven *local* economic development (LED), by being characterized as development not only "in" the community but also "by," "for," "from," and "of" the community. If our expectations of place-based development are in anyway similar to what we might expect of the CED process, then we will look for a very particular, largely endogenous dynamic. If we allow for a broader sourcing and conventional development process, we will settle for something akin to LED. The recognition and crafting of this choice is pivotal for rural, island, and regional development.

We have such great expectations of place: intellectually, materially, politically, emotionally, spiritually, and otherwise. We invest in the myth, the concept, the idea, the ideal, and its lived materiality. These and related themes are central considerations in this book: its diverse discourse happily straddles an array of disciplines and professional practices that converge in their focus on the pivotal role of place in rural community and regional development.

David J.A. Douglas

INTRODUCTION

CHAPTER 1

Development in Place: A View from the Periphery

Kelly Vodden, Godfrey Baldacchino, and Ryan Gibson

INTRODUCTION

Rural and remote regions hold cultural as well as economic and environmental significance for Canada and for the world. Rural workers and ecosystems continue to fuel natural resource and amenity-based economies while rural people and places occupy an important role in contemporary national identities and imaginations. Rural and remote communities throughout Canada and internationally are also hosts of social, cultural, and economic transformation. They are presented with the opportunities and challenges of initiating and maintaining sustainable economic development, often in the face of declining resources and traditional economies, shifting demographics, and the development of transportation, information, and communications technologies that have led to declarations such as the "death of distance" (Cairncross, 1997).

In response to the dynamics outlined by forces such as globalization, competition, and technological change, the current literature increasingly advocates place-based rather than sectoral and/or generic approaches to policy and planning (Goldenburg, 2008; Markey et al., 2008; Cheng and Mattor, 2010). Attention to place-based approaches has in turn led to explorations of representations of place, multiple and changing identities connected to development processes, and the role of cultural norms and social relationships in nurturing creativity, innovation, and resilience (Baeker, 2004; Stathopoulou et al., 2004; Lagendijk, 2011). The changes and challenges in rural and remote communities that this current literature addresses have shaped the core themes of this volume, in particular its focus on assets of and attachments to place and their implications for community resilience and sustainability.

Place Peripheral examines community and regional development in rural, island, and remote locales from a place-based approach. This edited volume addresses themes that are receiving considerable attention in Canada and internationally as researchers and public policy analysts alike strive to better understand and apply place and place-based strategies in rural and remote regions (see Barca, 2009; Bachleter, 2010; Bellefontaine and Wisener, 2011). The volume and its contributors examine place-based economic development strategies but move beyond a naive and narrow focus on commodification to recognize the broader and deeper significance, meanings, and attachments often associated with place. The chapters interrogate such relationships as may exist between sense of place, cultural and social development, environmental stewardship, and economic development.

This introduction argues for the importance of examining place and its role in development within the contemporary periphery, and thus outlines the timely and important contribution of this volume. It also reviews the organization of the volume and introduces the individual chapters.

THIS VOLUME AND ITS CONTEXT

The contributors to *Place Peripheral* investigate how rural and remote communities can face the challenges presented by globalization through governance, identifying and building upon local capacity in its various forms, and ongoing processes of place-making. Among the conclusions presented are that local governance and enhanced agency can aid in the pursuit of place-based social and economic development and policy formulation. *Place Peripheral* explores place-based development strategies and the conditions, including governance systems, that have led to their implementation, with varying results.

This volume consists of selected and edited chapters drawn from papers presented originally at the 2011 conference, "Culture, Place and Identity at the Heart of Regional Development," the North Atlantic Forum and Canadian

Rural Revitalization Foundation international event held in St. John's, Newfoundland and Labrador. The conference brought together Canadian and international researchers with policy-makers, community/regional development practitioners, industry, and artisans to share research findings and enhance our understanding of the role of place, culture, and identity in sustainable development for rural, remote, and coastal communities. An article by conference attendee and agriculture reporter Nancy Ralph explained, "The conference allowed delegates to create networks, share experiences and strategies and exchange their know-how. . . . Speakers at the conference encouraged delegates to let their community groups know it is important for them to work together to create new identities for their communities" (Ralph, 2011). This volume provides an opportunity for researchers, students, and practitioners to benefit from these lessons and experiences through a comparative and critical approach.

The contributions to this volume are both descriptive and analytical. They represent a carefully selected compendium of ideas and experiences that speak to the importance and value of place-based development, especially for so-called remote and peripheral island and rural communities. As illustrated in Figure 1, these experiences come primarily from the North Atlantic, including jurisdictions in Canada, the Republic of Ireland, Scotland, the Isle of Man, Finland, and Iceland, but also from western and central Canada and from the islands of Chiloé (in Chile) and Tasmania (in Australia).

This volume is also a companion text to *Remote Control: Governance Lessons for and from Small, Insular, and Remote Regions* (Baldacchino et al., 2009). Also published by ISER Books, *Remote Control* consists of selected papers from the 2005 North Atlantic Forum and Canadian Rural Revitalization Foundation international conference held in Twillingate, Newfoundland and Labrador. Like this complementary volume, *Remote Control* examined the impact of a seemingly borderless knowledge economy and concerns about a resulting cycle of decline for peripheral communities.

PLACING THE PERIPHERY

Increases in mobility and processes of globalization have generated significant interest in place and place-based development. Local cultures are

Figure 1: Case study locations in Place Peripheral.

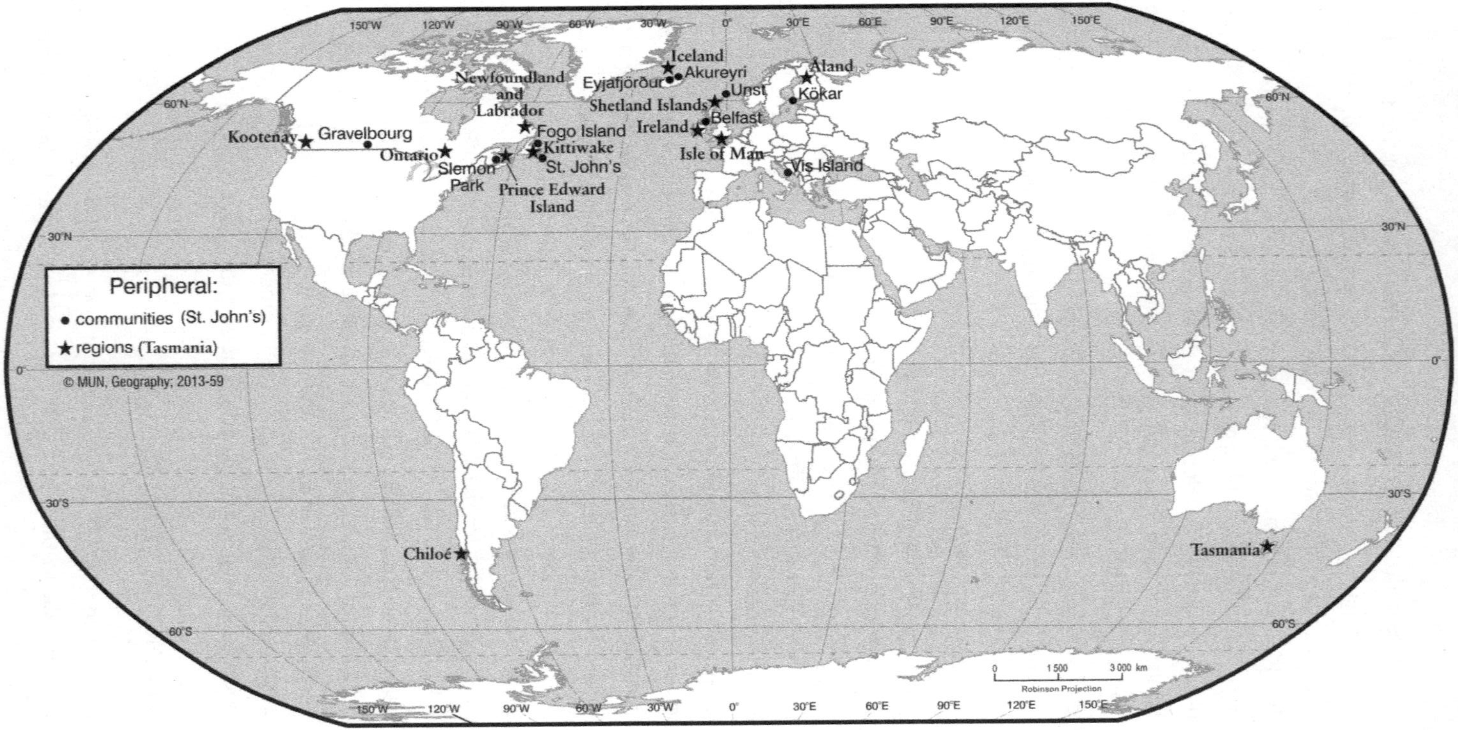

Peripheral:
● communities (St. John's)
★ regions (Tasmania)

© MUN. Geography. 2013-59

6

"threatened by the forces of global political, economic and social change" (Hay, 2006: 31); yet strong attachments to place remain (Lewicka, 2011). This sense of belonging and attachment is often particularly strong in rural and remote communities (Turcotte, 2005) — areas considered peripheries within their countries yet hosting characteristics that take on new meaning amid the onslaught of globalization that has created what Daniels et al. in Chapter 2 refer to as an "incentive to difference." In some cases, local languages and cultures have become important tools for economic development and political strategies to adapt to the changes associated with globalization (Wilson, 2007). As many of the chapters in this volume illustrate, tourism and the arts are crucial dimensions of the new rural economy (Halseth et al., 2009; Shannon and Mitchell, 2012). In other situations, stunning natural landscapes fuel strong local identities along with amenity-based development opportunities.

Identity politics continue to play themselves out in some of the most remote corners of the world where, for instance, industrial demands for natural resources conflict with long-standing traditions and ways of life and also with alternative visions for sustainable local economies (see, for example, Novaczek, Chapter 7). Dependency thinkers such as Frank (1967) and Allahar (1995) have long discussed these conflicts and the production of peripherality at multiple spatial scales through processes of exploitation, capital investment and disinvestment, and ensuing uneven economic and political relationships. Peripheral regions, these authors suggest, become dependent on and subservient to core regions. In the process, as Daniels et al. suggest in Chapter 2, peripheries become essentialized as "have-not" regions in need of continued external support and intervention. Centres assume the power to define regions in these terms, harnessing a discourse of difference to assert their own dominant position in contrast to the Other — the marginal, the needy, and the dependent (Corbin and Hunter, 2007; Gregory, 2004). As Brinklow points out in Chapter 10, these descriptors may then contribute to inferiority complexes within peripheral regions, further contributing to underdevelopment.

While sociologists have focused on dependency and world systems theory perspectives, using core–periphery relationships to describe and explain uneven development, economists and economic geographers have tended to describe peripheral regions in terms of low population density, lack of accessibility and economies of scale, and/or distance from nodes or "cores" where economic benefits and power over economic decisions are concentrated (Crescenzi, 2005; Krugman, 1998). Polese and Shearmur (2003), for example, define the periphery within the Canadian context as all parts of Canada further than a 90-minute drive from a major metropolitan centre. But surely the line between core and periphery is not so clear-cut. In recognizing limitations of the core–periphery dichotomy, others have identified the notion of the semi-periphery, for example (Wallerstein, 1979; Potter, 2001). Still others have questioned the value of such categories given blurred boundaries and changing circumstances, including deindustrialization of former core regions (e.g., Chirot, 1977; Collyer, 2014). Meanwhile, new categories of peripherality continue to be developed. Notably, a series of ultra-peripheral regions have been identified in Europe, mostly islands with "limited possibilities" (Fundo de Maneio, 2006: 11; Hudson, 2006).

In this volume we offer a counterpoint to these common narratives. While not denying the challenges that geography can present or the existence of patterns of wealth and power accumulation, we offer a more critical and current understanding of peripheries and their varied development paths. We pay particular attention to how people of the so-called periphery engage in place-making processes shaped by past trajectories of development and core–periphery relationships, but also by shifting circumstances and perceptions and by relationships between people and their surroundings that are more complex than structural explanations alone can capture. The cases provided in the chapters that follow offer examples of how the global and local come together, as well as insights into the complex and contested nature of place and place-based identities.

Research on innovation, the knowledge economy, and competitiveness emphasizes the continued importance of qualities of place to economic well-being, while sustainability scholars highlight the importance of local actions and practices for environmental outcomes (Bradford, 2005). Scholars in the 1990s drew our attention to social capital, based on social organization and relationships within and between communities, as an important contributor to development and collective action. More recently, place characteristics have been shown to influence demographic trends and the decisions made by increasingly mobile workers about whether to leave or stay in certain regions (Florida et al., 2010). Put simply, place still matters — perhaps more than ever.

Much of the literature on the role of place in contemporary development, however, has focused on urban centres as hubs and magnets of innovation and creativity: nodes in a networked world where significant flows of capital, people, ideas, and influence converge. The authors in this volume turn their attention to place in peripheral regions, viewing place from the periphery, especially island places. We do so while being aware that, for many people from rural remote and island locations, their homes are not the periphery at all. We concur with Tuan (1977): the very definition of a place is that it is a centre of meaning. Thus, places peripheral are also places central. This is particularly true when we take into account that experiences of place are both material and mental (Cars et al., 2002). As Gupta and Ferguson (1992) argue, "actual" places may be less important today while the idea of place grows more salient, including notions of home, remembered places, and places in the "near view."

Moreover, our attention to place and rootedness does not deny mobility or identities that transcend particular places. We see place and placelessness as coexisting, and concur with Squires (2012: 29) that "[i]t is time to move beyond the mobility versus place debate." Places can be both rooted and connected, dynamic and diverse. They contribute to and are affected by mobilities and by the many, often larger, forces that influence our daily lives (Bradford, 2005). Indeed, this volume contributes to a growing body of literature that conceptualizes our world not in terms of bland dichotomies (such as global versus local, rural versus urban, island versus mainland), or even of memorable sound bites (such as the global village), but rather as a globe of villages and place-based globalism (Douglas, 2005; Osterweil, 2005).

The arrival of the information age promises to bring peripheral regions closer both to each other and to centres of economic wealth and decision-making. Yet, as Massey (2006) warns, "time-space compression" is not a ubiquitous reality. Some people and places are more mobile and have greater access to flows of people, capital, knowledge, and information than others. In the crumpling of space, some locales have become even harder to reach, some people immobilized and further marginalized. A whole new layer of hegemonic "mobility regimes" and communication infrastructures is increasingly brought into play, typically affording more mobility to the rich and powerful and less mobility to the poor (Canzler et al., 2008; Sheller, 2013). The contributing authors to this volume explore the complexities of movement in and out of the periphery, in differing circumstances. Their chapters demonstrate the diverse ways in which place does — and does not — affect development processes in peripheral regions within the context of a more globalized, knowledge-intensive world.

Hayter et al. (2003) suggest that globalized resource peripheries warrant particular attention because they are "deeply contested spaces" with economic, cultural, environmental, and geopolitical dimensions different from those of core regions. Only through the examination of these intersecting dimensions in particular peripheral contexts can we begin to understand the nature and implications of these dynamics. Critical to this understanding is a willingness to look beyond a discourse of peripheries as victims to explore how people at the edge articulate place for themselves and deploy it critically in shaping their own futures.

Peripheral regions remain important as targets of interventions designed to fix "the regional problem." By examining differing ways in which place is incorporated into development policy and practice, the contributors to this volume compare and contrast approaches from various contexts and allow readers to reflect on how these policies and practices have influenced the development trajectories of peripheral regions across the North Atlantic and beyond.

ORGANIZATION OF THE TEXT

This volume is organized in two major parts. In Part I, "Understanding and Negotiating Place," we examine the notion of place as the foundation upon which place-based development efforts are conceived, built, interpreted, and negotiated. Part II, "Place-based Development in Practice," considers the ideas and lessons learned from specific places for creating more sustainable, livable communities and regions, and also explores some dangers and pitfalls observed from past experiences.

Part I: Understanding and Negotiating Place

Jennifer Daniels, Godfrey Baldacchino, and Kelly Vodden, in Chapter 2, continue setting the stage and tone by examining notions of place from various theoretical and disciplinary perspectives. They explore the reasons why place and place-making maintain currency among fears of homogenization under such forces as globalization, urbanization, and commodification, as well as the social and political ramifications of how place is defined and used. Even more critically, they examine the intellectual and material implications of not carefully considering the role of an expanded and nuanced notion of place that reaches beyond understandings of place as locale. Finally, the authors interrogate how identity is involved in place-making and in creating individual and collective sense(s) of place; they also explore how place is implicated and deployed in identity-making (including nation-building).

In Chapter 3, Godfrey Baldacchino further tackles the meanings embedded in two central concepts tackled by this volume: place and periphery. He outlines how advances in information and communication technologies have altered notions of core and periphery and forced a reconceptualization of the role and meaning of place as well as associated terms such as mobility, space, settlement, attractiveness, and even quality of life. He does so through a discussion of recent developments in five North Atlantic island jurisdictions. This critical, comparative review allows for description and discussion of different regional development strategies, challenges, and results.

Core–periphery is but one continuum across which place can be viewed. In the following three chapters, the authors illustrate this by examining place from the point of view of newcomers and long-time residents, of musicians and artists as well as the audiences for these artistic endeavours, and of residents of different age groups. Bojan Fürst, in Chapter 4, delves into the tensions that can arise in a rural or small island settlement with a relatively sudden influx of outsiders whose previous connections to their new communities and landscapes are often limited. He examines relationships between seasonal and permanent residents and between residents and their landscapes. Drawing from literature in geography, folklore, and architecture, together with photographs and interviews from Croatia and Newfoundland and Labrador, he explores how the meanings of terms such as "place," "space," and "landscape" change and manifest themselves in the context of small islands.

Again drawing from experiences in Newfoundland and Labrador, Deatra Walsh, in Chapter 5, illustrates the changing nature of place and place expression through the story of Hey Rosetta!, an indie-rock band that has risen to the top of Canadian and international stardom. The group's music and songs do not explicitly reflect their home province; yet, they connect music to place in other ways. In this chapter, Walsh critically analyzes television and music videos to understand how new musical and visual representations of Newfoundland and Labrador are contributing to renovated place associations and fuelling socio-cultural and economic development in the "New" Newfoundland.

In Chapter 6, Gordon Cooke, Sara Mann, and Jennifer Burns conclude Part I by discussing how characteristics and perceptions of place affect the education, location, and employment decisions made by young adults in rural settings within Ireland, Ontario, and Newfoundland. Their findings demonstrate differing perspectives on place within groups of young adults. Some young adults are highly motivated to acquire post-secondary education and subsequent related employment, even though it may require relocation to an urban centre. Among those who chose to remain in their hometowns, some were willing to accept lower levels of education and a higher level of occupational uncertainty as a result, while yet another group were adamantly career-focused. Policy implications are also discussed; these include an appeal for increased local education and training options for rural young adults, meant to entice them to remain in their communities.

The chapters in Part I show that places are created, interpreted, and reinvented by those who are part of them: the young and elderly, the new and old, the musician and the fisher, the municipal leader and the state decision-maker, the long-time resident and the recent immigrant. The contributors to this volume, together with other authors, argue that deliberate attention to place-making by residents, community groups, and institutions that influence the future of communities can enhance the value and qualities of place and, in doing so, foster a dynamic and resilient sense of place and identity (Baeker, 2004; Imbroscio, 2004). Place-based approaches to local development draw from local actors, knowledge, and resources, often in collaboration with non-local actors, to create locally relevant responses to socio-economic and environmental policy challenges. Typically, these challenges are complex and of long term, and therefore are more appropriately addressed through a holistic approach involving the collective efforts of multiple stakeholders than through top-down and/or sector-specific, siloed interventions (Policy Horizons Canada, 2011a, 2011b).

Part II: Place-based Development in Practice

Part II focuses on how place-making and place-based development move from theory into practice and policy. Examples of place-based initiatives at the local level include the celebration of local histories, traditions, distinctive foods and festivals, and co-operative ventures in response to such concerns as cultural homogenization, competition from international food supply chains, and related environmental impacts (Douglas, 2005). These ideas can also be incorporated into planning and policy interventions that draw from a deep and intimate knowledge of particular local circumstances and from the identity, meanings, and images of places, and that take into careful account the impacts of various alternatives on those who use and care about a place in the design of future strategies and management of local resources (Kruger and Williams, 2007).

The authors in this section draw on ideas and experiences, primarily from the North Atlantic, to illustrate the importance and value of place-based development, especially for so-called remote and peripheral island and rural communities. Moreover, they shed light on how place-based strategies have been employed and the policies, processes, and partnerships that have supported their implementation.

Through a comparative analysis of Chiloé (Chile) and Prince Edward Island (Canada), Irene Novaczek argues in Chapter 7 that much is to be learned from islands and their communities' attempts to develop more human-scaled, place-based local economies that provide a rich quality of life without compromising the integrity of local ecosystems — both important elements of place. In particular, she suggests that we look to "underdeveloped" islands of the global South for such lessons, while pointing out that analogous options are also available in countries dominated by globalized, industrial scale-economies. Her contribution demonstrates a diverse range of strategies that contribute to alternative, socially and ecologically sustainable modes of development, based on cultural and natural heritage and a highly developed sense of place. These include subsistence and artisanal food production, arts, culture, and carefully managed tourism industries organized as small and micro-enterprises, co-operatives, and non-profit organizations. In the face of damaged cultures and ecosystems and powerful industrial interests, Novaczek acknowledges, however, that the road to a diverse, alternative local economy is not an easy one.

In Chapters 8 and 9, Andrew Jennings and Christopher Fullerton respectively address an identified gap in the development literature regarding the contributions that arts and culture-based initiatives can make to rural revitalization. Jennings offers an example of how a small, apparently isolated community uses its unique assets and attractions to enrich life for locals and visitors. The chapter describes the distinctiveness of Shetland — an archipelago off the northeast Scottish coast, and how this is protected and promoted by Shetland Islands Council and in the work and ambitions of Shetland's cultural bodies, Shetland Arts and the Shetland Amenity Trust. Fullerton provides a case study of Gravelbourg, Saskatchewan, where local residents have pursued a wide range of arts and culture-related projects as part of a broader revitalization strategy. His research shows that these initiatives have strengthened the town's quality of place and improved its long-term attractiveness and viability as somewhere to live and work.

Laurie Brinklow continues to make connections between culture, identity, and place-based development in Chapter 10. She tells the tale of Tasmania's biennial Ten Days on the Island festival and its showcase of island cultures from around the world within the context of place-specific artistic and tourism development. In examining the 2011 festival, she considers the specific instance of a theatre piece created by island youth from opposite sides of the globe: Tasmania and Newfoundland. These youth, at antipodean extremes, collaborated to celebrate place, and contribute to our knowledge of "islandness" and to their own. Brinklow describes how the parallel cultural renaissances on both islands have capitalized on peripherality and pride of place to create rich cultures that are distinctive because of the very isolation previously used in negative portrayals of provincial backwaters. Local assets, strong leadership, and governance models that recognize the role of culture in reframing self-image in a positive light, as well as global connections, have had a role to play in these successes.

In Chapter 11, Gary Wilson examines place branding, a key component of many place-based development strategies. This chapter focuses on the Isle of Man, a small island jurisdiction in the British Isles and its "Freedom to Flourish" branding project. The case study challenges the assertion often made in the literature on place branding: that brand messages tend to be generic in nature and do not adequately capture the cultural characteristics of the places they seek to represent. Instead, Wilson argues, the "Freedom to Flourish" brand strikes a balance between recognizing the Isle of Man's indigenous culture and heritage and the needs of its dynamic, post-industrial economy and changing demographics.

Brendan O'Keeffe's Chapter 12 provides both an example of what is possible in implementing place-based policy and a sobering reminder of the challenges proponents of place-based development face, particularly in a time of austerity. O'Keeffe describes the well-known and much-lauded model of rural development through locally based partnership bodies in the Republic of Ireland. With dedicated support from the European Union for rural development partnerships and multi-sectoral planning, local partnerships delivered local development and implemented national policies and programs. O'Keeffe explains how, despite (and perhaps even in part because of) this growing and notable capacity, the state-funded (and thus, at least to some extent, state-driven) system began to impose increasing levels of formalism, standardization, and bureaucratization. Sadly, this is an all-too-familiar script, where central governments are willing to share the work of program and policy delivery but, as O'Keeffe points out, less so the power and decision-making. The Irish story has not ended, however, and O'Keeffe leaves us with some optimism in the current resistance to re-centralization and mobilization of a civil society that has been strengthened by 25 years of experience in taking control of development.

Sarah Breen, Sean Markey, Jennifer Daniels, and Kelly Vodden return to the Canadian context in Chapter 13 to conclude Part II by examining the extent and ways in which the notion of place-based development has been put into practice in British Columbia and Newfoundland and Labrador. Like Novaczek, Breen et al. discuss a wide range of place-based initiatives: in arts, culture, and tourism but also in environmental stewardship, the creation of wealth from industrial by-products, branding, and buy-local campaigns. This chapter pays particular attention to the delineation of territorial boundaries and how these boundaries affect regional identities and perceptions of place, which in turn are translated and mobilized for the purposes of regional collaboration and development. The authors conclude with policy insights regarding the potential of well-thought-out, place-responsive development approaches but also the very real challenges of adopting such approaches. These include, for example, traditions of individualism, sector-focused institutional structures, and economic restructuring, as well as the complexity and definitional obscurity associated with the very concepts, such as place and identity, the authors throughout this volume have engaged with.

CONCLUSION

The authors in this volume, through their rich comparative analysis and case studies from Chile to Iceland, and from Tasmania to the Isle of Man, demonstrate that sense of place and place attachment continue to flourish, and even to be renewed, in many peripheral areas. They also demonstrate that these ties can be a valuable resource that can be harnessed to improve quality of life for residents, to create and sustain vibrant cultures, and to boost socially and environmentally resilient local economies. The unique qualities of place within the cases presented in this volume have fostered a multitude of artistic, tourism, niche production, marketing, heritage, and environmental protection initiatives that have captured the attention of scholars, policy-makers, consumers, visitors, and potential residents within these supposed peripheries, as well as across the globe. As Brinklow suggests, citing *The Mercury,* a

Tasmanian newspaper (2011: 22), Tasmania and other locales discussed can be considered to be "no longer at the end of the earth but at the centre."

As with any resource, however, place — and more specifically, place-based identities and sense of place — can be squandered and mismanaged. The chapters in this volume offer examples of concrete and successful place-based development strategies, but also cautionary tales of conflicts over romanticized and invented traditions, of commodification of place for the benefit of the few, of place branding that silences the voices and over-rides the emotions and attachments of already marginalized citizens. Place remains problematic. A key challenge for place-based development raised in this volume, then, is the need to remain critical and careful about notions of the local and place-focused approaches as necessarily superior.

Place-based development relies on capacity and a degree of authority at the local level. In *Remote Control*, the preceding companion volume, Baldacchino et al. (2009) conclude that inhabitants of rural communities and peripheral regions located within larger jurisdictions often lack the capacity to pursue their desired development paths. Public policy and in-stitutions at all levels have a role to play in addressing these gaps and in capitalizing on the significant promise of place-based development. Shifts towards governance and sharing of power with local actors can reignite discussions of place, enhance local confidence, and energize the capacity and the role of place in local decision-making. But in many jurisdictions we observe a retreat from rural and from decentralized, collaborative, inte-grated governance approaches.

Along with the authors in this volume, we must continue to ask prob-ing questions about who and what is local, to acknowledge the multiplicity and dynamic nature of local identities and senses of place, and to focus not only on places in and of themselves, but also on connections between and within places, and between particular places and larger forces of change. How we define and answer each of these queries influences the processes and outcomes of place-based development in the periphery. If we do not engage with these questions and with place-based approaches to develop-ment, surely we put at risk the many distinctive and important contribu-tions and futures that *places peripheral* have to offer.

REFERENCES

Bachleter, J. 2010. *Place-based Policy and Regional Development in Europe.* Ottawa: Policy Horizons Canada.

Baeker, G. 2004. *Placemaking in Canadian Cities: Program Context and Research and Consultation Results.* Toronto: EUCLID Canada.

Baldacchino, G., L. Felt, and R. Greenwood, eds. 2009. *Remote Control: Governance Lessons for and from Small, Insular, and Remote Regions.* St. John's: ISER Books.

Barca, F. 2009. *An Agenda for a Reformed Cohesion Policy: A Place-based Approach to Meeting European Union Challenges and Expectations.* http://ec.europa.eu/regional_policy/policy/future/pdf/report_barca_v0306.pdf.

Bellefontaine, T., and R. Wisener. 2011. *The Evaluation of Place-based Approaches: Questions for Further Research.* Ottawa: Policy Horizons Canada.

Bradford, N. 2005. *Place-based Public Policy: Towards a New Urban and Community Agenda for Canada.* Ottawa: Canadian Policy Research Network.

Cairncross, F. 1997. *The Death of Distance.* Cambridge, Mass.: Harvard Business School.

Canzler, W., F. Kaufmann, and S. Kesselring, eds. 2008. *Tracing Mobilities: Towards a Cosmopolitan Perspective.* Aldershot: Ashgate

Cheng, A., and K. Mattor. 2010. "Place-based Planning as a Platform for Social Learning: Insights from a National Forest Landscape Assessment Process in Western Colorado." *Society & Natural Resources: An International Journal* 23, 5: 385–400.

Chirot, Daniel. 1977. *Social Change in the Twentieth Century.* New York: Harcourt Brace Jovanovich.

Collyer, F. 2014. "Sociology, Sociologists and Core–Periphery: Reflections." *Journal of Sociology* 50, 3: 252–68.

Corbin, C., and M. Hunter. 2007. "The Centre–Periphery Dialectic in Cape Breton: A Discourse Analysis." In D. Johnson, S.A. Royle, and S. Hodgett, eds., *Doing Development Differently: Regional Development on the Atlantic Periphery*, 172–85. Sydney, NS: Cape Breton University Press.

Crescenzi, R. 2005. "Innovation and Regional Growth in the Enlarged Europe: The Role of Local Innovative Capabilities, Peripherality, and Education." *Growth and Change* 36, 4: 471–507.

Douglas, D.J. 2005. "The Restructuring of Local Government in Rural Regions: A Rural Development Perspective." *Journal of Rural Studies* 21: 231–46.

Florida, R., C. Mellander, and K. Stolarick. 2010. *Should I Stay or Should I Go Now:*

The Effect of Community Satisfaction on the Decision to Stay or Move. Toronto: Martin Prosperity Institute.

Frank, A.G. 1967. *Capitalism and Underdevelopment in Latin America: Historical Studies of Chile and Brazil.* New York: Monthly Review Press.

Fundo de Maneio, Lda. 2006. "MACROUP: Report Elaborated in order to Support Experts' Work to be Presented at the Conference in Brussels." Final Version. Ponta Delgada, Azores.

Goldenberg, M. 2008. *A Review of Rural and Regional Development Policies and Programs.* Ottawa: Canadian Policy Research Networks.

Gregory, D. 2004.*The Colonial Present: Afghanistan, Palestine, Iraq.* Oxford: Blackwell.

Gupta, A., and J. Ferguson. 1992. "Beyond 'Culture': Space, Identity, and the Politics of Difference." *Cultural Anthropology* 7, 1: 6–23.

Halseth, G., S. Markey, and D. Bruce, eds. 2009. *The Next Rural Economies: Constructing Rural Place in a Global Economy.* Oxford: CABI International.

Hay, P. 2006. "A Phenomenology of Islands." *Island Studies Journal* 1, 1: 19–42.

Hayter, R., T. Barnes, and M. Bradshaw. 2003. "Relocating Resource Peripheries to the Core of Economic Geography's Theorizing: Rationale and Agenda." *Area* 35, 1: 15–23.

Hudson, R. 2006. "The EU's Ultra-Peripheral Regions: Developmental Considerations and Reflections." Paper prepared for the Conference on the Macroeconomic Situation of the European Ultraperiphery, Brussels, 15 Dec.

Krugman, P. 1998. "What's New about Economic Geography?" *Oxford Review of Economic Policy* 14: 7–17.

Lagendijk, A. 2011. "Regional Innovation Policy between Theory and Practice." In P. Cooke, B. B. Asheim, R. Boschma, R. Martin, D. Scwartz, and F. Tödtling, eds., *Policy Handbook of Regional Innovation and Growth*, 597–608. London: Edward Elgar.

Lewicka, M. 2011. "Place Attachment: How Far Have We Come in the Last 40 Years?" *Journal of Environmental Psychology* 31, 3: 207–30.

Markey, S., G. Halseth, and D. Manson. 2008. "Challenging the Inevitability of Rural Decline: Advancing the Policy of Place in Northern British Columbia." *Journal of Rural Studies* 24: 409–21.

Osterweil, M. 2005. "Place-based Globalism: Locating Women in the Alternative Globalization Movement." In W. Harcourt and A. Escobar, eds., *Women and the Politics of Place*, 174–89. Bloomfield, Conn.: Kumarian Press.

Polese, M., and R. Shearmur. 2003. "How Can We Halt the Demise of Canada's Peripheral Regions?" *Policy Options* 24, 5: 46–52.

Policy Horizons Canada. 2011a. "Location, Location, Location: Putting Evaluation in 'Place.'" Horizons Policy Brief (PH4-102/2011E-PDF).

Policy Horizons Canada. 2011b. *Bringing Place-based Tools to Policy Connecting Information, Knowledge, and Decision-making in the Federal Government Workshop Report.* Ottawa: Policy Horizons Canada.

Potter, R. 2001. "Geography and Development: 'Core and Periphery'?" *Area* 33, 4: 422–27.

Ralph, N. 2011. "Tap Strengths to Revitalize Community." *The Western Producer*, 27 Oct. http://www.producer.com/2011/10/tap-strengths-to-revitalize-community/.

Shannon, M., and C. Mitchell. 2012. "Deconstructing Place Identity? Impacts of a 'Racino' on Elora, Ontario, Canada." *Journal of Rural Studies* 28, 1: 38–48.

Sheller, M. 2013. "The Islanding Effect: Post-Disaster Mobility Systems and Humanitarian Logistics in Haiti." *Cultural Geographies* 20, 2: 185–204.

Smith, A. 2002. "Trans-Locals, Critical Area Studies and Geography's Others, or Why 'Development' Should Not Be Geography's Organizing Framework: A Response to Potter." *Area* 34, 2: 210–13.

Squires, G. 2012. "Beyond the Mobility versus Place Debate." *Journal of Urban Affairs* 34, 1: 29–33.

Stathopoulou, S., D. Psaltopoulos, and D. Skuras. 2004. "Rural Entrepreneurship in Europe: A Research Framework and Agenda." *International Journal of Entrepreneurial Behaviour & Research* 10, 6: 404–25.

The Mercury. 2011. "Editorial: Descend into the Chamber." 22 Jan. http://www.themercury.com.au/article/2011/01/22/33155_editorial.html.

Tuan, Y.-F. 1977. "Geography, Phenomenology, and the Study of Human Nature." *Canadian Geographer* 15: 181–92.

Turcotte, M. 2005. "Social Engagement and Civic Participation: Are Rural and Small Town Populations Really at an Advantage?" *Agriculture and Small Town Canada Analysis Bulletin* 6, 4.

Wallerstein, I. 1979. *The Capitalist World-Economy: Essays by Immanuel Wallerstein.* Cambridge: Cambridge University Press.

Wilson, G. 2007. "The Revitalization of the Manx Language and Culture in an Era of Global Change." *Proceedings for the 3rd Annual Small Island Cultures Conference*, July. Charlottetown, PEI: Institute of Island Studies, University of PEI.

PART I: UNDERSTANDING AND NEGOTIATING PLACE

CHAPTER 2

Matters of Place: The Making of Place and Identity

Jen Daniels, Godfrey Baldacchino, and Kelly Vodden

INTRODUCTION

> . . . *if there is anything to the notion of attachment to place, if cherishing a neighbourhood in which one has spent a significant part of one's life is a meaningful concept, if sense of place and identity are at issue, then the demolition of places large and small inevitably represents an immense cost in human terms.*
>
> Friedmann (2010: 156)

Place is a key factor influencing individual and social behaviour, modes of living, and well-being (Halseth et al., 2010). Place-based development frameworks address this empirical imperative by their sensitivity to the existing assets and challenges experienced in a place. Some scholars and development practitioners recognize that "competitive advantage" comes from assets and resources nested in place. Others are drawn to place and place-making in response to fears of homogenization under such forces as globalization, urbanization, commodification, and the general "horrors of placelessness" (Friedmann, 2010: 150).

And yet, how are notions of place operationalized in place-based development and what are the social and political ramifications of how place is defined and used? How might various conceptions of place inform understandings and practices of place-based development? Even more critically, what are the ramifications, both intellectual and material, of ignoring, or at best, not fully exploring, the role of a more expanded and nuanced notion of place? This chapter first explores these concerns through an investigation of various notions of place; it particularly examines how identity is involved in place-making and creating individual and collective sense(s) of place, and likewise, how place is involved in identity-making. It then considers the significance of these place- and identity-making processes for development policy and practice.

CONCEPTIONS OF PLACE

Coe et al. (2007: 16) suggest that place refers to "somewhere in particular," a location or space that has history and holds meaning. While place often is conceived of as a country, a region, a municipality, a neighbourhood, or some other spatially determined entity, several authors caution against simply collapsing place into space (e.g., Casey, 2001; Entrikin, 2001); understanding place requires acknowledging deeply embedded processes. Defining place and understanding connections between place and individual and collective identities is far from simple. In terms of empirically assessing place meanings and the emotional attachments to place, there are various approaches across disciplines. Friedmann (2010) describes a growing literature on place by diverse authors: from geographers to anthropologists, from psychologists and sociologists to landscape architects, planners, and philosophers (e.g., Bachelard, 1964; Chandler et al., 2003; Salamon, 2003; Davenport and Anderson, 2005; Escobar, 2008; Easthope, 2009).

Distinguishing between space and place, space is conceived of within geography as a highly abstract entity most commonly understood and applied in the form of cartographic representations and co-ordinate points, while place is a much richer concept, redolent with meaning and affect. Halseth et al. (2010) argue that "championing" place over space is by no means a recent concept in geography; nor is it new within research on place-based development. Understanding the policy implications of such a difference, however, remains largely unexplored. Accordingly, "space-based analyses tend to be transformed from their descriptive roots to proscriptive

objectives, and in the process they come to represent these trends and relationships as inexorable . . . driving us to futures we all must share and over
which we have limited influence" (Halseth et al., 2010: 3). Opening up
place meanings, then, is an important first step in exploring the potential
policy implications of analyses that are based on agency-in-place (rather
than space), thus also helping to avoid the observed deterministic pitfalls
of the latter (e.g., Baldacchino et al., 2009).

The construction of place is substantiated through multiple, concurrent processes, including economic, social hierarchical relations (e.g., gender, class, race), and biophysical factors (e.g., Massey, 1994; Harvey, 1996;
Escobar, 2008). Harvey (1996) argues that there is an inherent tension in
place construction through political-economic frameworks that conceptualize place as commodity. A place's assets, often argued as one component
of what makes a place unique, may be promoted by entrepreneurs and
local economic development actors in an attempt to ensure a continuation
of place with minimal personal, affective, or similar valorization (Harvey,
1996). Increasing mobility of capital in recent decades has intensified efforts to *sell* a place. Not only can this pit one place against another, in altogether unsustainable modes of competition; such a strategy of trying to
"differentiate [places] as marketable entities ends up creating a kind of seri-
al replication of homogeneity" (Harvey, 1996: 298). It is therefore fruitful
to critique attempts to (re)invent place with questions about the motivations to do so and with an eye on the implications of any resulting changes.

Massey (1994) and Cresswell (2002) emphasize the importance of mobility in the perception and performance of place, particularly in the context
of a globalized world. Mobility, Massey (1994) asserts, is fundamentally influenced by the movement of capital — money, as the idiom suggests, makes
the world go around — which determines who and what moves and does
not, influencing our individual and collective sense of place. But capital
alone is insufficient; it cannot adequately describe the differences, for example, between women's and men's experiences of place, or those between people of different race, culture, and sexual orientation. Cresswell (2002)
demonstrates that recent conceptualizations of place have gained increasing
traction in contemporary cultural theory through shifting focus from

"rooted" and otherwise essentialist place identities towards those that are more fluid, boundless, and indeed performative in nature. "Mobilities" scholarship in the last decade insists that identities are situated through networks of people, things, and ideas in flux, and that analysis should not start "from a point of view that takes certain kinds of fixity and boundedness for granted [but rather] start with the fact of mobility" (Cresswell, 2011: 551).

In terms of the biophysical element of places, Escobar (2008) posits that landscapes have agency, and maintains that the place assemblage is not simply a social construction. He argues that landscapes are not passive to the kinds of lives people and other beings make in them. Conversely, the external world is highly relevant in the "kind of distinctions humans make ... [and] different places have different things to offer humans to work with and live in and this has everything to do with how humans construct places" (Escobar, 2008: 42). Landscapes, and the biological and physiological entities contained therein, are key components of territory, which in turn, as Escobar (2008) argues, is the embodiment of people's uses, practices, and work in the world — and, ultimately, is the embodiment of their relationship with/in it. Places, then, are co-productions between people and environments. An important feature of place, as conceived by human geographers and post-colonial authors, is that place cannot be limited to geographic locality. It stands that the increasing interconnection and interdependence between places marks not "the end but [rather] the beginning of geography" (Paasi, 2004: 536). Thus, in human geography, place must be positioned in a context where "there is no pure 'local' just as there is no pure 'universal' as all things are interconnected and diffuse in meaning, intention and power" (Bowers, 2010: 204). Places are assemblages of relations. Ultimately, people (and other living things) are connected in ways that extend beyond a spatial location. At the same time, the global does not exist without the local, as every global phenomenon that exists is in some way rooted in a locality, with local origins and/or "touching down" points (Massey, 2004; Sassen, 2007). Thus, the relational and territorial are interconnected and do not present an irreconcilable dichotomy, as they are too often portrayed (e.g., Escobar, 2008).

One approach to understanding sense of place is through analysis of human–environment interactions. In their study of governance of the Niohrara River in Nebraska, for example, Davenport and Anderson (2005) demonstrate that examining residents and other river users' diverse perceptions of sense of place provided a framework for informing decisions. They identify four central tenets related to human–environmental relationships in the literature: (1) place manifests physical characteristics as well as social processes; (2) people assign meanings to and derive meaning from place; (3) some place meanings evoke strong emotional bonds, which influence attitudes and behaviours within the context of those places, and; (4) place meanings are maintained, challenged, and negotiated in the context of natural resource management and planning (Davenport and Anderson, 2005).

If places have multiple meanings that transcend the physical and the locational, then investigating these multiple meanings of place is critical to developing a more nuanced and better-grounded understanding of place politics (e.g., Cheng et al., 2003; Yung et al., 2003; Davenport and Anderson, 2005). In political ecology, the role of place is also increasingly seen as fundamental in tackling the complexity of socio-environmental problems. One of the central arguments here is the *environmental identity and social movement thesis*, which argues that "changes in environmental management regimes and[/or] environmental conditions have created opportunities or imperatives for local groups to secure and represent themselves politically" (Robbins, 2004: 15). Thus, understanding the conceptualizations of place, and the identities lurking within, is pivotal to these movements, providing an additional lens to investigate place in place-based development (e.g., Escobar, 2008; Howitt, 2001; Neumann, 2010). Howitt (2001) asserts that perceiving places as complex sites, produced by multiple scales of interactions between human and non-human agents, helps to unsettle and reframe resource development. Such a turn "for place" is subversive: it guides the examination of those power relations and assumptions that surround such loaded terms as "progress," "planning," "management," "capacity-building," and even "periphery," all in the name of that equally loaded term, "development."

PLACE AND IDENTITY

In their analysis of individual and social identity and of place meanings, Cheung et al. (2003) discuss the well-documented evidence of personal and collective identity construction through places. Individuals' deep-seated emotional and impassioned responses to particular resource and development policies, as well as the social and cultural meanings that may be shared by a group towards a particular place, are important markers of identity. They conclude that "natural resource politics is as much a contest over place meanings as it is a competition among interest groups over scarce resources" (Cheng et al., 2003: 87). Although place is also created through processes of day-to-day life and practice, this opens the discussion of place-making as deeply political work. Given the political stakes involved, these authors stress that negotiations around meanings of place must include a wide set of people, especially those who would normally not be included in management and development decisions.

Markey (2010) states that Canadian development policy and practice often adopt a neo-liberal perspective, such that individuals are deemed to be relatively autonomous and capable of acting independently from those people and places around them in their own rational best interest. Such policies completely disregard the role of identity and place on a person's or a group's decisions and well-being. In Aboriginal constructions of identity, for example, the "place of place [has a] vital link in the chain of meaning" (Bowers, 2010: 217), affecting people's decisions on how to conduct themselves and their ability to heal and learn, and to experience culture and fulfillment (e.g., Kelly and Yeoman, 2011). The research by Chandler et al. (2003) on suicide rates in Aboriginal communities demonstrates that identity construction plays a central role in personal persistence and cultural continuity, which can contribute to lower overall rates of youth suicide these communities.

Many studies of identity point to similar challenges and draw parallel conclusions as they relate to the multiplicity of identities. Bowers (2010) offers a conceptualization of identity as expressed in the Mi'kmaq saying *Msit Nogma*, that is, *All My Relations*. He states "this way of knowing deeply connects the local, familial, tribal, regional, global, and cosmic ecologies into a wholistic/ecology of identity" (Bowers, 2010: 206). Here, identity is grounded in the day-to-day — the places where we eat, sleep, relax, and perform ceremony (Bowers, 2010). Place identity, in this way, also can be viewed from the lens of individual/landscape co-production, and as an interconnected, intermeshed knot, where individual components cannot (or perhaps, should not) be treated in isolation. Bowers (2010) asserts, along with other authors (e.g., Howitt, 2001; Rose, 2004), the urgency of articulating this "deep ecology" of identity by reflecting on the practices within communities and grappling with the complexities and interconnectivity of, in this case, Indigenous ontologies. These complex performances or ontologies of place and identity are not exclusive to Aboriginal communities. Woods (2010), for example, describes an emerging literature on the practice and performance of rural identities.

One common theoretical approach to understanding human–environmental relations and the creation (or co-production) of places and place identities is through phenomenology: this proffers an investigation into how abstract spaces become places through people's interactions and experiences in the world (Buttimer, 1976; Harvey, 1996; Davenport and Anderson, 2005). A person's relationship with a space, particularly the relationship between one's body and the world, involves a baseness and a tactility that require phenomenologists to "reveal an attachment that is native in some way to the primary function of inhabiting" (Bachelard, 1964: 4). Here, Bachelard speaks to the experience of dwelling, using the house as an analogy. Through the act of inhabiting, we create a home, or a sense of belonging in the universe, and by rooting in the home we have access to the cosmos, or consciousness, of the world. Drawing from Relph (1976), Harvey emphasizes that this connection between humans and the earth — the intimate relationship to place(s) — is not simply a sentimental value or "extra" to be indulged after material problems are resolved. It is, indeed, "part of being in the world and prior to technical matters" (Harvey, 1996: 301). We couldn't agree more.

In elaborating on the concept of inhabiting, Buttimer argues that to dwell "implies more than to inhabit, to cultivate, or to organize space. It means to live in a manner which is attuned to the rhythms of nature, to see one's life as anchored in human history and directed toward a future, to build a home which is the everyday symbol of a dialogue with one's ecological and social milieu" (Buttimer, 1976: 272). The concept of *genre de vie*, or lifeway, closely follows a phenomenological approach in describing the connection between people's livelihood and culture and their biophysical setting (Buttimer, 2001). The relationship between self and place is not simply one of reciprocal influence; rather, it is one of "constitutive coingredience: each is essential to the being of the other. That is, there is no place without self, and no self without place" (Casey, 2001: 684).

A considerable literature, both scholarly and populist, gloats over the victimization of local places, and every other thing local, by rampant globalization. But if the latter has its origin in local places, then some of these entities (that is, particular places) are producing globalization and cannot be considered merely victims or consumers. And is this not "an imaginative failure; [one which] closes down the possibility of inventing an alternative local politics, an alternative local economic strategy, in relation to neoliberal globalization" (Massey, 2004: 100)? Throughout history, people have demonstrated a capacity to defend their "local" places while simultaneously reinventing them. As Harvey (1996) suggests, attempts to find, or promote the search for, the "authentic community" — interpreted as one that is grounded in a particular locality and its millenary traditions and that has completely and/or successfully resisted and defied global influences — is probably leading us down the proverbial blind alley. A greater understanding may be gained through an exploration of the hybridization and multi-scalar processes occurring in places, which have provoked in people a "capacity to insert and reinsert themselves into changing space relations" (Harvey, 1996: 318). Invention and reinvention are the stuff of human resilience; the specifics of place are both a cause and an effect of these dynamics.

PLACING PERIPHERIES

This argument is relevant to a more critical understanding of the place of the periphery in a world driven by agglomerations, networks, clusters, and scale economics. Here, we navigate between and among two popular conceptualizations of a globalized world. First is that vision celebrated by communication and information technology (IT) revolution, which has triumphantly declared the death of distance and the irrelevance of geography. We are now all connected, and all barriers have broken down in what has really become a global knowledge economy of "prosperous city regions" (Ohmae, 2001: 33). The second vision is that driven by hard-nosed economics, where major investments, capital flows, and IT-specializing universities still chase each other, with job seekers likely to follow. Large urban centres, equipped with institutional "thickness" (Amin and Thrift, 1994: 14–15) are the main beneficiaries of these trends, while rural and remote communities lose populations and political and economic power. Localities around the world — irrespective of size, resources, and endowments — need to learn how to navigate being both local and global players. Their task is to nurture livability in all its meanings. Failure to encourage place-based development could easily threaten the very sustainability of their communities, and would be evident in depopulation. People vote with their feet (Baldacchino, 2006a).

The task is not an impossible one. The sheer onslaught of globalization may have nurtured an anodyne reductionism to sameness, triggered by global cultural norms in some instances; but this is only part of the story. The same juggernaut has also provided an added incentive to difference. Cultures celebrate specific identities and rediscover (or invent) specific histories; moribund local languages receive a new lease of life; and all of these, somewhat perversely, are fuelled and supported by global tourism industries. The global reach of the World Wide Web has cut down the costs of marketing local products, leading to a renaissance of branded, "authentic" goods from specific places. Diasporas, widely dispersed and swayed by nostalgia, become important customers and cultural agents. Urban refugees, no longer willing to forgo quality-of-life issues in competitive urban labour markets, choose to move to places that are small, charming, and relatively safe.

Islands share many of the features attributed to remote rural regions: their aquatic delineation and often smaller populations and resource bases give the notion of periphery a stark geographical character (Baldacchino et al., 2009). And yet, just like remote rural regions, they are exploiting the "structural holes" that pervade the overarching global network (Burt, 1992; Sennett, 1998: 84). If theirs are also places whose future is "in play," they have done well by presenting themselves as places "to play," platforms of amusement, excitement, and relaxation in a hedonistic age (Sheller and Urry, 2003). But not only so: coupled with the resourcefulness of jurisdictional powers — many islands are self-contained administrative units — they have deployed the tools of governance to practise "agency in place," carefully identifying or crafting niches in ever turbulent markets. Their repertoire includes tourism — whether of the "sun, sea, and sand" variety in warm-water locations (e.g., Conlin and Baum, 1995), or the "ice, isolation, and indigenous culture" type of their cold-water cousins (e.g., Baldacchino, 2006b). Beyond that industry, islands also sport military, satellite, and communications installations; nature reserves; offshore banking industries; niche crafts and manufactures; and vibrant arts scenes. All celebrate location, though for altogether different reasons.

Clearly, being an island has its advantages. This is not just a function of the place-specific and revenue-generating repertoire of activities referred to above, but also of those elusive but determining quality-of-life factors (e.g., Dahlström et al., 2006). House prices on islands are usually lower than in metropolitan areas (though with some notable exceptions); cultural and historical heritage is important, as is the value of one's roots in the community. Indeed, islands typically contain tight and robust communities, which are warm, supportive, and welcoming when one belongs; but hard to penetrate if one does not (e.g., Cohen, 1987; Marshall, 2008).

And so, while regional and national development plans generated from metropolitan and administrative cores and rural scholars continue, top-down, to objectify and essentialize peripheries as "have-not" regions that need to be the targets of economic largesse to survive, some of these communities are reacting to this deficit syndrome, refusing to accept its assumptions or consequences. In other cases, communities and regions have adopted and perpetuated this narrative of deficit, whether it has been internalized or is used to further their own interests. While connectivities remain important and vital for survival, what may appear to be remote and marginal to some is very much the view from the centre for others. We all stand at the centre of our own worlds: valuing place is a significant conceptual turn towards asserting and fulfilling our right to belong.

DEVELOPMENT CAN ONLY BE (MORE OR LESS) PLACE-BASED

Place-based development, in many ways, is a reaction to more conventional forms of development, which have been pronounced in an almost universal application of those policies, programs, and practices deemed most appropriate by Western science and political-economic agendas. In this "rational" Western view, planning is controlled by planning experts, development institutions, and nation-states that govern largely from the top down (Coe et al., 2007; Escobar, 1995), often focusing on single-sector, and frequently large-scale, industrial projects (Markey et al., 2008). Meanwhile, local contexts, their subsequent historical contingencies, and the gamut of socio-cultural, political, and environmental specificities and relationships are temporarily suspended or even completely disregarded (Escobar, 1995, 2008).

In sharp and welcome contrast, place-based development is "a holistic and targeted intervention that seeks to reveal, utilize and enhance the unique natural, physical, and/or human capacity endowments present within a particular location for the development of the *in situ* community and/or its biophysical environment" (Markey, 2010: 1). Place-based strategies adopt a territorial approach to planning and development that encourages the integration of contextual endowments and potentials, such as the environmental, economic, social, and cultural characteristics of a locality (Amdam, 2002; Markey et al., 2008). Such a style of doing development differently is commonly associated with "bottom-up" or grassroots modes of governance, promoting the leadership, participation, and agency of local actors within development (Greenwood, 2009; Halseth et al., 2010; Markey et al., 2008; OECD, 2010; Reimer and Markey, 2008).

It can be argued that place-based development follows on the multiple traditions of community development practice and theory dating back at least to the 1950s (Chekki, 1989) and of area-based initiatives from the 1960s and 1970s (Matthews, 2012). Recent attention to place-based approaches can be largely attributed to the drastic restructuring of the economic, political, and social fabric of rural communities. But there have also been concurrent shifts in scholarly communities, with the more integrative and relational turn in economic geography, the rise of interest in "sustainable livelihoods," and the generally critical reviews of past approaches to development policy and theory (e.g., Barnes et al., 2000; Hettne, 1995; Markey et al., 2008; Markey, 2010; Sachs, 2003). Surely, place-based development offers a better alternative.

Four critical reasons why place needs to be taken into account in development policy and practice, certainly in a rural context, have been simply yet aptly proposed. First, place is where assets such as resources are located; second, services of all kinds — health, education, sanitation, justice, housing, welfare, recreation — are delivered in places; third, governance and decision-making around planning and development occur in places; and, finally, identities of who we are, individually and collectively, are formed and reinforced in places (Reimer and Markey, 2008). These are important arguments regarding why place matters in development, particularly in the face of standard and context-blind policies that have been indiscriminately applied, top-down, cookie-cutter fashion, to many rural areas (Markey et al., 2008). Is this one reason why rural depopulation has been so extensive worldwide in recent decades?

Yet, what place is, and by what it is constituted, is not immediately apparent within the place-based development literature. The characteristics of place-based approaches, including related local and community economic development literatures, are widely discussed (e.g., Haughton, 2002; Markey et al., 2005; Markey et al., 2008), indicating an obvious interest, in both academia and in practice, in the role of place in development; and yet, there is a lack of an explicit or consistent definition of "place" in this body of work. Such definitional obscurity is just one of the central reasons why place-based policies are often treated with suspicion or indifference (Reimer and Markey, 2008). Other key criticisms include: a danger of elitism and parochialism; an inability to engage or enforce a broader community and/or regional interests; an unreflexive promotion of local control as ideal, including the privileging of local governance mechanisms at the cost of broader (e.g., national and multinational) institutional and political relations; and a disregard for inter-community co-operation, as is especially required where regional identity does not align neatly with that of a community (e.g., Markey et al., 2009; Reimer and Markey, 2008).

What these criticisms may implicitly suggest is that a geographic locality, understood as a bounded, spatially or politically predetermined entity — such as a municipality — is synonymous with the "place" in place-based development. Place-based resource management, however, is not about removing mechanisms of non-local control over resource decisions. It is argued there is a need to collaborate across jurisdictional scales, and both knowledge-sharing mechanisms and collaborative relationships warrant greater academic attention, as suggested by collaborative and multi-level governance literatures (Emerson et al., 2011; Vodden, 2009; Hooghe and Marks, 2003). Thus, places and their particularities warrant being explored in their own right and in the context of their wider context and relationships (Cheung et al., 2003; Robbins, 2004; Sivaramakrishnan, 1998).

PLACE MATTERS

Clearly, place-based identities are highly contested, and so are contemporary views on the roles of place and identity, including the explanatory value of place in social theory (Entrikin, 2001). Place can be conceived as both a materially identifiable territory and a set of relations that extend in and beyond "local" actors, to imbricate decisions and relationships that reach far beyond the immediate geographical boundaries. Place meanings are maintained, challenged, and negotiated in the context of management, planning, and development; it follows that there is a dire need for research to explore how such development challenges, reinforces, and dismisses certain understandings of place, sense of place, and identity in place. An important reminder here is that place is in play: it is contestable, up for grabs, embroiled in all sorts of other (mainly incidental) conversations about resources, about local government, about social provision. Place can get lost in the shuffle: it can be implicitly or explicitly redefined; it can be colonized; it can be subsumed; it can be revalorized; it can be renamed; or it can slip off the agenda, unnoticed and unwept. Further exploration of these notions of place would surely help to open place-based development scholarship to alternative notions of place identities — notions that better capture the contextual richness of these places.

Deeper understandings of place are called upon to support and inform a more equitable and responsible development policy and practice. This requires of us "an act of geographic imagination . . . an ability to read landscapes — not simply as texts, but as complex records of interactions, interrelationships and change over time and space" (Howitt, 2011: 165). As development practitioners, policy-makers, and scholars, but also as affected community members, we all do well to recognize the settings of our work as places, in all their plurality, complexity, and diversity. This recognition needs to be squarely on the agenda in pursuing place-based development. Place matters, and in many more ways than we may realize.

ACKNOWLEDGEMENTS

The authors would like to acknowledge very helpful comments on an initial draft from David Douglas, Professor Emeritus, University of Guelph.

REFERENCES

Amdam, R. 2002. "Sectoral versus Territorial Regional Planning and Development in Norway." *European Planning Studies* 10, 1: 99–111.

Amin, A., and N. Thrift, eds. 1994. *Globalization, Institutions and Regional Development in Europe*. Oxford: Oxford University Press.

Bachelard, G. 1964. *The Poetics of Space*. Boston: Beacon Press.

Baldacchino, G. 2006a. "Small Islands versus Big Cities: Lessons in the Political Economy of Regional Development from the World's Small Islands." *Journal of Technology Transfer* 31, 1: 91–100.

———. 2006b. *Extreme Tourism: Lessons from the World's Cold Water Islands*. Oxford: Elsevier.

———, R. Greenwood, and L. Felt, eds. 2009. *Remote Control: Governance Lessons for and from Small, Insular, and Remote Regions*. St. John's: ISER Books.

Barnes, T., J. Britton, W. Coffey, D. Edgington, M. Gertler, and G. Nordcliffe. 2000. "Canadian Economic Geography at the Millennium." *Canadian Geographer* 44, 1: 4–24.

Bowers, R./Kisiku Sa'qawei Paq'tism. 2010. "Identity, Prejudice and Healing in Aboriginal Circles: Models of Identity, Embodiment and Ecology of Place as

Traditional Medicine for Education and Counselling." *AlterNative: An International Journal of Indigenous Peoples* 6, 3: 203–21.

Burt, R. 1992. *Structural Holes: The Social Structure of Competition.* Cambridge, Mass.: Harvard University Press.

Buttimer, A. 1976. "Grasping the Dynamism of Lifeworld." *Annals, Association of American Geographers* 66, 2: 277–92.

———. 2001. "Sustainable Development: Issues of Scale and Appropriateness." In A. Buttimer, ed., *Sustainable Landscapes and Lifeways: Scale and Appropriateness,* 7–34. Cork, Ireland: Cork University Press.

Casey, E.S. 2001. "Between Geography and Philosophy: What Does It Mean to Be in the Place-World?" *Annals, Association of American Geographers* 91, 4: 683–93.

Chandler, M.J., C.E. Lalonde, B.W. Sokol, and D. Hallett. 2003. "Personal Persistence, Identity Development, and Suicide: A Study of Native and Non-Native North American Adolescents." *Monographs of the Society for Research in Child Development* 68, 2: 1–129.

Chekki, D.A., ed. 1986. *Community Development: Theory and Method of Planned Change.* New Delhi: Vikas Publishing House.

Cheng, A.S., L.E. Kruger, and S.E. Daniels. 2003. "'Place' as an Integrating Concept in Natural Resource Politics: Propositions for a Social Science Research Agenda." *Society and Natural Resources* 16, 1: 87–104.

Coe, N.M., P.F. Kelly, and H.W.C. Yeung. 2007. *Economic Geography: A Contemporary Introduction.* Malden, Mass.: Blackwell.

Cohen, A. 1987. *Whalsay: Symbol, Segment and Boundary in a Shetland Island Community.* Manchester: Manchester University Press,

Conlin, M.V., and T. Baum. 1995. *Island Tourism: Management Principles and Practices.* Chichester, UK: John Wiley.

Cresswell, T. 2002. "Theorizing Place." In G. Verstraete and T. Cresswell, eds., *Mobilizing Place, Placing Mobility: The Politics of Representation in a Globalized World,* 11–32. Amsterdam: Rodopi.

———. 2011. "Mobilities I: Catching Up." *Progress in Human Geography* 35, 4: 550–58.

Dahlström, M., A. Aldea-Partanen, K. Fellman, S. Hedin, N. Javakhisvili Larsen, H. Johannesson, J. Manniche, G. Mattland Olsen, and T. Petersen. 2006. "How to Make a Living in Insular Areas: Six Nordic Cases." *Nordregio Report* 1.

Davenport, M.A., and D.H. Anderson. 2005. "Getting from Sense of Place to Place-based Management: An Interpretative Investigation of Place Meanings and Perceptions of Landscape Change." *Society and Natural Resources* 18, 7: 625–41.

Emerson, K., T. Nabatchi, and S. Balogh. 2011. "An Integrative Framework for Collaborative Governance." *Journal of Public Administration Research and Theory* 22: 1–29.

Escobar, A. 1995. *Encountering Development: The Making and Unmaking of the Third World*. Princeton, NJ: Princeton University Press.

———. 2008. *Territories of Difference: Place, Movements, Life, Redes*. Durham, NC: Duke University Press.

Entrikin, J.N. 2001. "Hiding Places." *Annals, Association of American Geographers* 91, 4: 694–97.

Friedmann, J. 2010. "Place and Place-making in Cities: A Global Perspective." *Planning Theory & Practice* 11, 2: 149–65.

Greenwood, R. 2009. "Doing Governance for Development: The Way Forward for Newfoundland and Labrador." In G. Baldacchino, R. Greenwood, and L. Felt, eds., *Remote Control: Governance Lessons for and from Small, Insular, and Remote Regions*, 280–94. St. John's: ISER Books.

Hägerstrand, T. 2001. "A Look at the Political Geography of Environmental Management." In A. Buttimer, ed., *Sustainable Landscapes and Lifeways: Scale and Appropriateness*, 35–58. Cork, Ireland: Cork University Press.

Halseth, G., S. Markey, B. Reimer, and D. Manson. 2010. "Introduction: The Next Rural Economies." In G. Halseth, S. Markey, and D. Bruce, eds., *The Next Rural Economies: Constructing Rural Place in Global Economies*, 1–16. Wallingford, Oxfordshire, UK: CABI Publishing.

Harvey, D. 1996. *Justice, Nature and the Geography of Difference*. Oxford: Blackwell.

Haughton, G. 2002. *Community Economic Development*. Norwich, UK: Routledge.

Hooghe, L., and G. Marks. 2003. "Unraveling the Central State, but How? Types of Multi-level Governance." *American Political Science Review* 97, 2: 233–43.

Howitt, R. 2001. *Rethinking Resource Management: Justice, Sustainability, and Indigenous Peoples*. London: Routledge.

Kelly, U.A., and E. Yeoman. 2011. *Despite This Loss: Essays on Culture, Memory, and Identity in Newfoundland and Labrador*. St. John's: ISER Books.

Markey, S. 2010. "Primer: Place-based Development." *Canadian Regional Development: A Critical Review of Theory, Practice and Potentials*. Canadian Regional Development/New Regionalism Working Paper, St. John's, NL.

———, G. Halseth, and D. Manson. 2008. "Challenging the Inevitability of Rural Decline: Advancing the Policy of Place in Northern British Columbia." *Journal of Rural Studies* 24, 4: 409–21.

———, ———, and ———. 2009. "Contradictions in Hinterland Development: Challenging the Local Development Ideal in Northern British Columbia." Community Development Journal 44, 2: 209–29.

———, J. Pierce, K. Vodden, and M. Roseland. 2005. Second Growth: Community Economic Development in Rural and Small Town British Columbia. Vancouver: University of British Columbia Press.

Marshall, J. 2003. Tides of Change on Grand Manan Island: Culture and Belonging in a Fishing Community. Montreal and Kingston: McGill-Queen's University Press.

Massey, D. 1994. Space, Place and Gender. Minneapolis: University of Minnesota Press.

———. 2004. "The Responsibilities of Place." Local Economy 19, 2: 97–101.

Matthews, P. 2012. "From Area-based Initiatives to Strategic Partnerships: Have We Lost the Meaning of Regeneration?" Environment and Planning C: Government and Policy 30, 1: 147–61.

Neumann, R.P. 2010. "Political Ecology II: Theorizing Region." Progress in Human Geography 34, 3: 368–474.

Ohmae, K. 2001. The Invisible Continent: Four Strategic Imperatives of the New Economy. New York: Harper Business.

Organization for Economic Co-operation and Development. 2010. OECD Rural Policy Reviews: Québec, Canada 2010. Paris: OECD.

Paasi, A. 2003. "Region and Place: Regional Identity in Question." Progress in Human Geography 27, 4: 475–85.

———. 2004. "Place and Region: Looking through the Prism of Scale." Progress in Human Geography 28, 4: 536–46.

Reimer, B., and S. Markey. 2008. Place-based Policy:A Rural Perspective. Ottawa: Human Resources and Social Development Canada.

Relph, R. 1976. Place and Placelessness. London: Pion.

Robbins, P. 2004. Political Ecology. Malden, Mass.: Blackwell.

Rose, D.B. 2004. Reports from a World Country: Ethics for Decolonisation. Sydney: University of New South Wales.

Sassen, S. 2007. A Sociology of Globalization. New York: Norton.

Sennett, R. 1998. The Corrosion of Character. New York: Norton.

Sheller, M., and J. Urry, eds. 2003. Tourism Mobilities: Places to Play, Places in Play. New York: Routledge.

Sivaramakrishnan, K. 1998. "Comanaged Forests in West Bengal: Historical Perspectives on Community and Control." Journal of Sustainable Forestry 7, 3 and 4: 23–49.

Vodden, K. 2009. "Experiments in Collaborative Governance on Canada's Coasts: Challenges and Opportunities in Governance Capacity." In G. Baldacchino, R. Greenwood, and L. Felt, eds., *Remote Control: Governance Lessons for and from Small, Insular, and Remote Regions*, 259–79. St. John's: ISER Books.

Woods, M. 2010. "Performing Rurality and Practising Rural Geography." *Progress in Human Geography* 34, 6: 835–46.

Young, T. 2001. "Place Matters." *Annals, Association of American Geographers* 91, 4: 681–82.

Yung, L., W.A. Freimund, and J.M. Belsky. 2003. "The Politics of Place: Understanding Meaning, Common Ground, and Political Difference on the Rocky Mountain Front." *Forestry Science* 49, 6: 855–66.

CHAPTER 3

Placing Identity: Strategic Considerations for Rebounding Peripheries

Godfrey Baldacchino

INTRODUCTION

One consequence of rampant globalization has been the resurgence, and in some cases invention, of local identity and difference in the face of the threat of glib and anodyne sameness. For small communities in islands and remote rural regions, a failure to undergo such a (re)positioning may initiate a vicious cycle of heavy depopulation, youth out-migration, growing and chronic unemployment, and an overall feeling of malaise and helplessness. This cycle of loss, gloom, and defeat is also a consequence of neo-liberal policies that have championed market forces and under-mined the role and legitimacy of the state in economic development, generally, and in supporting "uncompetitive" and "non-viable" projects, specifically. Economies of scale, and the virtues of urban clusters and ag-glomerations, have shifted interests and investments away from far-flung and non-strategic locales, leaving their local residents with the stark op-tion to either pack up and leave for greener pastures or stay but scramble for effective survival strategies. While circumstances and resources change with time and context, many such communities find themselves in a strug-gle to break out of the downward spiral induced by the "double whammy" of globalization and neo-liberalism, and hopefully succeed in replacing it by a virtuous mix of select visitations, in-migration, economic activities that generate employment and high local value added, and a general pride in place.

And yet, as noted in Chapters 1 and 2, the impact of globalization is messy and complex: former "centres" get downgraded to peripheries in a regional or international context, while peripheries benefit from a "time/space compression" (Harvey, 1990) that is a consequence of new information and communication technologies — such as satellite phones, global positioning systems, and broadband mobile and Internet communication services — that facilitate access, in spite of physical space constraints. Moreover, increasingly more people find themselves "seagulls," in permanent flux, moving from place to place, or having more than one home: evidence of nomadism, brain/brawn circulation, and cyclical migration patterns (Baldacchino, 2006a; Freeland, 2011; Peters, 1998). Meanwhile, research suggests that opportunities for employment and self-employment, along with the provision of basic and affordable infrastructural services — not just water and electricity, but health care, basic education, inexpensive and efficient transportation to/from economic and population centres, and wireless broadband provision — are critical to stem population decline, and may even contribute to population increase (Barthon, 2007; Royle, 2007).

The responses by various islands and remote rural regions towards "identity re-engineering" — a term long associated with strategic management discourse (Jackson, 1996) — have been diverse, and debates still rage as to the effectiveness of local, bottom-up, and democratic initiatives, as against those that are "top–down," planned and driven by state agencies and technical experts (Hooghe and Marks, 2001; Baldacchino et al., 2009). In an era of public retrenchment and divestment of state assets, a more bottom-up governance approach (discussed further by O'Keeffe in Chapter 12) comes across not necessarily as a preferred policy choice but as the default option in the face of the "eclipse of government" (Jordan et al., 2005).

FOUR STRATEGIC CONSIDERATIONS

An attempt at a comparative overview of these responses on the ground suggests that some or all of the following four strategic interlocked considerations for community viability are brought into play. These ideas are drawn from my ongoing interest in, and research on, the economic development challenges of peripheral jurisdictions, with a special focus on small islands (e.g., Baldacchino, 2006c, 2006d). They correspond to development strategies that seek to maximize the multiplier effects of boutique tourism, select in-migration, niche manufacturing, plus the opportunities presented in some instances by a single but significant windfall investment, which often takes over and rejuvenates assets that others may have abandoned.

The first response is to seek to develop an ecologically and culturally friendly tourism industry that appreciates local and small-scale assets, engages with the local community, and respects the cultural and natural ambience of place. As the global tourism industry continues to grow, it is also diversifying rapidly into various niches, and small-scale tourism fits well with what small communities off the beaten track can offer, preserving elements of authenticity, cementing local proprietary control over infrastructure, and avoiding the rampant commodification that tends to follow mass tourism invasions (Smith, 1998; Scheyvens and Russell, 2012).

The second response is to pursue another select tourist market: second-home residents and urban or lifestyle refugees, desirous to escape the "rat race" and the urban hustle and bustle, raise children in safe neighbourhoods, and otherwise keen to face the raw challenges of life "at the edge." Thanks to electronic connectivity, artists, professionals, and retirees have been seriously considering moving, or moving back, to places where the tempo of life is more natural and human (Baldacchino, 2010; Baldacchino and Pleijel, 2010). Crucial here is the reception afforded by the local inhabitants: welcoming societies register the highest levels of retention and integration of incomers, while xenophobia and subtle racism can turn them away (Baldacchino, 2006b, 2012; Marshall, 2008). Fürst discusses these challenges further in Chapter 4.

A third response involves the production and promotion of well-branded, good-quality, high value-added, and locally sourced products, services, and natural assets geared for niche export markets, including the tourists and new residents mentioned above. As Novaczek (Chapter 7), Jennings (Chapter 8), and others in this volume suggest, these goods ideally align with and reinforce the qualities of a just as well-branded locale that celebrates an enviable quality of life (Punnett and Morrison, 2006; Pounder, 2010; Zhang, 2010; Khamis, 2010).

Fourth, and finally, are responses to the opportunities provided by an injection of new investment: a phoenix-like, resurgent flagship industry, possibly replacing a moribund or redundant one, such as a hotelier or an educational institution taking over defunct or surplus military barracks (see Prince Edward Island and Unst below). Such initiatives, at times, are mired in controversy, given that the stakes are high and the activities involved may hover on the limits of legitimacy (Palan, 2003). They also typically require a major injection of capital and, given their size, are always at risk of being appropriated and driven by non-local owners and interests. And yet, where successful, the transformation in the economic fortunes of the hosting community can be tremendous (see Chapter 8 on the Shetland Islands by Jennings).

FIVE CASES OF REGIONAL DEVELOPMENT

This chapter reviews experiences with these four interlocked strategic considerations for sustainable development in relation to five exemplars of peripheral locales that are, at the time of writing, experiencing some sense of revival and growth. These are located on five different island jurisdictions in the North Atlantic, in decreasing population size: Belfast, Northern Ireland; Slemon Park, Prince Edward Island, Canada; Akureyri and the Eyjafjörður region, North Iceland; Unst, Shetland Islands, Scotland; and Kökar, Åland Islands, Finland.

The material presented here, and its ensuing analysis, is derived from my own personal knowledge (I have visited and stayed at all five sites since 2008); my familiarity with projects that have explored rural and regional development in these and other regions (Baldacchino et al., 2009; Dahlström et al., 2006); and other critical sources, including official documents and local informants. Where possible, I have corroborated my analysis with, and tested my observations on, other local resource persons.

The five cases have also been selected because they manifest a range of approaches to regional development: from the classical state-driven injection of massive amounts of public financing and corporate baits like subsidies and tax relief incentives (as in the Belfast case), to the much more modest and less visible but more finely targeted grants to small businesses (as in the Kökar case). They also reflect different shades of peripherality: from the capital of a country within the United Kingdom to the small island periphery of what is itself a small island jurisdiction in the Baltic Sea.

Case #1: Belfast, Northern Ireland

At its peak, Harland & Wolff employed 35,000 people at its shipyard in the city of Belfast (now with a population of 275,000) to make the ships that linked Britain to its empire, as well as the doomed *Titanic*. In 2003, the firm officially registered as a small business, with a staff complement of 135. This shipyard, with its two giant gantry cranes, sits in what is now called Titanic Quarter, in Northern Ireland (land area 13,800 km^2; population 1.8 million; sub-national jurisdiction). The Titanic Quarter is a waterfront regeneration project, including apartments, a riverside entertainment district, and a major *Titanic*-themed attraction developed on reclaimed land in Belfast Harbour (www.titanic-quarter.com/). Since 2005, it has also become the home to the Northern Ireland Science Park (a hi-tech science park affiliated closely with Queen's University Belfast and the University of Ulster) as well as the Paint Hall, now converted into a film studio used during the production of films and television series. This is the biggest property development scheme ever undertaken in Northern Ireland, and was embraced with gusto by all official place promotion agencies in Belfast, including the Belfast Tourist Board and Belfast City Council; the Northern Ireland Executive pitched in with financing in 2008 in the guise of a "counter-recessionary stimulus" (Neill, 2010: 315–19). The shipyard has obtained a new lease on life by building wind turbines; and close by Bombardier is setting up a site to build wings for new aircraft. Offering lower costs and desirable skills, Northern Ireland still depends considerably on public-sector spending; being discussed is a cut in the basic corporation tax rate, from Britain's 26 per cent to something close to the Republic of Ireland's 12.5 per cent. This policy measure could lure foreign direct investment, especially now that the sectarian troubles that plagued Northern Ireland seem to have largely become history (*The Economist*, 2011). The city "has been transformed since the cessation of widespread political violence" (Bairner, 2006: 159). "A sustained reduction in unemployment, economic growth and house price increases have reflected Belfast's post-conflict renaissance just as readily as the global recession has exposed the fragility of construction-led growth. Rates of segregation have stabilized and new consumption spaces and élite developments further reflect the city's engagement with globalization and economic liberalization" (Murtagh, 2010: 1119).

Case #2: Slemon Park, Prince County, Prince Edward Island (PEI), Canada

The history of Slemon Park originates in 1940 with the decision to open a base in Prince Edward Island (land area 5,700 km^2; population 150,000; province) to support the British Commonwealth Air Training Plan during World War II. In 1948, the RCAF Air Navigation School was established to provide pilot and navigator training. Starting in 1949, houses, roads, and a school were built. In 1968, 413 Transport and Rescue Squadron, operating out of what was then renamed Canadian Forces Base (CFB) Summerside, was set up as the prime search and rescue unit on Canada's east coast.

The closure of CFB Summerside was announced by the Canadian government in 1989, and in April 1992 the former CFB Summerside property was transferred to its current owner, Slemon Park Corporation, a commercial and residential property management and development company.

PEI has developed Slemon Park into a "successful tax-free zone for aerospace companies" (Carroll, 2000: 11). It is now the location of various companies and training organizations in aviation, aerospace, police and security training, and other commercial activities. The former Officers' Mess for CFB Summerside serves as the front desk and conference facility for the Slemon Park Hotel and Conference Centre (Slemon Park Corporation, n.d.). Indeed, that the island province has a manufacturing sector at all has been due in no small part to "the aeronautics industry located in Summerside's Slemon Park" (Murphy, 2001: 11). At least nine companies — including Honeywell Engines — provide around 900 well-paid jobs (Aerospace PEI, 2013). Because of its earlier history as a Canadian Forces Base, the Slemon Park facility possesses all of the accoutrements needed by a modern aerospace cluster. The 1,500-acre business park includes a working airport with two runways and numerous well-maintained hangars (Innovation PEI, 2013). The province's higher education college has a facility at Slemon Park and trains graduates in various engineering and aerospace-related skills that are prized and sought by the industry (Holland College, PEI, 2013).

Case #3: Akureyri and Eyjafjörður, North Iceland

Iceland has become today a highly "urbanized" island state, with only 7.7 per cent of the population classified as rural dwellers in 2012 (Hagstofa Íslands, 2003; Statistics Iceland, 2013). Some two-thirds of the entire population of around 318,000 lives in the Reykjavík metropolitan area in the southwest, and only one town — Akureyri in northern Iceland — outside this area has more than 10,000 inhabitants. This rapid urbanization has occurred in spite of four-year regional development plans put into place since 1978 by the national government. Migration from the Icelandic countryside and provincial towns to the capital area is considered to be a very serious problem. Rural Iceland is isolated from other areas by peninsulas, vast areas of wilderness, and often inclement weather; it is far from markets, both within Iceland and abroad, resulting in higher costs for the transportation of people and products; it tends to have shortages of both skilled labour and business know-how; and it suffers from a brain drain because most youth leave to seek education, employment, or just adventure, and often don't return (Bjarnason and Thorlindsson, 2006). The amalgamation of various small rural municipalities has been one rational strategy to achieve some economies of scale in community services and thus to help prevent rural depopulation and decline (Eythórsson, 2009).

In 2004, a Regional Growth Agreement (RGA) was established to enhance the Eyjafjörður region, where Akureyri is located (land area 4,300 km²; population 22,000; region, with nine municipalities) — a rural region of Iceland dependent on crop farming, raising livestock (especially sheep), horse breeding, fishing, commerce, and, increasingly, tourism. To increase its attraction as a popular place to live and to encourage economic growth and competitiveness, four "clusters" were conceived, in line with the doctrine of Michael Porter (1998): food innovation (mainly fishing, but also agriculture and the processing of agricultural produce); education and research (with elementary schools, two secondary schools, and one university — the University of Akureyri — established in 1987, now with three faculties); health (with the largest hospital in Iceland outside Reykjavik, plus health-related services); and tourism (seasonal, and mainly rural) (Sigursteinsdóttir, 2008).

Eyjafjörður is well known in Iceland for relatively milder and better weather and is renowned for good-quality food. The region has the best ski resort in Iceland, and is generally conceived as a good place to live. Compared to other rural regions in Iceland, a much higher ratio of people who move away do return to live in the Eyjafjörður region. There are frequent daily flights to and from the capital region, which is 385 km to the south: this facilitates business trips and meetings, and makes it possible for part of the workforce to commute between regions on a weekly basis (Jóhannesson, 2006; Dahlström et al., 2006).

While Akureyri was the manufacturing town of Iceland, this sector was heavily downsized when firms belonging to a large employer — Sambandið (Cooperative Union) — were sold or went bankrupt. Various important markets in Eastern Europe were lost with the collapse of the Soviet Union in 1991, and stronger competition from cheaper imports resulted after Iceland's decision to join the European Free Trade Association and the European Economic Area in 1993 squeezed out local products. However, Samherji, a vertically integrated fishing company, has grown rapidly: based in Akureyri since 1983, it is now by far the largest fishing company in Iceland with operations in nine countries, a fishing fleet of nine ships, and 790 employees, many (such as crew members) well paid (Samherji HF, 2013).

While the RGA was concluded in 2007, it generated sufficient momentum to enable the Eyjafjörður region to persevere with private-sector funding and support (Sigursteindottir, 2008). Meanwhile, the steep hill that runs down from the Akureyri thermal swimming pools to the city centre is "Arts' Alley": it includes various art galleries, the Akureyri School of Visual Arts, design and handcraft shops, workshops, the Akureyri Art Museum, and the Akureyri Cultural Centre (*Icelandic Times*, 2010; Visit Akureyri, 2013).

Case #4: Unst, Shetland Islands, Scotland

RAF Saxa Vord was an early-warning radar station operated by the Royal Air Force. It was located on the island of Unst (land area 121 km^2; population around 650; part of municipality), the most northerly of the Shetland Islands, in the north of Scotland. It served as a vital part of Britain's air defence network during the Cold War, and was closed by the UK Ministry of Defence in 2006, when it employed 100 locals, in spite of requests to postpone the closure (BBC, 2005). Then, it was expected that "the departure of service personnel and their families will see the island's population drop by a quarter to 500" (BBC, 2006). (The population was 1,067 in the 1991 census, and 720 at the 2001 census). Unst airport had also closed in the year 2000. Job loss between 1999 and 2007 was estimated at 175, or 42 per cent of all employment (Unst Community Plan Consultation, 2010: 1).

The radar facility was bought the following year by Military Asset Management (MAM), a private company owned by the Scottish Highland entrepreneur, Frank Strang. Recognizing that military bases tend to be situated in remote rural areas, and that their closure could have devastating socio-economic consequences for local communities, MAM was set up to transform closing bases into self-sustaining, profitable enterprises, encouraging and fostering economic regeneration in the process. Saxa Vord is being redeveloped into what is being hailed as Britain's first "residential natural and cultural heritage activity centre" (Saxa Vord, n.d.). The facility currently includes a hotel, 20 self-catering holiday houses, a 16-bedroom bunkhouse, leisure facilities, a restaurant, bar, and a guided walks/evening talks program. Locals are employed whenever possible, and there is direct local involvement in the business. For example, Sonny Priest, owner of Unst's Valhalla Brewery, manages and supplies the bar at Saxa Vord, and has relocated the brewery to the site (Valhalla Brewery, n.d.).

The Shetland Island Council is one of 32 councils that organize local government in Scotland. It is now the major employer in Unst; however, the 600 plus island residents are resourceful, as witnessed by other entrepreneurial ventures. The island is the home of PURE, an operational community-owned renewable hydrogen energy system (Pure Energy Centre, n.d.). A mussel farm started harvesting mussels in 2009 (Fishupdate.com, 2007) and farmed salmon is thriving (*Shetland Times*, 2011), having also survived an ownership transfer of late (Bevington, 2013). And there is Steven Spence, Unst's fiddler, who exports fiddles and other instruments from Unst, and who accepts commissions to compose fiddle tunes for special occasions (Spencies Tunes, 2013).

Among Unst's recent incoming population, consider Mike Smith, who "escaped" to Unst to retrain after a career with the Royal Air Force. He has since completed a degree in Environment and Heritage Studies and built a house. He is passionate about renewable energy systems and energy saving, and has incorporated these into his house design. Mike is the Community Powerdown Officer with the Unst Partnership, the community development trust (The Unst Partnership, 2013). Unst comes across as "one of the few remaining places in Scotland which still has a real community spirit. The schools on Unst offer an outstanding level of education, crime is a rarity, leisure facilities are second to none, and people live and work in a safe and clean environment." There is, one could argue, no better place to escape the debilitating rush and stress of modern life (Unst.org, 2013).

Case Study #5: Kökar, Åland Islands, Finland

The Åland archipelago is a home-ruled, demilitarized, and Swedish-speaking jurisdiction located in the northern Baltic Sea, enjoying political autonomy within the state of Finland. It consists of a main island surrounded by various smaller islands, of which around 60 are inhabited. The population is around 27,000, 90 per cent of whom live on the main island and around its capital city, Mariehamn. The remaining 10 per cent are scattered among six municipalities — Brändö, Föglö, Kökar, Kumlinge, Sottunga, and Vårdö — situated in the archipelago region and not connected to the main island by road or bridge; their links with the main island and the world depend on a network of car ferries (Alandstrafiken, 2010). The proportion of archipelago-to-main island dwellers has fallen from 10.8 per cent in 1980 to 7.8 per cent in 2011. But the introduction of regular, all-year-round ferry services (capable of vehicle transportation) in the early 1970s — free of charge to residents of the archipelago — has coincided with a significant "brake" in the rate of population out-migration from the archipelago (ÅSUB, 2012; Baldacchino and Pleijel, 2010).

Kökar (land area: 58 km², 263 inhabitants; municipality) consists of several small islands, is Åland's second smallest municipality by population size, and is the one furthest away from the jurisdictional hub of Mariehamn. Yet, Kökar is doing well by most counts. In-migration is almost as high as out-migration, and births are only just trailing behind deaths. Moreover, only 5 out of the 150 economically active residents are reported as unemployed; people keep busy and earn a living by exploiting the short but hectic tourist, second-home, and pleasure craft season, and by engaging in other activities for the rest of the year. Indeed, there are 254 weekend cottages for about 500 summer residents, so the resident population triples during the busy summer. There are also some 45,000 tourist visitations annually, one fourth of whom come with their own pleasure craft. The Kökar commune is a major year-round, and the largest, employer, providing community work for 23 employees who in turn provide a basic but decent suite of social services: a library with 8,800 volumes, daycare (20 places), school (with six teachers for 31 students from grades 1–9, aged 7 to 15) (Kökar Åland, 2013), senior care, a health care clinic with a full-time nurse, and a physician who visits once a month. Private-sector economic activities include shipping, a bank branch, and the provision of supplies. Most economic activity is locality based. The Kökar commune website (Kökar Åland, 2013) refers to some 30 local, and locally owned, businesses, most of which wholeheartedly practise "portfolio diversification," providing more than one key activity or service. These businesses include: a hotel and restaurant, grocery, supermarket, museum (Kokar Museum, 2013), bicycle rental, kayak rental, room rental, camping ground, tour guides, and an apple orchard with 1,000 trees plus farm shop whose local produce includes cider, salsa and chutney. The "core" (full-time and part-time) economically active population is around 100 persons, with some 40–50 others added on during the peak summer months, taking care of the needs of thousands of hotel guests, guest-house residents, cottage renters, campers, and hikers. The informal economy is strong and vibrant — the locals fish and hunt birds and moose; they practise reciprocity and co-operation; and those employed as seamen/women bring back many useful goods from their working trips. Local people have been able to plug into EU structural funding to co-finance small infrastructural works (like extending a jetty or restaurant). Only short-term and seasonal jobs have been thus created, but this is not surprising, given the very low rate of unemployment. Both residents and business people identify the absence of "training opportunities" on the island as a most serious obstacle to the further advancement of local economic development (Baldacchino and Pleijel, 2010: 104).

The island already hosts an "Artist Residence" facility. This connects readily with its vibrant culture. Apart from five resident landscape-inspired artists (such as Satu Kiljunen), there have been various musicians (old and young), a choir, and rock bands such as Skrå. Almost everybody on Kökar has been reported as "doing music" in some form (Karlsson, 2007). The artist-in-residence facility already welcomes some 20 artists a year; and some 20,000 students have visited the facility over the last decade (Kokar Kultur, 2013). Some urban refugees — such as architects Jens Karmert and Marina Karlman and their two children (Ålandstidningen, 2009) — have been tempted to settle on Kökar, restoring one of its empty old houses.

DISCUSSION: SIX THEMES

Some key themes emerge in this comparative case study that help us to identify what may be important insights into strategies for sustainable development. The themes follow from a close examination of each of the cases discussed, in light of inspiration from the select scholarship reviewed above but also framed by this author's experience and views of sustainable development options for, and by, the periphery.

In such analysis, one must remember that it is certainly difficult to apply the regional development policies of larger and more populated locales to remote and sparsely populated regions. Trying to do so can easily end in frustration. Such an outcome may appear self-evident; nevertheless, it remains a tempting proposition to consider models that have proven themselves elsewhere and apply them religiously, hoping to secure a similar positive effect. Cluster strategies, for example, even though they are predicated on scale economies, have become popular and trendy options in various settings, as seen in the case of North Iceland. But, beyond the fine-sounding rhetoric, a cluster in such cases may often refer loosely to the collaboration and networking of stakeholders (Huijbens et al., 2014).

Here, then, is a review of six interlocking and interdependent policy themes whose significance materializes from the analysis of the previous cases. Together, these themes propose a suite of initiatives that can be taken by state actors, private businesses, and individuals, and at different scales, to craft and maintain a sustainable identity-in-place. None of these themes is new; and none should come as a surprise to the informed reader. Perhaps the novelty here lies mainly in their appearing together as a mutually reinforcing and co-dependent set of measures.

1. *Social capital and social networks* clearly play an important role in terms of people's ability to make a living in remote island regions: for example, often these are the routes by which people find out about, and land, jobs; or find suitable schools for their children; or find out about housing (typically more affordable than in larger urban centres) available for sale or rent. Hence, the critical need to be able to fit into a local community, something that tends to be done well by returning migrants and less so by newcomers with no history of association with the place. These networks and interrelationships facilitate a broad measure of odd jobs, temporary contracts, barter, self-employment, and other forms of informal sector entrepreneurship that can be important for economic survival or for supplementing one's income from other, regular or semi-regular sources. This is all the more critical in seasonal economies where economic activity could be restricted to a few summer months. Different forms of art and culture are themselves components of these small-scale but socially well-integrated enterprising activities. These activities are also democratically run and locally inspired, not dependent on state-driven measures and top-down funding programs.

2. An *institution of higher learning*, such as a university or technical college, can deliver a very strong contribution to local development. The facility provides opportunities to the many local youth for further education or training, preventing early departure to the metropole; its academic staff can support research and development activities in the region; and other practitioners (especially from the private sector) can contribute to the teaching and research effort on campus. Such an institution is typically

also one of the largest local employers and a magnet for luring well-qualified personnel and their families to the region: all the more successfully when spouses are also offered suitable employment. Nowadays, as the Northern Ireland, PEI, and North Iceland examples testify, it is no longer necessary to justify economies of scale in institutions of higher learning: various small island communities operate colleges or universities (including, in the North Atlantic, the Faroe Islands and Greenland), or branch campuses thereof (as in Shetland).

3. A *relatively large private-sector venture* usually becomes a dominant employer quite easily in these small labour markets. (And, effectively, in the absence of a dominant private employer, the state takes over that just-as-dominant role.) Such a venture typically will take over some of the assets remaining from a previous investment, usually moving it in a different commercial direction but still maintaining some connection with the locale's economic history and labour skill set. Service and new processing industries are more likely to emerge as competitive opportunities in lieu of traditional manufacturing activities. A flagship corporate player — as with Samherji in Akureyri or Military Asset Management in Unst — also helps to make a locale visible and better known. Dominant positions within the local economy are risky, however, since they engender high levels of dependency on what could be a quasi-monopoly provider of employment. Local communities are often concerned about this, as demonstrated by the cases of resistance to large-scale development in Chiloé and Prince Edward Island presented in Chapter 7 of this volume, and may wish to exercise some local influence on the venture (for example, via part shareholding or through local state pressure), but this is not always possible. The employer may rise to the occasion by becoming a model local firm, proudly employing local personnel as a policy priority (which also leads to low staff turnover), but such human resource policies may not fly if the company is not, or is no longer, locally controlled. Turmoil can result when and if such an employer decides to relocate or downsize in the inevitable search for profit. Perhaps this is a risk and dependency that small island or remote rural communities need to live with; the alternative is not to have such significant investment at all. While a large private-sector venture can be a boon and a

foundation for a local economy, the importance of small and medium-sized business ventures in these communities also warrants recognition and is highlighted by other chapters in this volume.

4. *Tourism* is no panacea for regional development; it is, however, a clear economic opportunity for remote regions with significant natural and cultural assets. Small-scale, locally owned tourism services — modest accommodation units, restaurants, travel agents, car rentals, property rentals — can provide significant monetary injections, and to a broad local constituency. And members of the extensive locale's diaspora are likely to visit, often and for long periods. But small places are very fragile to a tourism industry driven by profit and growth: remoteness needs to be looked at strategically as a factor that can permit a small-scale yet sustainable tourist operation. So-called local tourism "products" need to be nested comfortably within the existing cultural mesh of the place, rather than superimposed as alien implants.

5. Other increasingly important infrastructural assets for livable peripheral communities in the twenty-first century are *transport and communication technologies*. These include: regular, reliable, safe, and affordable ferry and/or air communications to metropolitan centres, as well as fast broadband speed to connect to the Internet. The former also makes it possible for most potential visitors to experience and participate in the local service economy as tourists. The latter makes distance education and tele-working a possibility (among other things), and thus not obliging resident students or workers to relocate or to spend as much time travelling.

6. While social capital, education, employment, transport, and connectivity are all critical features for livelihood, quality of life and quality of place (concepts elaborated on by Novaczek in Chapter 7 and Fullerton in Chapter 9) extend beyond these. As the examples above and others provided throughout this volume demonstrate, livable communities offer opportunities for creativity, fun, entertainment, relaxation, and other activities, for children, youth, adults, and seniors. *Artistic endeavours* — music, sculpture, drama, painting, singing, ceramics, food preparation, theatre, dance — as well as sport, provide a depth and meaning to life and energize communities, contributing to their lure as attractive places to live. Gardens, swimming

pools, saunas, community halls, churches, family reunions in their different ways bring people together and help them to celebrate, live, and replen-
ish their pride in place.

CONCLUSION

Our understanding of not just the meaning of place but also how we wish
to experience it has changed dramatically, even within one generation. Of
course, as material beings, we still need to be somewhere — "everything
takes place" (Hubbard et al., 2002), even though highly skilled personnel
and those who are considered of "high net worth" could perhaps today be
citizens anywhere. Our engagement with the specific draws in ever wider
contexts and different scapes that are fluid, irregular, and ultra-territorial
(Appadurai, 1996). Modern media and technology, for instance, allow for
an "augmented relationality" (Thrift, 2005: 9) that makes "glocalization"
(Robertson, 1995) not just a distinct possibility but often an expectation,
even for "bare life" (Agamben, 1988). A multitude of both specific, place-
based engagements and across-place mobilities continues to contour the
core rubric of our lives.

Place, of course, remains a problematic resource: peripheral rural and
island communities cannot lift themselves out of their specific geographic
entanglements. But such a materiality is always nuanced by individual and
social constructions of place, built on experiences, impressions, expectations, and relationalities that form, and are in turn formed by, emotional
geographies that can resonate as livable, vibrant communities. This is why
such communities craft and reinforce their self-identities as they seek to
maximize local benefits and characteristics, while strategically enhancing
and expanding connectivities. This spurt is not new, and there is considerable hype surrounding these endeavours: after all, migration has been synonymous with the histories of most island and other remote settlements
(Connell, 2007), and corporate hyperbole seems to suggest that every
grand "place branding" project simply cannot but succeed.

For those working for, in, and with peripheral communities, one key
objective would be to position and align their locales on the life-cycle,
recreational, artistic, or professional trajectories of many who would

consider visiting, but not necessarily stay. These places can serve as ports of call, refuelling stations, "entrepôts" (Warrington and Milne, 2007), and "spaces of flows" (Castells, 1989: 146), offering their "betweenity" to many more than would want, or be able, to settle there (Baldacchino, 2010a: 170). A vibrant cultural mix can be created between residents and visitors of various stripes: tourists, contract employees, itinerant artists, diaspora returnees, second-home residents, incoming entrepreneurs, urban refugees (e.g., Baldacchino, 2010b). There remain significant opportunities for an identity-in-place in an unsettled yet connected world.

ACKNOWLEDGEMENTS

Earlier versions of this paper have been presented at the North Atlantic Forum held in St. John's, NL, Canada (October 2011) and at a conference organized by Island Dynamics in Unst, Shetland, Scotland (April 2012). I am grateful to Michael Clair, Françoise Enguehard, Rob Greenwood, and Adam Grydehøj for logistic and organizational support; to Harry Baglole, Edward H. Huijbens, Bjarne Lindström, Christian Pleijel, Stephen A. Royle, and two anonymous reviewers for critical and constructive comments on earlier drafts; and to Kelly Vodden and Ryan Gibson for editorial commentary. The usual disclaimers apply.

REFERENCES

Aerospace, Prince Edward Island, Canada. 2013. "Aerospace: The Sky Is No Limit." http://www.aerospacepei.com/.

Agamben, G. 1998. *Homo Sacer: Sovereign Power and Bare Life*. Stanford, Calif.: Stanford University Press.

Ålandstidningen. 2009. No. 238, 17 Oct. Mariehamn, Åland.

Appadurai, A. 1996. *Modernity at Large: Cultural Dimensions of Globalization*. Minneapolis: University of Minnesota Press.

ÅSUB. 2012. Invånarantalet 31.12.2011. Mariehamn: Statistics and Research Åland. http://www.asub.ax/files/invanare11.pdf.

Bairner, A. 2006. "Titanic Town: Sport, Space and the Re-imag(in)ing of Belfast." *City and Society* 18, 2: 159–79.

Baldacchino, G. 2006a. "The Brain Rotation and Brain Diffusion Strategies of Small

Islanders: Considering 'Movement' in Lieu of 'Place.'" *Globalisation, Societies and Education* 4, 1: 143–54.

———. 2006b. *Coming To and Settling On Prince Edward Island: Stories and Voices: A Report on a Study of Recent Immigrants to PEI*. Charlottetown: University of Prince Edward Island. http://www.islandstudies.ca/sites/vre2.upei.ca.island-studies.ca/files/u2/Settlers_to_PEI.pdf.

———. 2006c. "Innovative Development Strategies from Non-Sovereign Island Jurisdictions: A Global Review of Economic Policy and Governance Practices." *World Development* 34, 5: 852–67.

———. 2006d. "Managing the Hinterland Beyond: Two, Ideal-Type Strategies of Economic Development for Small Island Territories." *Asia-Pacific Viewpoint* 47, 1: 45–60.

———. 2010a. *Island Enclaves: Offshoring Strategies, Creative Governance, and Sub-national Island Jurisdictions*. Montreal and Kingston: McGill-Queen's University Press.

———. 2010b. "Island Brands and 'the Island' as a Brand: Insights from Immigrant Entrepreneurs on Prince Edward Island." *International Journal of Entrepreneurship and Small Business* 9, 4: 378–93.

———. 2012. "Immigrants, Tourists and Others from Away: 'Come Visit, but Don't Overstay': The Welcoming Society of Prince Edward Island." *International Journal of Culture, Tourism & Hospitality Research* 6, 2: 145–53.

———, R. Greenwood, and L. Felt, eds. 2009. *Remote Control: Governance Lessons for and from Small, Insular, and Remote Regions*. St. John's: ISER Books.

——— and C. Pleijel. 2010. "European Islands, Development and the Cohesion Policy: A Case Study of Kökar, Åland Islands." *Island Studies Journal* 5, 1: 89–110.

Barthon, C. 2007. "Bridge Impacts on Islands off the Coast of France." In G. Baldacchino, ed., *Bridging Islands: The Impact of Fixed Links*, 219–37. Charlottetown, PEI: Acorn Press.

BBC. 2005. "Delay Call over Unst RAF Closure," 28 July. http://news.bbc.co.uk/2/hi/uk_news/scotland/4724889.stm.

———. 2006. "Last Signal for Unst Radar Base," 1 Mar. http://news.bbc.co.uk/2/hi/uk_news/scotland/4760954.stm.

Bevington, P. 2013. "Salmon Jobs safe." *Shetland News*, 1 Oct. http://www.shetnews.co.uk/newsbites/7412-salmon-jobs-safe.

Bjarnason, T., and T. Thorlindsson. 2006. "Should I Stay or Should I Go? Migration Expectations among Youth in Icelandic Fishing and Farming Communities." *Journal of Rural Studies* 22, 3: 290–300.

Carroll, T. 2011. "Economic Sovereignty for Prince Edward Island." *Policy Options* (Dec.): 7–11. http:/archive.irpp.org/po/archive/dec00/carroll.pdf.

Castells, M. 1989. *The Informational City: Information Technology, Economic Restructuring, and the Urban Regional Process*. Oxford: Blackwell.

Connell, J. 2007. "Island Migration." In G. Baldacchino, ed., *A World of Islands: An Island Studies Reader*, 455–82. Charlottetown, PEI and Luqa, Malta: Institute of Island Studies, University of Prince Edward Island and Agenda Academic.

Dahlström, M., A. Aldea-Partanen, K. Fellman, S. Hedin, N. Javakhisvili Larsen, H. Johannesson, J. Manniche, G. Mattland Olsen, and T. Petersen. 2006. *How to Make a Living in Insular Areas: Six Nordic Cases*. Nordregio Report, 1.

The Economist. 2011. "Getting Back to Business," 2 July, 48.

Eythórsson, G.T. 2009. "Municipal Amalgamations in Iceland: Past, Present and Future." In G. Baldacchino, R. Greenwood, and L. Felt, eds., *Remote Control: Governance Lessons for and from Small, Insular, and Remote Regions*, 170–83. St. John's: ISER Books.

Fishupdate.com. 2007. "Shetland: New Mussel Farm for Unst." http://www.fishupdate.com/news/archivestory.php/aid/6331/Shetland:_New_mussel_farm_for_Unst.html.

Freeland, C. 2011. "Immigration Undergoes a Sea Change." *Globe and Mail*, 6 Oct. http://www.theglobeandmail.com/report-on-business/commentary/chrystia-freeland/immigration-undergoes-a-sea-change/article2193717/.

Hagstofa Íslands. 2003. *Landshagir: Statistical Yearbook of Iceland 2003*. Reykjavík, Iceland: Hagstofa Íslands.

Harvey, D. 1990. *The Condition of Postmodernity: An Enquiry into the Origins of Cultural Change*. New York: Wiley-Blackwell.

Holland College, PEI. 2013. "Programs." http://www.hollandcollege.com/programs/#app.

Hooghe, L., and G. Marks. 2001. *Multi-Level Governance and European Integration*. Lanham, Md.: Rowman & Littlefield.

Hubbard, P., R. Kitchin, R. Bartley, and D. Fuller. 2002. *Thinking Geographically: Space, Theory and Contemporary Human Geography*. New York: Continuum.

Huijbens, E., H. Johannesson, and G.T. Johannesson. 2014. "Clusters without Content? Icelandic National and Regional Tourism Policy." *Scandinavian Journal of Public Administration* 18, 1: 63–85.

Icelandic Times. 2010. "A Piece of Everything in Akureyri." Issue No. 2. http://www.icelandictimes.com/section.php?id=1554&id_art=1558.

Innovation PEI. 2013."Aerospace." http://www.innovationpei.com/aerospace.

Jackson, B.G. 1996. "Re-engineering the Sense of Self: The Manager and the Management Guru." *Journal of Management Studies* 33, 5: 571–90.

Jóhannesson, H. 2006. "Vaxtarsamningur Eyjafjarðar." University of Akureyri Research Institute. http://www.klasar.is/index.php?pid=92&cid=50.

Jordan, A., R.K. Wurzel, and A. Zito. 2005. "The Rise of 'New' Policy Instruments in Comparative Perspective: Has Governance Eclipsed Government?" *Political Studies* 53, 3: 477–96.

Karlsson, M. 2007. "Vad behövs i musiklivet?" [What is needed in the music scene?]. Åbo Akademi, Finland. http://web.abo.fi/meddelanden/forskning/2007_13_musik.sht.

Khamis, S. 2010. "An Image Worth Bottling: The Branding of King Island Cloud Juice." *International Journal of Entrepreneurship and Small Business* 9, 4: 434–46.

Kökar Åland. 2013. "Kökar Is Different." http://www.kokar.aland.fi/en/startsidatur/turism-eng.

Kökar Kultur. 2013. "Artist Residences in the Finnish Archipelago." http://www.kokarkultur.com/.

Kokar Museum. 2013. "Rundtur i muséet." http://www.kokar.ax/en/startsidatur/turism-eng/attractions/the-local-folklore-museum.

Marshall, J. 2008. *Tides of Change on Grand Manan Island: Culture and Belonging in a Fishing Community.* Montreal and Kingston: McGill-Queen's University Press.

Murphy, S.J. 2011. "Rural Planning and Community Development in Prince Edward Island." Master of Urban and Rural Planning thesis, Dalhousie University.

Murtagh, B. 2010. "Desegregation and Place Restructuring in the New Belfast." *Urban Studies* 48, 6: 1119–35.

Neill, W.J.V. 2010. "Belfast: Rebranding the 'Renaissance City' from 'The Troubles' to Titanic Quarter*." In J. Punter, ed., *Urban Design and the British Urban Renaissance*, 305–21. New York: Routledge.

Palan, R. 2003. *The Offshore World: Sovereign Markets, Virtual Places, and Nomad Millionaires.* Ithaca, NY: Cornell University Press.

Peters, J.D. 1998. "Nomadism, Diaspora, Exile: The Stakes of Mobility within the Western Canon." In H. Naficy, ed., *Home, Exile, Homeland: Film, Media, and the Politics of Place*, 17-41. London: Routledge.

Porter, M. 1998. "Clusters and the New Economics of Competition." *Harvard Business Review* 76, 6: 77–90.

Pounder, P. 2010. "Branding: A Caribbean Perspective on Rum Manufacturing

Competitiveness." *International Journal of Entrepreneurship and Small Business* 9, 4: 394–406.

Punnett, B.J., and A. Morrison. 2006. "Niche Markets and Small Caribbean Producers: A Match Made in Heaven?" *Journal of Small Business & Entrepreneurship* 19, 4: 341–53.

Pure Energy Centre. n.d. "Pure Energy Centre: Experts in Renewables." http://www.pureenergycentre.com/pureenergycentre/Index.php.

Robertson, R. 1995. "Glocalization: Time-Space and Homogeneity-Heterogeneity." In M. Featherstone, S. Lash, and R. Robertson, eds., *Global Modernities*, 25–44. London: Sage.

Royle, S.A. 2007. "Islands off the Irish Coast and the 'Bridging Effect.'" In G. Baldacchino, ed., *Bridging Islands: The Impact of Fixed Links*, 203–18. Charlottetown, PEI: Acorn Press.

Samherji. 2004. Ársskýrsla 2003. Aðalfundur, 29 Apr. Akureyri, Samherji.

Samherji HF. 2013. "The Company." http://www.samherji.is/en/the-company.

Saxa Vord. n.d. "Shetland Holidays at Saxa Vord Resort, Unst." http://www.saxavord.com/.

Scheyvens, R., and M. Russell. 2012. "Tourism and Poverty Alleviation in Fiji: Comparing the Impacts of Small-and Large-Scale Tourism Enterprises." *Journal of Sustainable Tourism* 20, 3: 417–36.

Shetland Times. 2011. "One of Last Few Locally-owned Salmon Farms Sold to Norwegian Operator," 26 Apr. http://www.shetlandtimes.co.uk/2011/04/26/two-locally-owned-salmon-farms-sold-to-norwegian-operator.

Sigursteinsdóttir, H. 2008. "Akureyri's Regional Growth Agreement." In H.W. Tanvig, ed., *Innovation Systems and Rural Development*, 30–42. Proceedings from 10th annual conference, Nordic-Scottish University for Rural and Regional Development. Forest & Landscape Working Papers No. 27, University of Copenhagen, Faculty of Life Sciences.

Slemon Park Corporation. n.d. "Slemon Park: A Great Place to Work, to Live and to Learn." http://www.slemonpark.com/.

Smith, V.L. 1998. "Privatization in the Third World: Small-Scale Tourism Enterprises." In W.F. Theobald, ed., *Global Tourism*, 2nd ed., 205–15. London: Butterworth Heinemann.

Spencies Tunes. 2013. "Commission Shetland Fiddle Music: A Unique Timeless Gift." http://www.spenciestunes.com/.

Statistics Iceland. 2013. "Population Statistics." http://www.statice.is/Statistics/Population.

Thrift, N. 2005. "From Born to Made: Technology, Biology and Space." *Transactions of the Institute of British Geographers* 30, 4: 463–76.

Unst.org. 2013. "Relocate." http://unst.org/web/relocate/.

Unst Partnership. 2010. *Unst Partnership Plan Consultation*. Summary Report. http://unst.org/web/unstpartnership/files/2011/01/Ideas-Day-Report-22.10.10.pdf.

———. 2013. "Aims." http://unst.org/web/unstpartnership/aims/.

Valhalla Brewery. n.d. "Valhalla Brewery: Almighty Ales from Britain's Most Northerly Island." http://www.valhallabrewery.co.uk/web.

Visit Akureyri. 2013. "Arts Alley." http://www.visitakureyri.is/en/things-to-do/culture/arts-alley.

Warrington, E., and D. Milne. 2007. "Island Governance. In G. Baldacchino, ed., *A World of Islands: An Island Studies Reader*, 327–428. Charlottetown, PEI and Luqa, Malta: Institute of Island Studies, University of Prince Edward Island and Agenda Academic.

Zhang, J.J. 2010. "Brand(ing) Kinmen: A Tourism Perspective." *International Journal of Entrepreneurship and Small Business* 9, 4: 407–33.

CHAPTER 4

Newcomers at the Gates: Place and Space in Small Island Context

Bojan Fürst

> *An island, if it is big enough, is no better than a continent. It has*
> *to be really quite small, before it feels like an island.*
> D.H. Lawrence (1961 [1926]: 722)

A COWBOY ON FOGO ISLAND

On a perfect October day on Fogo Island, drizzly, windy, and with the kind of cold that sticks to your bones, I met a cowboy. Not a strapping, Hollywood version of a cowboy embodied by Clint Eastwood or captured on William Albert Allard's Kodachromes: banish the thought. This cowboy was a large, portly, and loud middle-aged Alberta gentleman, a cattle ranger — as he described himself — with a passion for keeping his government accountable, which is why he was on Fogo Island in the first place. He wanted to check where exactly his hard-earned tax dollars are ending up and assuage at least some of his misgivings about the whole equalization payments scheme (whereby fiscal disparities among the Canadian provinces are to some degree minimized).

Our Alberta cowboy, travelling across the island of Newfoundland and making a stop at the picturesque fishing town of Tilting on Fogo Island, had a sinking feeling that the federal transfer payments worked rather too well; the Newfoundland fishers he met had decent housing, good roads, worked only during the fishing season, and in general seemed laid back and happy in ways an Alberta cattle ranger couldn't afford to be. The whole thing vexed him.

It is hard to blame him for feeling perplexed. He found himself in a place different from anything he would find familiar. He may have just as well travelled to another planet. The fact that he never left his own country 'only added to his sense of confusion.

And even though his appearance in Tilting was a stroke of luck for the author of this narrative (this introduction pretty much wrote itself), our cowboy was by no means an isolated case of a lost fellow Canadian on Fogo Island shores and desperately in need of an interpreter.

But why would that be so? What is so special about small islands? Why would anyone take the trouble to travel long distances only to find oneself in strange and incomprehensible places? And who are these islanders whose laid-back lifestyle is so easy to envy? What happens to the islands themselves when those not of the islands decide to make them their own?

This chapter looks at interactions between newcomers and permanent residents in small island contexts on Change Islands and Fogo Island in Newfoundland, Canada, and Vis and Biševo islands, Croatia. Implications of these interactions for island identities and development are explored, including the leisuring or commodification of landscapes that often occurs as newcomers find themselves on small islands in search of the remote and authentic. The findings presented here are a part of a larger study looking at the perceptions and policies towards small islands as peripheral places (Fürst, 2014). The data for the study were collected through a series of 43 semi-structured interviews as well as informal conversations with island residents, policy-makers, and scholars with expertise in each of the study areas, along with secondary and primary sources analysis and photography-aided observation. The larger study and this chapter employ island studies as a theoretical framework, elaborated on below. This approach allowed for an intriguing interplay between theoretical discussions and islanders' own perceptions of islandness and island life as it is lived.

ILL-DEFINED ISLES

Smallness is a state of mind.

Epeli Hau'ofa (1993: 7)

It seems rather obvious. In a memorable anecdote from his travels to the Aran Islands, Tim Robinson tells us about his first island day: "On the day of our arrival we met an old man who explained the basic geography: 'The ocean,' he told us, 'goes all around the island'" (Robinson, 2012).

Add an adjective such as "small" to a word "island" and things become more complicated.

There is what appears to be an easy way out. Depraetere (1991: 1) defines islands as "pieces of land permanently surrounded by water with a land area of at least 0.1 km²." That helps us in deciding how small an island should be for it to still be an island; but it doesn't help us in defining how small an island needs to be for it to be a small island.

As with the terms "place" and "periphery" discussed in Chapters 1 and 2, we are confronted with a plethora of definitions of islands and, in particular, small islands (Hache, 1998); virtually all those coming from governmental and international agencies and governing bodies focus on easily measurable aspects of islands such as area, population, or distance from mainland while taking into account political and economic aspects of islandness as seen from a mainland perspective. All of those definitions are quite remarkably unhelpful if one is trying to actually define what a small island is. For that, I suspect, a better place to start is the quotation from D.H. Lawrence at the beginning of this chapter, because it seems that how one feels about islands matters more than an island's land area or its distance from a mainland shore.

The sense of edge, of "geographical precision" (Baldacchino, 2005: 35), or of "obstinate separateness" (Edmond and Smith, 2003: 4), has been a defining feature of what constitutes an island. However, when one starts talking to the islanders, that sense of islandness, of separateness and edge, emerges as being more complicated. Hache (1998: 48) points out that "the human notion of what is insular, and what is not, is a flexible one, in space as well as in time." Croatian geographer Vera Graovac (2004: 185), coming from a country where islands are so revered that they are enshrined in the national constitution as places of special importance to the state, writes that islandness is "in essence a complex idea. . . . It is as much a state of mind as it is an objective reality."

We pay homage to Lawrence, keeping in mind the insistence that island studies should be about "[t]he study of islands on their own terms" (Baldacchino, 2006: 7) and the notion that insularity could be defined as "the assertion of islanders of their island condition" (Hache, 1998: 51). So, I would like to propose a definition of small islands that allows us to step away from a purely geopolitical definition of water-bounded entities and enter a realm of ideas: *any island inhabited by people who feel they live on a small island is a small island.*

Such a looser, more subjective definition allows us to ask all sorts of questions that don't require geographic and statistical precision, but take advantage of ambiguity and explore complex relationships entered into by those who choose to inhabit a small island for at least some time. While looking for answers to those questions, I enlist the help of people who have a strong attachment to the Change Islands and Fogo Island off the northeastern coast of Newfoundland in Canada, as well as the islands of Vis and Biševo in Croatia, Europe. Over the past three years, through more than 40 formal interviews and countless informal conversations, I feel that I am starting to get a sense of the relationships between the newcomers and those who consider themselves islanders.

WHAT IS SO SPECIAL ABOUT SMALL ISLANDS ANYWAY?

> *It is quiet. It's very peaceful. And everybody knows everybody.*
> *Except [winking at me] some of them strange fellows that are*
> *coming now [laughter].*
>
> Fisher on Change Islands, Newfoundland

In a world chronically suffering from increased uniformity, islands, especially those smaller and remote, are rapidly acquiring the status of the last authentic places. Architect Norberg-Schulz (1979: 5) writes that "the spaces where life occurs are places. . . . A place is a space which has a distinct character. Since ancient times, the genius loci, or 'spirit of place,' has been recognized as the concrete reality a man [*sic*] has to face in his daily life."

However, what we face in our daily life has changed quite dramatically over the last three decades. Robinson (2012), writing about the Aran Islands off the coast of Ireland, calls that change "the material destructiveness of modern life." A little less dramatic is Massey (1999: 146), who adopts Harvey's terminology when she calls that change, which is in many ways rooted in current rapid advancement of communication technologies and distributive production processes, "time-space compression" (Harvey, 1990: 261). Massey asks the obvious question: "How, in the face of all this movement and intermixing, can we retain any sense of a local place and its particularity?" (Massey, 1999: 146). As noted by Vodden et al. (Chapter 1), Massey warns against simplification of the causes of time-space compression because "different social groups, and different individuals, are placed in very distinct ways in relation to these flows and interconnections" (Massey, 1999: 146).

It is also worth keeping in mind that viable, healthy places change all the time. As Harvey points out, "[s]ocieties change and grow, they are transformed from within and adapt to pressures and influences from without. Objective but socially given conceptions of space and time must change to accommodate new material practices of social reproduction, new ways of assigning value" (Harvey, 1996: 222).

While that may very well be so, both the increased mobility and the search for authentic places are often a privilege of those who can afford it. "[S]ome people move more than others, and . . . some have more control than others. It is that the mobility and control of some groups can actively weaken other people. . . . The time-space compression of some groups can undermine the power of others" (Massey, 1999: 150).

If we agree with Coppes (2008: 25) that "a place is . . . a qualitative, total phenomenon, which we cannot reduce to any of its parts or properties without losing its concrete character," it comes as no surprise that in a world that "institutionalize[s] placelessness" (Ghenoiu, 2008: 91) islands and island experiences are becoming the rarest of all things — seemingly naturally well-defined authentic places suddenly within reach of those who can afford to visit places remote and on the margins of global flows of people, capital, and cultures. But that, too, is a recent phenomenon.

Gillis (2001: 39) reminds us that the desirability of remoteness is quite recent. "Not so very long ago," he writes, "remoteness, like backwardness, was something to be overcome. . . . The scarcity of remoteness has driven up its value and encouraged a kind of cultural counterfeiting" that takes various forms. Gillis notes repeatedly that remoteness today has both a spatial and temporal quality. "We tend to think of isolated villages and island communities as old regardless of their age," he continues. "In our mobile society, it is connection to the past rather than to the place that is most sought after" (Gillis, 2001: 40).

That search for the remote and authentic often leads to a romancing and commercialization of place that suddenly needs to be protected and "saved" for those urbanites looking for a mythical place of rest and a life in the slow lane (Coppes, 2008: 28). It is not surprising that, with their precise geographic boundaries, a perceived and real sense of place and community, and the promise of a romanticized timelessness, small islands are increasingly becoming destinations of choice for those craving remoteness. "Boundedness makes islands graspable, able to be held in the mind's eye and imagined as places of possibility and promise" (Edmond and Smith, 2003: 2).

More often than not, those who seek the promise of islandness have significant disposable income to play with and, as a rule, are more interested in a romanticized idea of island living than the actual reality of lived island existence. As Lawrence (1961 [1926]: 725) ironically points out: "[w]e begin all our attempts to regain Paradise by spending money." The results are rather predictable.

A growing number of people can afford to travel to, or buy property in, remote and rural places without a need, interest, or ability to live an actual island life. And so, the island landscapes, among the most desirable of all landscapes, are undergoing a process of "leisuring" (Bunce, 2008) and commodification. That process requires that a version of islandness be preserved for the enjoyment of those whose lives do not depend on the island. As a native of Vis Island in Croatia succinctly put it: "To us, this is a place we live in. To others, it is a place for a vacation and the two are not always compatible."

Gillis (2001) and Bunce (2008) insist that the "leisuring" and commodification of previously productive island landscapes are direct results of global and urban forces outside of islanders' control. Hay (2006: 30), writing about island metaphors, goes further and says that the representation and exploitation of the island locale "without genuinely engaging with it should be revealed as the persistence of a colonial cast of mind . . . islanders [are] entitled to view all promotions of metaphorical senses of islands as acts of post-colonial appropriation. . . . Island metaphors . . . render irrelevant the realness of island lives . . . they are continental as well as colonial, constructions." But they are powerful and profitable constructions deliberately and effectively used to attract those seeking remoteness and authenticity on the shores of small islands, often nurtured by island-based tourism agencies themselves. Cresswell (2004) and others similarly point out that the image of authentic places is often produced for consumption, at the exclusion of some who may not be seen or see themselves within this image. While arguably increasingly common, this view of authenticity lies in stark contrast to the authenticity described by Relph (1976) as sincere and reflective of an awareness of and sense of responsibility to a place.

Finding examples of manufactured authenticity and "cultural counterfeiting" is not difficult. The Croatian government and Newfoundland and Labrador provincial government both employ the practice of creating temporal and spatial remoteness as a marketing ploy. The Croatian National Tourism Board has opted for a temporal remoteness slogan in a recent promotional campaign (CNTB, 2011). The viewer sees a screen filled with a hand holding and then removing a series of photographs of stunningly beautiful island landscapes revealing the natural scene that looks exactly like a photograph. All of this is accompanied with a generic "Mediterranean" music, which is just about as authentic as the famed "Mediterranean" diet. The voice-over at the end declares Croatia "a Mediterranean as it once was." There is not a trace of either the contemporary world or of local inhabitants in the entire advertisement.

Newfoundland and Labrador's Department of Tourism, Culture and

Recreation decided that distancing Newfoundland from the rest of North America is the winning strategy (NLDTCR, 2010). After 45 seconds of happy Newfoundland faces, postcard-perfect landscapes, enchanted children, wooden boats, colourful houses, and laundry on the line, the remoteness and distance from the modern world is explicitly emphasized: "Where is this place exactly?" asks the voice-over. "As far from Disneyland as you can possibly get."

Does "cultural counterfeiting" work? Some would find it hard to argue that it does not, given the growing number of visitors to places remote and islanded. In Croatia, over 56 million overnight stays in 2010 and year-over-year growth of virtually every tourism indicator the government bothers to track can be attributed, at least partially, to successful marketing campaigns (Republika Hrvatska, Ministarstvo turizma, 2011). Newfoundland and Labrador has similarly recorded an increased number of visitors, especially those who arrived on the island by air (Tourism Research Division, NL Department of Tourism, 2012).

Who are these people making their presence felt on islands around the world, enticed by sleek marketing campaigns and making personal pilgrimages in search of the remote, authentic, and islanded?

NEWCOMERS AND ISLANDERS

> *When you have lived in a certain way for generations, it is hard to think outside of the box. The influence of us coming seems to be helping. Not that we are getting Christmas cards or anything.*
> A newcomer and permanent resident in Canada

In his study of interactions between various island inhabitants on Lake Superior's Madeline Island in Wisconsin, USA, Gibbons distinguished between three types of islanders: long-, medium-, and short-term islanders. He arrived at that particular division assuming that "[o]ne strove to be a real islander, and the best way to illustrate that authenticity was through a display of commitment to the island identity, often through the amount of time one spent on the island, and whether one made one's living on the island" (Gibbons, 2010: 171–72).

This is problematic. The amount of time spent on an island does not necessarily make one an islander. Massey argues that a long history of a place and our presence in place is not what matters on its own but rather, she says, the place "is constructed out of a particular constellation of social relations, meeting and weaving together at a particular locus" (Massey, 1999: 154).

As discussed by Daniels et al. in Chapter 2, Buttimer (1976: 277) draws an important distinction between being physically present in a place and actually living in a place:

> To dwell implies more than to inhabit, to cultivate, or to organize space. It means to live in a manner which is attuned to the rhythms of nature, to see one's life as anchored in human history and directed toward a future, to build a home which is the everyday symbol of a dia- logue with one's ecological and social milieu.

That kind of a careful, layered identity is difficult to build and it eventually creates a different kind of knowledge that Pocius (2000: 7) calls "experiential series of familiar places . . . a series of emotionally based meaningful spaces."

Identity, in this case, is truly relational: newcomers cannot bestow the status of "islanders" on themselves. This can only happen if newcomers are accepted as a part of the common layered history. There is an art to living on an island and it is a complicated one to master. Stratford (2008: 160) wisely points out that "islandness is a complex expression of identity." Péron (2004: 330) argues that "islandness engenders closeness, solidarity, scrutiny, and capacity to accommodate and be tactful." She continues: "[there is] a real art de vivre, sharing an ethos that is both private and com- munal. . . . Island communities are also characterized by subtle internal divisions between inhabitants." To navigate such a layered and complex set of social networks and, as Baldacchino suggests in Chapter 3, to "fit in" within them, is a daunting task that requires a high level of tolerance and acceptance of others as they are. It is possibly D.H. Lawrence who best ar- ticulated, if somewhat jadedly, that island way of being, in his short story "The Man Who Loved Islands":

It is doubtful whether any of them really liked him, man
to man, or even woman to man. But then it is doubtful if
he really liked any of them, as a man to man, or man to
woman. He wanted them to be happy, and the little
world to be perfect. But anyone who wants the world to
be perfect must be careful not to have real likes or dis-
likes. A general goodwill is all you can afford. (Lawrence,
1961 [1926]: 727)

Gibbons's classification of island residents into three categories comes
across as a bit too neat, too cleanly cut for what is essentially a messy set of
social relations layered over time. Gibbons, however, offers another classification that emerged earlier in his study among the islanders themselves
— one that that divides "islanders" into locals, summer people, and tourists
— though he promptly dismisses it as "colloquial taxonomy" (Gibbons,
2010: 172). This may indeed be an example of populist wisdom devoid of
nuances, but it actually works reasonably well and it closely reflects the
opinions of the islanders interviewed for this study. They distinguish between three broad categories of newcomers arriving on their shores.

Before examining those three categories more closely, a word of caution: one needs to avoid the trap of simplifying an island's socio-historical
dynamics and the islanders–newcomers interactions to the point of carica-
ture. Péron (2004: 338) reminds us that "[a]n island is the home of a living
and mobile society"; and Massey (2007: 2) points out the obvious yet often
overlooked fact that "[v]isiting is a practice of engagement, an encounter
with others." So, keeping in mind that we are using a broad brush to paint
a complex scene, let us look at those three groups of island newcomers.

Visitors are transient newcomers who stay for a relatively short time
and may or may not return. They don't own any property on the island and,
as individuals, they have little impact on islanders' everyday lives. The cowboy from the beginning of this chapter is a visitor. In small numbers, the
visitors are relatively easy to deal with even when obnoxious. Often, they
are a source of amusement for the locals. Academic researchers, graduate
students, journalists, and visiting dignitaries could also be classified as visitors, albeit with potentially more significant impact on some aspects of

islanders' lives. Collectively, these visitors can have an enormous impact on the economy, the environment, and socio-cultural life through the development of mass and seasonal tourism (McElroy, 2003). Not least of those impacts is an eventual resignation among some islanders who decide "to play the tourist game of being custodians of 'another world', conforming to the image of being the last survivors of a bygone civilization. For this purpose, they have to keep alive a past that they would have happily consigned to oblivion, were it not so profitable to play the custodian role which they have been allocated" (Péron, 2004: 336)

The second category of newcomers is *seasonal residents*. They usually own property on the island. They could be former islanders looking for a connection to "home," but seasonal residents often have no previous connection to the island they choose for their summer home. Their livelihoods are almost never in any way connected to the islands and their island homes are purely summer residences. This is how one of the seasonal residents describes the time he spends on an island:

> When I am here, I do a lot of kayaking, a lot of hiking. I have dogs and I take them out on trails for walks. I like to go out fishing when the fishing season is opened if I can get some of the locals to take me out in a boat. I do lots of photography and just sit on my deck, read and look at the scenery.

Seasonal residents can have a significant impact on the island. "Newcomers to remote areas are often the ones to resurrect the old crafts and folk art long after the locals have abandoned them" (Gillis, 2001: 48). They can also demand and be more effective at obtaining services for the island that sometimes can have long-term benefits for the permanent residents if such demands result in new and improved roads, ferry terminals, ferry services, or broadband Internet access. At their worst, seasonal residents can become "sophisticated rusticators [who are] indulging in a fantasy of returning to the simple life in the bosom of nature" (Gillis, 2001: 45). "Islandness moves people to value the special qualities of islands and protect them, often in response to globalization and modernization" (Stratford, 2008:

171). In their attempt to preserve those island qualities they see as authentic, seasonal residents can hinder local initiatives and antagonize islanders whose lives depend on a productive relationship with the land and sea surrounding them.

Somewhat paradoxically, seasonal residents often see themselves as an essential instrument of progress as well as stewards of heritage and environmental preservation on small islands. In the words of one seasonal resident:

> When you are an island community, you sometimes, I don't want to say develop tunnel vision, but there is a perception of things from the island point of view and sometimes it's not really inquiring . . . you know . . . I think seasonal people bring different things here that people haven't normally experienced. They are interested to see them and sometime may even adopt them. Kayaking is an example. People are fascinated when I go out . . . and it's rough. They always comment: "Looks interesting, but you'll never catch me in one of those things." They are interested in seeing it done, but are reluctant to adopt it.

While the example above may be simplistic, there are situations where "tunnel vision" may indeed cause stagnation: "an identity too closely linked to a dominant activity seems to provide a degree of sense of place and identity, but tends to reinforce the strong bonds of exclusionary social networks that restrict creativity and visionary agenda" (Dale et al., 2008: 278).

The third type of newcomers is the one least often encountered, but they often have significant impact on islands. These are the "come from aways," those who chose to permanently live on an island. They are often retired and reasonably well off. They also tend to take a very strong interest in island affairs and become involved with various community groups and organizations in order to demonstrate their commitment to the island, but also to improve their own social lives.

Newcomers who settle on islands as *permanent residents* can indeed be valuable assets to their new communities. They often bring specific skill sets, such as understanding of government or business environments, project proposal writing and management, and the willingness to employ those skills on behalf of their community. They are willing to run in municipal elections and represent island interests on the mainland. Often, newcomers who settle on an island as permanent residents have a previous connection to the island, but have been away for most of their adult lives. Sometimes, they have no previous connection to the island at all, which makes their integration into the social networks of island life very difficult, despite their formal involvement with the community. That can lead to newcomers feeling unappreciated and undervalued. Once the natural beauty and the charm of life on a remote island wears off, the reality of island life sets in. One newcomer and a permanent island resident had this to say:

> It is very, very difficult to intellectually live here. It is hard to have friends who can relate to your life experiences because their life experiences have been focused on the fishery and putting food on the table. . . . It is a completely different way of looking at the world. I am sounding elitist and I don't mean to be that way. It is a very insulated community.

Some newcomers who decided to become permanent island residents also indicated that summer is a particularly difficult time, for this is when they feel that their commitment to the island is put to the test. They sometimes feel that they have to make a difficult choice of minimizing the contact with the visitors and seasonal residents, who do share their life experiences, in order to demonstrate their commitment to the island.

Péron (2004: 330) warns that "[b]eing forever attentive to the fine-tuning of personal relationships is a requirement for those who wish to survive as members of a small island community." So it should come as no surprise that even when they achieve certain levels of familiarity, intimacy, and community acceptance, newcomers permanently residing on islands still report confusion and alienation after experiencing social undercurrents they have no knowledge of, even after years of living on the island. One permanent newcomer described arriving home after attending a celebration

at a house of a local island friend and "dissecting" the evening with a partner: "You ask yourself: 'What was all that about?'" The question might be
legitimate, but it betrays the lack of understanding of those subtle divisions
that exist within the community and that, because of their tacit nature, are
difficult to learn.

So, if we divide newcomers into visitors, seasonal residents and permanent residents, what about locals? How do they fit into island dynamics?

Hay (2006) offers us a definition of place as a bounded geographical
entity with an investment of human attachment, loyalty, and meaning. After
all, "places acquire much of their permanence as well as much of their distinctive character from the collective activities of people who dwell there,
who shape the land through their activities, and who build institutions and
social relationships within a bounded domain" (Harvey, 1996: 310).

Local residents are the self-proclaimed custodians of their islandness.
It is only with the layers of their collective actions and memories that
islands acquire the particular set of characteristics and the aura of authenticity that newcomers wish to partake in. There is a harsh unpredictability
in island life. A fisher on Change Islands muses:

> You've got to be a certain kind of person to put up with
> being too uncertain. We always live on the edge. Always
> live on an edge, wondering. You always hang by a tread
> all the time, eh. And that's what you've got to continue
> doing.

It can be a hard pill to swallow for newcomers, especially those who invest
time, capital, and goodwill, to know that the agency of bestowing the title
of an islander rests exclusively with the islanders themselves. That is, perhaps, as it should be. Becoming a part of a shared story is not an easily
accomplished task. Ghenoiu (2008: 93) writes that "[t]he idea of place . . . is
a culturally contingent organization of meanings and associations meant
to establish a seemingly durable, coherent human habitat." To be able to
understand and correctly interpret that web of meanings and associations
requires genuine commitment. "A place has to be sensible and legible to its
occupants," he continues, "but it also has to resonate more deeply with

their conceptions of themselves and of their world" (Ghenoiu, 2008: 93). Newcomers may indeed struggle to find that resonance between their island worlds and those they left behind.

On the other hand, the locals can hardly ignore the influx of newcomers. The encounters can be invigorating. Both the locals and newcomers I spoke to easily recalled stories of sharing of ideas and opportunities to see the world through someone else's eyes. A fisher on Change Islands talked about watching newcomers restoring and painting old fishing stages and stores bright, ochre red and realizing that these precariously perched wooden sheds on stilts used for storing fishing gear are actually quite pretty. He restored his own stage as a result and he is not the only one. In fact, the whole community is now dotted with red, freshly painted stages and stores — so much so, that one local resident of neighbouring Fogo Island, with a mix of envy, sarcasm, and bemusement, referred in an interview to Change Islands as "gingerbread island." There are similar stories on Vis Island, Croatia, where a local resident reflecting on a recent renovation of an old, abandoned stone home said: "You know, they [newcomers] do come here because it is so beautiful, but we just take it for granted." That particular sentiment can be observed in virtually any environment. As van Nes (2008: 115) points out, "the more normal our living environment looks, the more it is taken for granted. It is only when something disturbing or uncommon changes occur that people first tend to react to it."

The interactions are not always positive or synergistic. There are continuous tensions in the relationships between locals and newcomers, possibly the result of cultural misunderstandings and social faux-pas, but also an outcome of bold landscape interventions, such as: rising property values that become unaffordable to people whose families have lived on the islands for generations; increased cost of living; heightened demand on often inadequate ferry services. Locals harbour suspicions about newcomers whose behaviour may seem secretive or baffling; and the other way round. This is a sentiment expressed both in Croatia and in Newfoundland, especially among younger local residents. While I haven't encountered hostility towards newcomers in any of the islands I visited, the caution and reluctance to engage with each other are definitely present. A local Change

Islands resident articulated that sentiment as a question: "Why are they here? Some of them, they are okay, but others? What is their agenda? We don't know that." When one considers that islanders are more accustomed to watching people leave their shores rather than arrive with the mind to permanently settle there, that is a fair question. What are these newcomers looking for?

Péron (2004: 334) offers at least a partial explanation: "Against the background of rapidly increasing personal mobility and globalization of the world economy," she writes, "the island can be considered to be the quintessential physical place." Or at least, an island can be perceived as such, and quite a few newcomers express what Norberg-Schulz (1971: 9) described as "a need to grasp vital relations in . . . environment, to bring meaning and order into a world of events and actions."

And while, for some, island experiences are a sort of pilgrimage to an imaginary world far removed from the every day, others are driven by curiosity and a sense of adventure. Some, like our cowboy or a land speculator who was recently seen driving around Fogo Island, do indeed have ulterior motives for visiting. Others come to the islands with a sense of purpose. Gillis (2001: 43) argues that "[i]n this century, islands have become, for better or worse, the prime location of remoteness, a reflection of global economic, political, and cultural processes that often seem beyond their control. They have become satellites of the continents." The satellites are now within reach of those privileged enough to be able to access a place geographically remote.

The issues of rising property taxes and real estate prices, pressures on municipal infrastructure, and speculative land purchases are forcing local island governments to seek stricter controls and exercise greater vigilance when it comes to land purchases for seasonal residences or for pure speculation. On Croatian islands in particular, inappropriate and often illegal construction of residential structures has been a problem for decades. Losses of agricultural land and fishing grounds to tourism infrastructure — marinas, golf courses, large hotels, resort complexes — are also seen as issues that are rapidly changing the physical appearance of some small islands. As geographer Michael Bunce (2008) points out, this kind of "leisuring" of rural and coastal landscapes is happening around the world. Small islands just happen to be among the most desirable of those landscapes with the added mystique of remoteness.

CHANGING ISLAND LANDSCAPE

> *But it was the islanders' world, not yours.*
>
> D.H. Lawrence (1961 [1926]: 726)

The leisuring or commodification of landscape is easy to observe, even though it can take on radically different forms. On Change Islands, it was a benign exercise that required a bit of lumber and red paint, and it was readily accepted by the locals whose own stages and stores might have been, once upon a time, an ochre shade of red. The landscape of Fogo Island is going through radical transformation with the construction of an exclusive inn and a set of artist studios. Newcomers, often foreign nationals, on Vis Island in Croatia are buying 800-year-old stone houses — if the owners can be tracked down — and turning them into rental properties or seasonal residences. What all these highly visible interventions in island landscapes have in common is that they are changing the countryside to "a place for living, not for making a living" (Lowenthal, 1997: 183). That shift from a productive to leisure landscape is enormously important.

Maybe nowhere is that shift more obvious than on Fogo Island, where artist studios and, for island context, a very large and upscale inn above the community of Joe Batt's Arm are changing the landscape the islanders built and cultivated over the past 400 years. Such bold landscape interventions are not necessarily evil in and of themselves. In fact, architecture has been used before to revitalize communities and provide a new vision and new direction that often signified a clear break with the past: the Eiffel Tower in Paris, the Opera House in Sydney, and the Guggenheim Museum in Bilbao come to mind as examples, but also the provincial art gallery, museum and archives building, The Rooms, in St. John's, Newfoundland, which dramatically altered the city skyline and was, in fact, designed as a visual and symbolic competitor to the Basilica (Latta, 2005: 29).

Is the Fogo Island project, initiated by a former islander who returned to the island with significant resources, going to accomplish the same for an island of some 2,500 permanent residents? That remains to be seen. The project aims to bring to the island a top-paying, select group of guests looking for an "authentic experience" and an opportunity to learn from the islanders and resident artists about a life completely foreign to their own. But, beyond that, it also seeks to build on the local sense of connectedness to the wider world and continue, rather than preserve, vibrant cultural expressions found on Fogo Island. It is attempting to ensure that the island creates what Massey (1999: 154) calls an extroverted sense of place "which includes a consciousness of its links with the wider world, which integrates in a positive way the global and the local." While reviewing interviews with residents of Fogo and Change Islands, it is easy to detect a healthy amount of skepticism at the beginning of the project and a slow change towards approaching something of a buy-in on the part of the community. There is certainly a lot of excitement.

That project will bring with its success (or failure, for that matter) a host of issues that islanders will have to deal with. People of radically different cultural, economic, and social backgrounds will be brought together on an island that one can drive across in half an hour. That could be invigorating, but it could cause conflict.

The situation is not much different on the island of Vis in Croatia. The islanders there are also pursuing tourism along the principles of sustainability and boutique offer, so they decided they don't need another hotel in the main town of Vis. Instead, they converted an empty building in the town centre into a satellite campus for a private university out of the national capital, Zagreb. The dynamics of about 200 undergraduate students a year, outside of the tourist season, in a community of 1,500 and an island of less than 3,700 people could prove just as taxing for the local residents as two dozen multi-millionaire guests ensconced on Fogo Island.

With the influx of visitors and seasonal and permanent residents, it is inevitable that the physical and cultural landscapes of small islands will change. That is a good thing. Alive, vibrant communities change all the time. Small islands are often called fragile and it's true that they are highly responsive to economic and demographic fluctuations. But islanders tend to be very comfortable with who they are. "Islands have also been described as places in which resourcefulness and innovation are hallmark traits" (Stratford, 2008: 163). That much is true. However, it is important to remember that all of the islands included in this study are in fact experiencing a demographic decline. "[I]sland life cannot be taken for granted" (Baldacchino, 2008: 42).

PARTING WORDS

> *The people who owned this house that we bought went to Brant-*
> *ford, Ontario. I remember sitting at this table and saying to the*
> *woman: "Aren't you going to miss this. Working here and seeing*
> *this view?" And she said, and she was bitter I think: "There is*
> *nothing here that is a life for us anymore. We have to move." If*
> *the young people all leave here, there is no future. All the eco-*
> *nomic spin in the world [won't help you]. If you want to have a*
> *viable community, you've got to have a demographic of young*
> *children and young couples.*
>
> Seasonal island resident, Newfoundland

Bunce (2008) warns that the leisuring of rural, coastal, and island landscapes creates new distributions of power that once again favour those who already have the means to impose their will over the working and cultural landscapes that are built on generations of community relations. Hay (2006: 33) echoes that warning:

> The integrity of place can be threatened on both axes —
> by brutal "making-over" of physical place that pays scant
> heed to historical or communal place meanings; and on
> the vertical axis when the thread of story and the seam-
> less progression of time is snapped. The greatest threat
> to the integrity of place, on both axes, stems from the
> technological intrusiveness of dynamic global capital,
> intrusions that conduce to a loss of diversity and partic-
> ularity.

There are lessons islanders can teach us: lessons around sustainable development; the habit born out of necessity to at least attempt to live within one's means; lessons around social and cultural cohesion that is built one layer at the time; lessons of cautiously welcoming change. And we should also pay heed when writer Anela Borčić (2009), dedicated to her island of Vis, tells us — in the original Vis dialect of the Croatian language — a simple truth many islanders the world over know: "ni bogât oni ku ima puno, nego oni komu je potriba mãlo" ("rich is not the one who has a lot, but the one who needs little").

Péron (2004: 335) writes that "[g]oing to an island means seeking to rediscover and rebuild oneself as an individual." That is probably the most powerful aspect of the island allure — the promise that we can remake ourselves — and for that alone islands may be indispensable. Péron continues by warning that "in a world dominated by galloping time and human movement, the need for the island experience has never been more widespread; yet, the material basis of the island experience is seriously threatened" (Péron, 2004: 335).

If the resident elites of island newcomers remake those places without regard for the needs and wants of local residents, then they will destroy the very thing they profess to love. At the end of the day, islanders have proved many times over that they are willing to engage in dialogue and adopt new ideas and new ways of doing things; ultimately, this is the path to any successful development. It is what Massey (1999: 156) calls "a global sense of identity." She adds:

> It is a sense of place, an understanding of "its character", which can only be constructed by linking that place to places beyond. A progressive sense of place would recognize that, without being threatened by it. What we need, it seems to me, is a global sense of the local, a global sense of place.

These conversations must be held around many kitchen tables if islands are to thrive as distinct places. Coppes (2008: 30) reminds us that "places are constructed by people doing things and in this sense are never finished but constantly being performed." Newcomers, visitors, and policy-makers, and even clueless cowboys, all have a seat at those tables.

REFERENCES

Baldacchino, G. 2005. "The Contribution of 'Social Capital' to Economic Growth: Lessons from Island Jurisdictions." *The Round Table: Commonwealth Journal of International Affairs* 94, 1: 31–46.

———. 2006. "Editorial: Islands, Island Studies, Island Studies Journal." *Islands Studies Journal* 1, 1: 3–18.

———. 2008. "Studying Islands: On Whose Terms? Some Epistemological and Methodological Challenges to the Pursuit of Island Studies." *Islands Studies Journal* 3, 1: 37–56.

Borčić, A. 2009.*Garbîn, zao vjetar.* Zagreb. VBZ.

Bunce, M. 2008. "The 'Leisuring' of Rural Landscape in Barbados: New Spatialities and the Implications for Sustainability in Small Island States." *Geoforum* 39, 2: 969–79.

Buttimer, A. 1976."Grasping the Dynamism of Lifeworld." *Annals, Association of American Geographers* 66, 2: 277–79.

Coppes, J. 2008. "Revisiting the Invisible Hiding Place." *Architecture and Phenomenology* (Autumn): 23–38.

Cresswell, T. 2004. *Place: A Short Introduction.* Oxford: Blackwell.

Croation National Tourism Board (CNTB). 2011. "Croatia: The Mediterranean as It Once Was." http://www.youtube.com/watch?v=TBQRZjL1GVQ&feature=related.

Dale, A., C. Ling, and L. Newman. 2008. "Does Place Matter? Sustainable Community Development in Three Canadian Communities." *Ethics, Place and Environment* 11, 3: 267–81.

Depraetere, C. 1991. "NISSOLOG: Base des Données des îles de plus de 100 km²." Presentation at 17th Pacific Science Congress, Honolulu. MSDOS computer program and unpublished manuscript, Centre de Montpellier, France: Editions de l'OSTROM.

Edmond, R., and V. Smith. 2003. "Editors' Introduction." In R. Edmond and V. Smith, eds., *Islands in History and Representation*, 1–18. New York: Routledge.

Fürst, B. 2014. "Islands of Sun and Ice: Perceptions and Policies in Small Island Settings." MA thesis, Memorial University of Newfoundland. http://research.library.mun.ca/8379/1/thesis.pdf.

Ghenoiu, E. 2008. "Charles W. Moore and the Idea of Place." *Fabrications: Journal of the Society of Architectural Historians of Australia and New Zealand* 18, 2: 90–119.

Gibbons, M.S. 2010. "Islanders in Community: Identity Negotiations through Sites of Conflict and Transfer of Power." *Island Studies Journal* 5, 2: 165–92.

Gillis, J.R. 2001. "Places Remote and Islanded." *Michigan Quarterly Review* 40, 1: 39–58.

Graovac, V. 2004. "Islands on the Verge of Extinction: The Example of Zadar Islands." *Geoadria* 9, 2: 183–210.

Hache, J.-D. 1998. "Towards a Political Approach to the Island Question." In G. Baldacchino and R. Greenwood, eds., *Competing Strategies of Socio-economic Development for Small Islands*, 31–68. Charlottetown, PEI: Institute of Island Studies, University of Prince Edward Island.

Harvey, D. 1990. *The Condition of Postmodernity: An Enquiry into the Origins of Cultural Change*. Cambridge, Mass.: Blackwell.

———. 1996. *Justice, Nature and the Geography of Difference*. Cambridge, Mass.: Blackwell.

Hau'ofa, E. 1993. "Our Sea of Islands." In *A New Oceania: Rediscovering Our Sea of Islands*, 2–16. Suva, Fiji: School of Social and Economic Development, University of the South Pacific.

Hay, P. 2006. "A Phenomenology of Islands." *Islands Studies Journal* 1, 1: 19–42.

Latta, P. 2005. "Contested Space: A Place on the Way to Collaborative Government?" *Ethnologies* 27, 2: 17–42.

Lawrence, D.H. 1961 [1926]. "The Man Who Loved Islands." In *The Complete Short Stories*, vol. 3, 722–46. New York: Viking Press.

Lowenthal, D. 1997. "European Landscape Transformations: The Rural Residue." In P. Groth and T.W. Bressi, eds., *Understanding Ordinary Landscapes*, 180–88. New Haven: Yale University Press.

Massey, D. 1999. *Space, Place and Gender*. Minneapolis: University of Minnesota Press.

———. 2007. "Is the World Getting Larger or Smaller?" OpenDemocracy News Analysis. http://www.opendemocracy.net.

McElroy, J.L. 2003. "Tourism Development in Small Islands across the World." *Geografiska Annaler* 85B, 4: 231–42.

Newfoundland and Labrador Department of Tourism, Culture and Recreation (NLDTCR). 2010. TV ad: Place Names. http://www.youtube.com/watch?v=aX-JNYi4ByXc.

Norberg-Schulz, C. 1971. *Existence, Space and Architecture*. New York: Praeger.

———. 1979. *Genius Loci: Towards a Phenomenology of Architecture*. New York: Rizzoli.

Péron, F. 2004. "The Contemporary Lure of the Island." *Tijdschrift voor Economische en Sociale Geografie* 95, 3: 326–39.

Pocius, G.L. 2000. *A Place to Belong: Community Order and Everyday Space in Calvert, Newfoundland*. Montreal and Kingston: McGill-Queen's University Press.

Relph, R. 1976. *Place and Placelessness*. London: Pion.

Republika Hrvatska, Ministarstvo turizma. 2011. *Analiza turističke godine 2010*. Zagreb. http://www.mint.hr/UserDocsImages/110530-analiza-2010-w.pdf.

Robinson, T. 2012. *Stones of Aran: Pilgrimage*. Dublin: Lilliput Press (digital edition).

Stratford, E. 2008. "Islandness and Struggle over Development: A Tasmanian Case Study." *Political Geography* 27, 2: 160–75.

Tourism Research Division, NL Department of Tourism, Culture and Recreation. 2012. Department of Tourism, Culture and Recreation (TCR) Year-To-Date (YTD) Tourism Highlights December 2011. St. John's NL. Retrieved from http://www.tcr.gov.nl.ca/tcr/publications/2011/Tourism_performance_2011_YTD_December_2011.pdf.

van Nes, A. 2008. "The Heaven, the Earth and the Optic Array: Norberg-Schulz's Place Phenomenology and Its Degree of Operationability." *Architecture and Phenomenology* (Autumn): 113–34.

CHAPTER 5

Music in the Development of Place: Hey Rosetta! and the "New" Newfoundland

Deatra Walsh

INTRODUCTION

In January of 2010, the Canadian Broadcasting Corporation (CBC) debuted its newest television pilot, *The Republic of Doyle*. Set and shot in St. John's, Newfoundland, the comedy-drama about a private investigation father-and-son duo, rose to instant success. The show is known for its imagery of greater St. John's, as it often blurts out cityscapes of vibrantly coloured row houses, busy streets, local watering holes, and rolling ocean in between its scenes. Set to the distinct sound of Newfoundland's folk-rock group Great Big Sea hailing "oh yeah," it portrays a prosperous and bustling metropole rife with crime that needs solving.

That *The Republic of Doyle* encourages and embodies place-based development is undeniable. It is based upon and sells the specificities of St. John's, as well as larger cultural nuances of Newfoundland and Labrador. In so doing, it fuels economic development by ensuring that production is local. *ROD*, as it is known, directly and indirectly employs up to 200 local people (MacEachern, 2012) and has a GDP investment return of 2.9 per cent based on provincial projections (Government of Newfoundland and Labrador, 2012). As show co-creator, executive producer, and star Allan Hawco aptly described it:

> Investing in the film and television industry, investing in
> the cultural community, is not just good business — be-
> cause the economic impact is scrutinized and the payoff
> is obvious — but outside of business, you're contributing
> to the cultural identity of the place. (MacEachern, 2012)

This chapter draws on the sentiment expressed within Hawco's statement that the show *contributes to* cultural identity as inspiration to examine how culture and creative industries (i.e., film and music) influence place-based development as an iterative process. While *ROD* is a prime example of both tangible and intangible place-based development, another Newfoundland success story, the six-piece indie-rock band Hey Rosetta!, is also making contributions to development in new and exciting ways.

Formed in 2005, Hey Rosetta! has made its mark as one of Canada's leading bands, with a growing international following. While they are a Newfoundland-based band (and the band members do make their home in St. John's), they cannot be considered a "Newfoundland band" (Walsh, 2011), nor do they produce "Newfoundland music," which is characterized by Irish, folk, country, and Celtic influences (Rosenberg, 1997; Best, 2007). Despite this, Hey Rosetta! is contributing to what Jim Overton (1996) has described as a cultural renaissance. Most recently, their fusion of song and imagery in the music videos for singles "Yer Spring" and "Bandages" pro-vide images of a diverse and thriving Newfoundland. The audiovisual syn-ergy (Gow, 1992) here works to endow place with music, and in this case the new indie-rock sound of Hey Rosetta!, but it also endows the music, or rather the lyrics, with place. These processes create what I refer to as reno-vated place associations — particularly for people from or with connections to Newfoundland and Labrador — that fuel place-based development.

The chapter is divided into six sections. In the first section, I briefly review the relationship between music and place. I then link this relation-ship to place-based development and turn to illustrate how music in New-foundland and Labrador has historically been connected to both place and development. This provides an opportunity to introduce Hey Rosetta! as the new fresh sound of the province, and the country. The focus then shifts to the audiovisual world of music videos and their ability to create what

Steve Jones (1988) refers to as a digital narrative. I then ruminate on the digital narratives portrayed in the two Hey Rosetta! music videos — arguing that they contribute to renovated place associations. I then bring this discussion back to my introductory comments on *The Republic of Doyle*.

MUSIC, PLACE, AND DEVELOPMENT

Musical practices, as in the production of song (writing, instrumentation, and recording) and the act of singing, are also place-based practices. Songs are often written to reflect and represent places, either as experienced, remembered, anticipated, or mythologized (Leyshon et al., 1995). John Denver's "Take Me Home, Country Roads" has garnered American and international success as a theme song for the state of West Virginia (and West Virginia University), but has also been appropriated by others intent on using it to express their own sentiments and relationships to place. Writing about country and bluegrass singers in Thailand, Jane Ferguson (2010: 228) shows that their rendition of Denver's tune is actually a practice to "point to and romanticize a Northern Thai rural aesthetic, one that they insist is distinct from Bangkok-sanctioned Thainess." Ray Charles's cover of Hoagy Carmichael and Stuart Gorell's 1930 hit "Georgia on My Mind" brought the song, and Charles, to international success and helped embed the place of Georgia in the minds of his audiences. As biographer Michael Lydon (2004: 188) writes, "Georgia . . . evokes the universal yearning for home" and the "sunset colours of Ray's voice, the strings and chorus, underscore its nostalgic appeal." As of 1979, "Georgia on My Mind" became the state song of Georgia in 1979, with Charles there to perform it before a joint audience of the state house and the senate (Druesedow, 2008).

In Canada, folk-country singer/songwriters Gordon Lightfoot, Stompin' Tom Connors, and Stan Rogers are well known for songs written of and for places. Lightfoot was in fact commissioned by the Canadian government to represent the county in song at its centennial in 1967. The product, "The Canadian Railroad Trilogy," reflects a historical evolution of the country through a sonic painting of landscape that perhaps only Lightfoot could achieve. Ryan Edwardson (2003) argues that Lightfoot is not necessarily known for Canadian place-based associations in his songwriting, but his popularity prompted the Centennial Commission to get him to write about place. Rogers, also known for his place-based lyrics, was particularly apt at imagining places through song. While Rogers's songs have reconstructed places to which he has never been, other songwriters have constructed places that do not exist. Using the example of Jimmy Buffet's "Margarita-ville," Bowen (1997) shows that, despite its non-existence as an actual place, the mythology surrounding it is pervasive, thus demonstrating that a non-place (i.e., without physicality) could be any place.

Music and songs are not simply "representations of and for something extra-musical" (Anderson, Morton, and Revill, 2005: 640). They are also about the act of doing, singing, and embodying song in place (see Cohen, 1995; Anderson et al., 2005). In other words, they occur *in* places, and in so doing, connect singers and the songwriters themselves to music and place through the act of singing. These acts illustrate what Daniels et al. and Fürst in Chapters 2 and 4 of this volume refer to as the performance of place and identity. Alison Schnable's (2012) ethnographic research with two youth gospel choirs in a New Jersey Baptist church — Bethel Baptist Church — shows, for example, that through singing practice, choir members establish solidarity with others in the congregation, but also with wider racial communities. The act of singing also connects them to the city of Trenton in which the church is located and its history as a deindustrialized low-income black community. As Schnable (2012: 284) writes, church members:

> prize the fact that many of Bethel's families have belonged to the church for multiple generations. Others express pride in the church's historical role in Trenton's black community. Despite the suburbanization of its members, Bethel still understands itself to be a fixture of the city of Trenton, and the performances of the choirs are oppor-tunities to express this symbolically.

As both representations of and experiences in place, musical practices contribute to development and place-based development in particular. Within cultural tourism, music tourism or music-based tourism has be-come a popular niche within cultural tourism (Gibson and Connell, 2005), an offshoot of place-based development. Music tourism occurs when people travel "because of music" (Gibson and Connell, 2005: 1), either as pilgrimages to sites of music development and production, or to the birthplaces/ residences of musical icons. The earlier example of Jimmy Buffett music enthusiasts searching for the elusive Margaritaville could be an example of music tourism, although perhaps more apt examples include the hundreds of thousands of visitors who go to Graceland, in Memphis, Tennessee (where Elvis Presley lived and died, and about which Paul Simon wrote in his song, "Graceland"), or Liverpool, UK (home of the Beatles) (see Leaver and Schmidt, 2009). Music festivals can also fall under the music tourism rubric, as festival-goers often attend with the intent of connecting to particular musical styles within and unique to place. In much the same way that visiting sites of musical history are emotionally charged events for consumers (Leaver and Schmidt, 2009), so too is the act of experiencing a particular type of music at a festival venue.

Music tourism, as connected to heritage and history, is in many ways premised upon a backward gaze. Visiting Elvis's home or searching out artifacts from the Beatles' heyday are acts of nostalgia (Leaver and Schmidt, 2009). Attending Celtic music festivals, as in the case of Matheson's (2008) research, or travelling to Cape Breton in Atlantic Canada, for example, to embrace its Gaelic musical heritage (see cluster article), also rely on heritage as the driver of development. But, as the work of Gibson and Connell (2003) shows, music tourism can also be forward-looking, constructive, and iterative.

Because music is so intimately connected to tourism, and because music is consumed both immaterially (through experience) and materially (buying CDs or downloading tracks), it enables the commodification of place, and not always at the expense of "authenticity" or through cultural counterfeiting (as per Fürst in the preceding chapter). And, as examples such as the music videos of Hey Rosetta! discussed here but also the festivals and Lerwick cultural quarter of the Shetland Islands (Chapter 8) or Tasmania's Ten Days on the Island (Chapter 10) demonstrate, music enables production in place. From a development perspective, then, music produces economic and social outcomes in a variety of backward- and forward-looking ways that are beneficial to communities.

NEWFOUNDLAND AND LABRADOR: AN EVOLUTION OF PLACE-BASED MUSIC AND MUSIC PRODUCED IN PLACE

Newfoundland and Labrador has had a long and varied history of conquer and conquest, disappointment and hope. It would be impossible to cover the depth and breadth of this history here, but others have (Noel, 1971; Cadigan, 2009). From its historically Aboriginal roots to its flirtation with Norse settlement and on to its status as a European fishing station later turned permanent English, Irish, and French settlement, the province has historically been cosmopolitan, rife with controversy, and largely inhospitable to its suitors. Those who remained were said to be survivors. In its more recent historical past as a British colony that reluctantly joined the Canadian federation in 1949, controversy and survival remain key aspects of the Newfoundland and Labrador tapestry. It took two referendums to determine whether or not there was going to be a tenth Canadian province. These were particularly divisive, and arguably detrimental to relations among the local population. The Confederation campaign was, however, successful and the province entered into the agreement in poverty and, according to its patriarch, then Premier Joe Smallwood, in serious need of development, advancement, and improvement (Letto, 1998). From this moment on, it is sufficient to say that the politics of identity took particular root. These politics evolved into a heritage narrative of necessary mobility amid economic despair (Walsh, 2011) and a strong sense of nationalism (Hiller, 1987; Overton, 1996; Marland, 2010), which Baker (2012) argues can be more aptly described as patriotism.

As a result of this history and the narrative(s) that surround it, New-foundlanders and Labradorians are well known for writing and producing music with intimate connections to identity and place, in particular to the "island." Rooted in a blend of folk, country, Irish, and Celtic genres, "Newfoundland music," as it has come to be known, speaks to themes of identity, and national identity in particular (Keough, 2007), economic hardships, and the relationship of all of these things to the decision to either stay in the province or leave (Walsh, 2011). Singers and songwriters who have committed these themes to song, and expressed an intimate connection to place, are numerous. Folk-rock icon Ron Hynes is known for his place-based lyrics and his ability to vocalize the experience of place in song. Comedic songwriting trio Buddy Wasisname and the Other Fellas have also penned place-based connections, and again, the importance of their island home, through ballads such as "Salt Water Joys" and "Song for Newfoundland." The band Ryan's Fancy, a trio of Irish and English immigrants to Canada, has also been responsible for driving folk music appreciation in the province. One of the group's members, the late Dermot O'Reilly, wrote the song "West Country Lady" for the community of Torbay in Newfoundland. And, for 38 years, the Newfoundland Folk Arts Society has run the Newfoundland and Labrador Folk Festival in St. John's as a way to celebrate the folk music tradition in the province.

While most certainly connected to and reflecting place, these musicians and their songs are also reflections on Newfoundland and Labrador culture. This music–culture relationship has changed; it has evolved with contestation. Music and song rely on a dialectic process that is also, in the words of Deleuze and Guattari (1987), rhizomatic. In other words, they rely on each other with neither being at the root of the other per se. They change and develop in tandem. Claiming that there is a distinctive sound associated with a place, or that a particular type of music originated in one place, or even that a particular genre can best describe place, is a risky endeavour. And, although Newfoundland music is given form as a distinct genre, it is, in fact, the result of a culmination and combination of other influences brought here by people through their geographic mobility and assisted by such technology as the radio, print media (Osborne, 2007; Webb, 2008), and most recently, the Internet. Newfoundland music, and the culture it reflects, is the product of hybridity (see Chafe, 2007), constantly evolving and forever changing.

Much more recently, new musical influences have entered Newfoundland and Labrador and, in particular, the St. John's music scene. Bands such as the ska-funk ensemble Funky Dory, the reggae rock band The Idlers, and the afro-beat inspired group Mopaya have ignited the enthusiasm of local audiences, and have led local writers to suggest that Newfoundland and Labrador's "world" music scene is rapidly taking shape (Rollmann, 2011). St. John's is also now home to several new music festivals including the annual Wreckhouse Jazz and Blues Festival as well as the biannual Sound Symposium, which together bring new talent, influences, and musical exchanges to the province. The city has also been suggested as Canada's new indie-rock capital (Lee, 2009), with Hey Rosetta!, the band featured in this chapter, at its core. With three albums out and distribution rights across the globe, Hey Rosetta! has been busy taking their music on the road, touring extensively throughout the United States, Europe, Australia, China, and Canada and in doing so connecting Newfoundland and Labrador and its indie-rock music with the world.

REIGNITING THE MUSIC VIDEO

Hey Rosetta!'s music is not lyrically about Newfoundland and Labrador, as has been the case for many of the musicians found in what Rosenberg has called the Canon of Newfoundland music (Rosenberg, 1994). There are, in fact, very few references to place within their songs (see Walsh, 2011). Local journalist Kevin Kelly has argued that their songs do not "necessarily have a sense of place" (Kelly, 2008: 25) and that the band could be from anywhere. Lead singer and songwriter Tim Baker was quoted in 2008 as saying that journalists' pursuit of the Newfoundland angle is persistent (Lien, 2008: 7); yet he did not see the band as carrying any Newfoundland torch (Kelly, 2008). Rather, Baker said: "We just live here and grew up here and there isn't a lot more to it than that. I wish there was sometimes, because people want to hear that" (Kelly, 2008: 25). While this may have been the case in their earlier work and in these earlier self-reflections, a different message emerges through the visual representations of their work via music videos.

The fusion of film and music has occurred since the early twentieth century. The modern music video, as Aufderheide (1986) notes, dates back to the 1960s and the work of Richard Lester with the Beatles, but it was not until the American cable station Music Television (MTV) launched its promotional video clips in the early 1980s to promote artists and their music that the notion of a music video took root. Shortly after, rock videos came on stream and quickly gained popularity (Gow, 1992). Writing on the subject, Joe Gow (1992: 2) notes that by the 1990s the term "music video," which previously did not exist, had entered the "vocabulary of American popular entertainment."

The music video emerged largely to serve industry purposes (i.e., to sell more records) (Aufderheide, 1986). In the early production days of the 1980s, many music videos were developed as aesthetic pieces (Brawyn, 1996), but quickly they became less about art and more about advertising and commercialization. Despite this obvious commercial drive, Aufderheide (1986: 63) writes that:

> Music videos are authentic expressions of a populist industrial society. For young people struggling to find a place in communities dotted with shopping malls but with few community centres, in an economy whose major product is information, music videos play to the search for identity amid an improvised community.

Although the commercialized music video that "advertises" still remains a dominant form and is, in fact, a product of television airtime regulations, more artistic and aesthetic videos are part of the repertoire. And, with new technological "publishing" venues such as YouTube, musicians are not bound by these regulatory (or indeed industry) constraints. The artistic music video, then, could be argued to be more the domain of established artists who can afford to take risks (e.g., Peter Gabriel, Lady GaGa) but also of independent artists whose work is driven by aesthetics (Hibbert, 2005). I consider Hey Rosetta! to fall in the latter category.

HEY ROSETTA!: ART AND PLACE IN VIDEO

Two of Hey Rosetta!'s recent music videos offer rich material from which to ponder relationships among music, place, and cultural (re)production. I draw on two videos produced to visually reflect the songs "Yer Spring" and "Bandages" (see Hey Rosetta!, n.d.), both from the band's 2011 album release *Seeds*, as an analytical point of departure. Noah Pink, based out of Halifax, directed both videos and both were shot in and around St. John's. I use elements of content, discourse, and narrative analysis to draw out themes from the song lyrics and the visual representations that accompany them — the digital narratives — and link these themes to broader cultural and heritage narratives in Newfoundland and Labrador. This analytical approach and the results help illustrate my case for the development of renovated place associations, which I describe as new or altered understandings of place, intentionally or unintentionally created through art. They are renovations because they put a new face to old constructions of cultural reference, but still rely on them as their foundations.

The first video, "Yer Spring," begins with Hey Rosetta! performing at a local "homecoming" show at the Delta Hotel in St. John's in December 2010, and then takes the viewer back and forth from this show to a series of four different scenes. These include a series of people holding sparklers in various places around St. John's, young people and children practising for a performance of the Nutcracker at the city's Arts and Culture Centre, people and band members at a house party, and mummers dancing at the annual St. John's Christmas mummers' parade.

With the exception of the band's performance and the sequencing of various people holding sparklers, the video itself was not premeditated or planned but it does have thematic coherence. As director Noah Pink (personal communication, 24 July 2012) described it, he simply took his camera everywhere on a trip to St. John's and filmed what he saw. He then tried to match these images with the creative thrust of the song.

The song itself begins somewhat slowly and melodically, but with a steady background beat. Here Baker sings:

> long we were searching
> these serpentine streets for the signs of a spark
> fucking around in the dark
> then long we were held
> in the thrum and the desperate heat of the clubs
> drinking deep from that cup[1]

As we hear these first lyrics, we begin a journey to decipher the meaning of Pink's audiovisual synergy (Gow, 1992), which continues over the duration of the video. At two separate points in the video (and in the song), the speed of the music increases; it becomes louder and has more drum and guitar accompaniment. At these two intervals the images shift back and forth rapidly between the different scenes (e.g., the band playing, performers and mummers dancing). While the viewer is digesting this visual barrage, s/he is also met with the audio stimulation of the lyrics themselves. And, with the exception of the reference to the "spark" and the images of individuals holding sparklers throughout, there are very few other obvious and explicit connections between the audio and visual cues. The lyrics, it seems, appear only to be linked tangentially to the visuals. Pink (personal communication, 24 July 2012) says this was because this is simply not a traditional music video with images that literally reflect the song itself, nor is it a video just with shots of the band playing live.

Hey Rosetta! lead singer and songwriter Tim Baker describes the song as representative of a search that often fails. Inspired by the band's constant presence in bars and clubs, and their questioning of why people are there, he said that the song is "kind of about drinking in the hopes of finding something and then realizing that you're just hurting yourself." He added that it is also about religion: "trying to find . . . that rebirth or regeneration or hope in religion and having that fail you as well" (Lien, 2011). Although seemingly depressing (Baker himself admitted this potential interpretation), the song, when layered over the images of St. John's, and combined with the elements of cultural renaissance, takes on a different tone. In fact, one begins to wonder whether there is some esoteric meaning here that associates the song with place. It is as if, through the music video, the song actually endows space *with* meaning, and thus contributes to a sense of place. As geographer Yi-Fu Tuan has written: "What begins as undifferentiated space becomes place as we get to know it better and endow it with value" (1977: 6). The song adds value in this sense. But equally, through the music video, the portrayal of place gives new meaning and value to the lyrics of the song, which at its inception were not about place. Take, for example, the verse:

> doctor unbandage my eyes
> i feel the light and i'm ready to be out in it
> doctor uncover my ears
> I hear the chorus weeping, i see the people singing:
> doctor unbandage my eyes

i feel the light and i'm ready to be rising!
doctor uncover my ears!
I hear the chorus weeping! i see the people singing:

let the loser up.
let's get him up.[2]

While these lyrics were originally written to reflect a call or, as Baker describes it, "supplication" (Lien, 2011), a re-reading of them through the lens of the music video allows for an interpretation that can reflect a cultural heritage narrative of Newfoundland and Labrador: that of the underdog rising and a population living in hope (Maines and Bridger, 1992; Walsh, 2011). In 1982, then Premier Brian Peckford said during his election victory speech: "I am more convinced than I have been any time in the past that Newfoundlanders and Labradorians speak [with] one voice when we all say one day the sun will shine and have-not will be no more." (CBC News, 2008). At the time, Peckford was referring to the fact that the province was receiving equalization payments from Canada. However, he campaigned on the fact that this would no longer be the case and that, eventually, Newfoundland and Labrador would be economically stable within the Canadian federation. It was not until November 2008 that the province finally did become a "have" province — largely as a result of oil revenue. At the time, then Premier Danny Williams was quoted as saying:

> For 60 years we've been part of the great Canadian federation and we have been recipients of equalization payments from the Canadian government. Over the years we have been ridiculed for that. At times, we've been presented as the poor cousins in Canada. Now we can hold our heads high and feel very good about it. . . . I consider it to be a very significant day for all the people of the province and I want to share this moment with them. (CBC News, 2008)

Baker's sentiment expressed through the lyric "doctor unbandage my eyes / I see the light and I'm ready to be out in it!" could most certainly embody a collective sentiment of freedom applicable to the Newfoundland narrative upon reaching a "have" status. But beyond economics, a cultural element to this "light" reflects increased diversity, a vibrant arts scene supported by new and alternative musical styles, as well as a sense of renewal and, as writer Lisa Moore (2011: 24) described it, cultural reinvention. The Newfoundland and Labrador of today can be viewed in stark contrast to the province of more than 20 years ago — then reeling from the closure of the northern cod fishery.

This cultural re-reading of the video is not implausible, nor is its strong reflection of place accidental. Speaking about the vision behind the video, Pink (personal communication, 24 July 2012) says it was made for the fans as a celebration of them and where the band is from, and that the emergent set of images came as a result of his feeling as an outsider coming into St. John's. He says so many things about the video were fortuitous, something that perhaps can only happen in St. John's.

The audiovisual narrative of connecting culture, heritage, and place emergent in "Yer Spring" comes through more strongly in the video for "Bandages," also directed by Pink. "Bandages" begins with lead singer Tim Baker standing alone in front of an abandoned building at the west end of St. John's harbour. He is holding only a guitar and, after asking whether they're ready to start the video, he begins to play and sing:

> it will come around
> but everything is now
> i know everything is right now
>
> and the loneliness is a lot
> the nothing weighs a ton
> i mean the nothing weighs a fucking ton

Baker remains alone playing guitar and singing in several different locations around St. John's until approximately one minute into the video, where is he joined by fellow bandmate Romesh Thavanathan, who is also playing the guitar. Here, Baker sings the lyric "that half of the bed" as they stand between a divider at Memorial University's food court. Following this scene, they are joined by the rest of the band and a choir in the Basilica Cathedral of St. John the Baptist, located in downtown St. John's. At this point, Baker sings, with a choral accompaniment:

> if you get these bandages off
> you can stand, you can walk
> leave these towels and gauze
> you'll get up, you'll get out
> into the sun

In the next frame, we see the band playing in a kaleidoscope-type structure and we immediately recognize that the weather has shifted from cloudy and gloomy to sunny (this was not, however, planned, according to Pink). At this point Baker sings "that's where we belong," meaning in the sun, and continues:

> we've been abed too long
> all our weaknesses are growing strong
>
> but the winter always ends
> with water on your lips
> the April rain comes swinging in

Throughout these verses, the band continues to play and Baker sings in various places around St. John's, ending up along the Rennie's Mill River on a sunny day with the sound of the moving water in the background, singing the last lyric about the April rain. We are then taken back into a candlelit basilica with a youth choir behind the band as Baker sings the chorus again: "get these bandages off . . ." Various other places appear as Baker sings out the chorus until the band ends up at what used to be a café and bookstore on Signal Hill Road, where the message in the song becomes clear: that times will indeed be better and the sun will shine after all. As their online bio and description of the song indicates, "Bandages" reminds us that "even when things seem hopeless, 'the winter always ends'" (Hey Rosetta!, n.d.). Indeed, Baker sings towards the end of the song about the sun, "cause come she will, oh come she will."

While not written to represent Newfoundland and Labrador's heritage narrative, the sentiment of the song and its direct reference to the sun coming after a long winter and a rainy April (both of which are common in the province) do mark a material connection to place, but perhaps more importantly, a symbolic connection with the long entertained hopes for a "new" Newfoundland, proudly holding its head high, as spoken presciently by Brian Peckford back in 1982.

CONCLUSION

This chapter argues that the audiovisual synergy of the Hey Rosetta! music videos for "Yer Spring" and "Bandages" reflects and produces renovated place associations — new understandings of place based on old cultural constructions — for the province of Newfoundland and Labrador. Such understandings can fuel place-based development. The province has historically been considered "have-not" compared to the rest of Canada, in perpetual economic trouble and culturally backward. What we see in these videos can be argued to be an extension of the imagery found in the Newfoundland of the CBC series *The Republic of Doyle*, as well as that represented and reflected in the award-winning provincial tourism ads put out by the province's government (CBC News, 2012) — that is, a vibrant and prosperous province. The song lyrics for both "Yer Spring" and "Bandages," while not explicitly about place, economy, or identity, can be re-read in light of the music videos (i.e., the digital narratives) to reflect all three. The re-reading I have done here suggests that these songs can be understood as expressions of eventual economic, cultural, and social prosperity by virtue of the videos. The audiovisual synergy communicates the vulnerability and struggle of the proverbial phoenix that will rise from the ashes. In many ways, this *is* Newfoundland and Labrador's new collective heritage narrative — and part of its cultural reinvention (Moore, 2011), namely: it was a struggle for a long time, but look at us now. The degree to which the representation and reality of prosperity extend to the entire province is, however, questionable. It is often argued that new infusions of oil and gas money, which are largely driving the provincial economy, do not extend beyond the "overpass" — a highway perimeter just outside the greater St. John's area. The degree to which this is true can be debated, as many Newfoundlanders and Labradorians are profiting not only from well-paid oil and gas employment here in the province, but also from lucrative employment opportunities in western and northern Canada and other, international locales. They are not all living on the Avalon Peninsula. For now, representations and constructions of the "new" Newfoundland, as portrayed in *The Republic of Doyle* and in the Hey Rosetta! videos, seem to be resonating with people living in the province, as well as with the national and international community of expatriates. Future research could explore the ways in which the imagery of *ROD* as well as Hey Rosetta! contribute to cultural identity construction and place-based development outside of St. John's and into other rural and urban areas across the province.

NOTES

1. "Yer Spring" written by Tim Baker and performed by Hey Rosetta!. Lyrics reproduced with permission.
2. "Bandages" written by Tim Baker and performed by Hey Rosetta!. Lyrics reproduced with permission.

REFERENCES

Anderson, B., F. Morton, and G. Revill. 2005. "Editorial: Practices of Music and Sound." *Social & Cultural Geography* 6: 639–44.

Aufderheide, P. 1986. "Music Videos: The Look of Sound." *Journal of Communication* 36, 1: 57–78.

Baker, J. 2012. "As Loved Our Fathers: The Strength of Patriotism among Young Newfoundlanders." *National Identities* 14, 4: 367–86.

Best, K. 2007. "Hip-Hop on the East Side: A Multi-Sited Ethnography of Breakdancing and Rap Music from St. John's and Grand Falls, Newfoundland." *Newfoundland and Labrador Studies* 22, 1: 315–34.

Bowen, D.S. 1997. "Lookin' for Margaritaville: Place and Imagination in Jimmy Buffet's Songs." *Journal of Cultural Geography* 16, 2: 99–108.

Brawyn, G. 1996. "Never Mind the Broadcast: In Search of the Art of the Music Video." *Popular Music and Society* 20, 3: 95–117.

Cadigan, S.T. 2009. *Newfoundland and Labrador: A History.* Toronto: University of Toronto Press.

CBC News. 2008. "Have-Not Is No More: N.L. off Equalization," 3 Nov. http://www.cbc.ca/news/canada/newfoundland-labrador/story/2008/11/03/have-not.html.

———. 2012. "NL Tourism Campaign Wins National Advertising Award," 24 Jan. http://www.cbc.ca/news/canada/newfoundland-labrador/story/2012/01/24/nl-tourism-award-cassies-124.html.

Chafe, P. 2007. "Rockin' the Rock: The Newfoundland Folk/Pop 'Revolution.'" *Newfoundland and Labrador Studies* 22, 1: 345–60.

Cohen, S. 1995. "Sounding Out the City: Music and the Sensuous Production of Place." *Transactions of the Institute of British Geographers* 20, 4: 434–46.

Deleuze, G., and P.F. Guattari. 1987. *Thousand Plateaus: Capitalism and Schizophrenia*. Minneapolis: University of Minnesota Press.

Druesedow, J. 2008. "Georgia on My Mind: Reflections on Three Georgia Songs." *Music Reference Services Quarterly* 10, 2: 75–85.

Edwardson, R. 2003. "'Of War Machines and Ghetto Scenes': English-Canadian Nationalism and the Guess Who's 'American Woman.'" *American Review of Canadian Studies* 33, 3: 339–56.

Ferguson, J.M. 2010. "Another Country Is the Past: Western Cowboys, Lanna Nostalgia, and Bluegrass Aesthetics as Performed by Professional Musicians in Northern Thailand." *American Ethnologist* 37, 2: 227–40.

Gibson, C., and J. Connell. 2003. "'Bongo Fury': Tourism, Music and Cultural Economy at Byron Bay, Australia." *Tijdschrift voor Economische en Sociale Geografie* 94, 2: 164–87.

——— and ———. 2005. *Music and Tourism: On the Road Again*. Clevedon, UK: Channel View Publications.

Government of Newfoundland and Labrador. 2012. "A Prosperous Economy and Renewable Energy Future Fuelled by Budget 2012." http://www.releases.gov.nl.ca/releases/2012/ibrd/0424n04.htm.

Hey Rosetta! n.d. "Bio." http://www.heyrosetta.com/info.html.

———. n.d. "Video." http://www.heyrosetta.com/video.html.

Hibbert, R. 2005. "What Is Indie Rock?" *Popular Music and Society* 28, 1: 55–77.

Hiller, H.H. 1987. "Dependence and Independence: Emergent Nationalism in Newfoundland." *Ethnic and Racial Studies* 10, 3: 257–75.

Jones, S. 1988. "Cohesive but Not Coherent: Music Videos, Narrative and Culture." *Popular Music & Society* 12, 4: 15–29.

Kelly, K. 2008. "The National Rise of Hey Rosetta!" *Newfoundland Herald*, 15 June, 23–25.

Keough, S. 2007. "Constructing a Canadian National Identity: Conceptual Explorations and Examples in Newfoundland Music." *Material Culture* 39, 2: 43–52.

Lee, C. 2009. "Music: Newfoundland Rocks." *The Globe and Mail Online*, 21 Aug.

Leaver, D., and R.A. Schmidt. 2009. "Before They Were Famous: Music-based Tourism and a Musician's Hometown Roots." *Journal of Place Management and Development* 2, 3: 220–29.

Leyshon, A., D. Matless, and G. Revill. 1995. "The Place of Music." *Transactions of the Institute of British Geographers* 20: 423–33.

Letto, D. 1998. *Chocolate Bars and Rubber Boots: The Smallwood Industrialization Plan*. Paradise, NL: Blue Hill Publishing.

Lien, E. 2008. "Call of the Wild." *The Scope*, 22 May–5 June, 6-7.

———. 2011. "Track by Track with the New Hey Rosetta! Album, Seeds," 4 Feb. http://thescope.ca/music/track-by-track-with-the-new-hey-rosetta-album-seeds.

Lydon, M. 2004. *Ray Charles: Man and Music*. London: Routledge.

MacEachern, D. 2012. "Dollars for 'Doyle.'" *The Telegram*, 11 June. http://www.thetelegram.com/News/Local/2012-06-11/article-3004871/Dollars-for-%26lsquoDoyle%26rsquo/1.

Maines, D.R., and J.C. Bridger. 1991. "Narrative, Community, and Land Use Decisions." *Social Science Journal* 29: 363–80.

Marland, A. 2010. "Masters of Our Own Destiny: The Nationalist Evolution of Newfoundland Premier Danny Williams." *International Journal of Canadian Studies/Revue Internationale d'Études Canadiennes* 42: 155–81.

Moore, L. 2011. "Notes from Newfoundland." *The Walrus* 8, 4: 22–29.

Noel, S.J.R. 1971. *Politics in Newfoundland*. Toronto: University of Toronto Press.

Osborne, E. 2007. "Fiddling with Technology: The Effect of Media on Newfoundland Traditional Musicians." *Newfoundland and Labrador Studies* 22, 1: 187–204.

Overton, J. 1996. *Making a World of Difference: Essays on Tourism, Culture and Development in Newfoundland*. St. John's: ISER Books.

Rollmann, H. 2011. "African Beats Heating Up Newfoundland Dance-Floors." *The Independent*, 26 May. http://theindependent.ca/2011/05/26/african-beats-heating-up-newfoundland-dance-floors/.

Rosenberg, N.V. 1994. "Canadianization of Newfoundland Folksong: Or the Newfoundlandization of Canadian Folksong." *Journal of Canadian Studies* 29, 1: 55–73.

———. 1997. "Overview of Newfoundland Music [re Traditions and New Trends]." *Journal of New England Folk Almanac* 6, 7: 7–8, 26.

Schnable, A. 2012. "Singing the Gospel: Using Musical Practices to Build Religious and Racial Communities." *Poetics* 40: 278–98.

Tuan, Y.-F. 1977. *Place and Space: The Perspective of Experience.* Minneapolis: University of Minnesota Press.

Walsh, D. 2011. "Newfoundland: From Ron Hynes to Hey Rosetta!" In G. Baldacchino, ed., *Island Songs: A Global Repertoire*, 65–80. Lanham, Md.: Scarecrow Press.

Webb, J.A. 2008. "Repertoire and Reception: Radio and Music in St. John's, Newfoundland, 1930–1945." *Journal of Canadian Studies* 42, 2: 117–39.

CHAPTER 6

Education and Employment Choices among Young Rural Workers in Canada and Ireland:
A Tale of Two Studies

Gordon B. Cooke, Sara L. Mann, and Jennifer K. Burns

INTRODUCTION

The quality and quantity of employment opportunities have become polarized throughout the industrialized world (Betcherman and Lowe, 1997; Boulin, Lallement, and Michon, 2006; OECD, 2006): some individuals can access "good-quality" employment, while many others are only able to access poorer-quality jobs in terms of remuneration, benefits, and/or duration and security. Accessing good-quality employment can be particularly difficult in rural areas, which have historically had weaker and less diverse economic conditions (e.g., Alasia, 2003, 2010; Barca et al., 2012; OECD, 2006), especially for those without valued skills and/or experience. We believe that younger workers in rural communities face starker choices than older and urban job seekers because, on average, they have had fewer chances to acquire the skills and experiences needed to access good jobs.

This chapter explores the choices of rural youth with respect to education and employment, drawing from two related but separate exploratory studies. The first involved interviews with youth in various rural communities in Ireland and the two Canadian provinces of Newfoundland[1] and Ontario. The second study consisted of interviews and focus groups with youth in six areas of rural Ontario. The studies are similar, except the latter focused more on so-called "vulnerable" workers (Vallée, 2005), who face particular barriers acquiring good-quality employment. In these two studies, we focused on the pursuit of skills and knowledge achieved via post-secondary education, which is primarily available in urban centres. We examined choices for obtaining employment available locally, in the closest urban centres, and further beyond. Given the combination of out-migration and aging populations faced by many rural communities, as noted in the previous chapters of this volume, a better understanding of these choices is critical for place-based development efforts.

This research examines the factors that influence the acquisition of good-quality employment by rural youth, as well as the decision to remain in, or leave, one's rural hometown. To aid in this analysis we use Cooke's (2012) typology of three possible career paths: "High Fliers," "Mid Fliers," and "Upstream Swimmers." *High Fliers* are young adults who are willing, or even keen, to migrate from their rural hometown, often to pursue an education, because they aspire to enter a professional occupation. *Mid Fliers* are also interested in upgrading their skills/education, but without leaving their hometown. *Upstream Swimmers* are on a non-academic path and seek available local employment.

LABOUR MARKETS IN NEWFOUNDLAND, ONTARIO, AND IRELAND: URBAN VS. RURAL DIMENSIONS

The evolution of employers' labour strategies has resulted in different treatment being meted out to different types of workers (Betcherman and Lowe, 1997; Verma and Chaykowski, 1999). While a lucky few are able to acquire a job with good pay, benefits, and other favourable working conditions, others are only able to access "secondary market" jobs with poorer working conditions in terms of hours of work, pay, benefits, and lower job security (Boulin, Lallement, and Michon, 2006; Vallée, 2005). The challenge, for individuals, is to hold sufficient power to be able to obtain or negotiate attractive employment prospects. Not surprisingly, acquiring education and/ or experience is critical, since more highly educated/skilled individuals tend to command stronger leverage, and so enjoy better working conditions than others (Cooke, 2007; OECD, 2005; Lin, 2008).

Ireland and Newfoundland share a similar rural history. Although Felt (2003) cautions against drawing too many parallels, there is a shared past of rural stagnation coupled with out-migration of young people. For much of the late twentieth century, both islands had relatively weak economies and chronically high levels of unemployment (Felt, 2003; Fortin,

2000). In the early 1990s, however, Ireland emerged as a "Celtic Tiger," with much better employment levels and rising wages and living standards (Murphy, 2000). Newfoundland has similarly experienced an economic turnaround over the past decade, and has been growing faster than Ontario, Canada's traditional economic engine (Government of Newfoundland and Labrador, 2010; Industry Canada, 2010). Ontario's industrial sector had been struggling before (Lin, 2008), and its economy in general was disproportionately impacted by the recent global economic crisis (RBC, 2009, 2011).

Unfortunately, as noted by Walsh in Chapter 5, the effects of the boom in Newfoundland have not reached rural parts of the province to the same extent as the capital region (e.g., Government of Newfoundland and Labrador, 2010). In rural Ireland, the boom between 1992 and 2008 seemingly did provide vastly improved economic opportunities for rural citizens, although not enough to eliminate the historical urban–rural gap, since urban employment conditions were booming as well (Bank of Ireland, 2010; Brereton et al., 2011). On the whole, the forecast is looking relatively optimistic for Newfoundland, but less so for its rural workers, while both Ireland and Ontario potentially face more sluggish recoveries.

The economic reality in rural Canada is that unemployment rates tend to be higher, bouts of unemployment last longer, employment opportunities are more limited, and labour force participation is lower (Alasia, 2010; CCL, 2006; OECD, 2006). Conversely, employment growth is generally substantially higher in urban areas, and also more likely to contain professional and other knowledge economy jobs (Alasia and Magnusson, 2005). The Irish experience is similar in rural and western areas compared to the eastern capital region and surroundings (Walsh, 2006), although the unemployment gap temporarily disappeared in the latest recession, according to 2010 data (Government of Ireland, 2012).

Overall, employment quality tends to be poorer and with fewer and less diverse options in rural locations (CCL, 2006; Matthews, Pendakur, and Young, 2009; NLFL, 2009). Moreover, stronger economic conditions provide greater returns on investment in education for those in urban areas (Alasia, 2003). Thus, it is no surprise that rural populations are lagging and aging faster relative to urban populations in Canada (Alasia, 2010; Bryant and Joseph, 2001). This has occurred because Canadians have been migrating from rural to urban locations for many decades (Bryant and Joseph, 2001), with younger individuals more likely to out-migrate than older ones (Bernard, Finnie, and St-Jean, 2008). Canadian workers would be less likely to out-migrate if local labour conditions were better, all else being equal (Bernard, Finnie, and St-Jean, 2008), but if a rural population is aging and economic activity is low, there is a strong incentive for young workers to out-migrate. Their departure then exacerbates the demographic challenges within that community. The situation is somewhat different in Ireland, where a recent trend has seen urbanites settling in *nearby* rural locations to enjoy the lifestyle benefits while retaining urban employment (Bullock et al., 2011), and hence stemming or even reversing the long-standing pattern of rural population decline (Stead, 2011).

Rural populations are not homogeneous, since the size of each community and distance from an urban centre vary sharply, as do the prevailing economic and social conditions (Bryant and Joseph, 2001). Nonetheless, research (e.g., Matthews, Pendakur, and Young, 2009; Shucksmith et al., 2009) suggests that the economic realities facing rural workers across Canada, Ireland, and other industrialized nations share basic features. Those workers face a decision to move for work (i.e., to out-migrate) due to a relative lack of local employment options, versus staying and enjoying the lifestyle they presumably prefer (Shucksmith et al., 2009). In response to this risk of unemployment, underemployment, and out-migration, various levels of government have implemented development initiatives to address regional disparities via direct job creation and improving infrastructure to stimulate economic activity (Barca et al., 2012; Betz and Partridge, 2013). O'Keeffe (Chapter 12, this volume) provides multiple examples of such rural development programs in the Irish context.

ECONOMIC AND EDUCATIONAL REALITIES FACING YOUNGER AND/OR RURAL WORKERS

As noted above, young people with limited experience and/or education often have difficulty acquiring a good job (e.g., OECD, 2005; MacDonald,

2008). One key factor that affects access to and the completion of post-secondary studies is the availability of education options. Some rural students might have access to a local community college, but few have access to a nearby university campus (Looker and Lowe, 2001). Rural youths also face specific problems adjusting to post-secondary programs, such as living away from home, coping with urban life, dealing with public transportation systems, and finding suitable housing. Thus, geographic realities can affect youth participation in post-secondary education or even the completion of high school (Hango and de Broucker, 2007). The proportion of 25- to 54-year-olds in Canada who have attended post-secondary education is above 60 per cent in urban areas, yet under 50 per cent in rural areas (CCL, 2006), suggesting that rural youth are less likely to study beyond high school and start, let alone complete, a university degree (Andres and Looker, 2001). Other possible barriers to post-secondary education include a lack of child-care options, inability to pay college fees, and inadequate transportation (McAleavy, Collins, and Adamson, 2004). While these finance-related barriers seem to exist in Canada, Cooke (2012) found that funding for post-secondary students in Ireland was perceived to be generous enough to allow young adults to attend local or distant post-secondary institutions. Moreover, high school dropout rates are typically higher in Canadian rural areas than in urban ones (CCL, 2006). In Ireland, secondary school (i.e., high school in Canada) graduation rates equal or exceed 90 per cent, but only about 50 per cent of these individuals pursue post-secondary education (OECD, 2011). While the proportion of Irish residents who have completed post-secondary education has risen sharply over the past three decades, graduation rates remain lower among those from rural areas (Morgenroth, 2007).

A number of the young people who stay in rural areas in Newfoundland are school dropouts (Mulcahy, 2007). These youth tend to move from part-time seasonal work to some form of social assistance, particularly when resource sector employment declines. Ironically, where rural economic opportunities exist, they can contribute to a higher dropout rate by pulling students (particularly males) out of the classroom and luring them into the workforce. In these cases, young rural adults may obtain short-term, high-paying, and even stable jobs, but these jobs are often vulnerable to the booms and busts of resource economies. Rural youth are more likely than their urban counterparts to be called upon to leave school prematurely to make up shortfalls in their family budgets (CCL, 2006). Unfortunately, the short-term economic benefits gained from leaving school prematurely in order to work are typically offset by the limited employment opportunities available in the long term (CCL, 2006). This helps perpetuate labour market segmentation since there are often fewer advancement opportunities in these jobs, especially for rural workers with lower skills/education levels (MacDonald, 2008; MacDonald and Marsh, 2001). Conversely, out-migration from a rural area, while not without negative effects, can be a path to economic prosperity and increased social status (Kelly, 2009).

Corbett (2009) suggests the social positioning of individuals within rural communities also shapes their education and/or employment choices. Nixon (2010) and Locke (2010) recognized the important role that parents and relatives play as a social influence in career path decisions. Other factors accounting for the urban–rural divide include negative teacher–pupil relations, lack of intellectual and social support resulting in a loss of interest, perceptions that qualifications were irrelevant for their future plans, and inadequate career planning and advice (McGrath, 2001). In turn, these factors perpetuate self-doubt and angst towards education, particularly if one's social circle shares an unease and unfamiliarity with post-secondary education (Looker and Lowe, 2001; McAleavy, Collins, and Adamson, 2004; MacDonald, 2008). Many young people follow the career paths of their parents, at least directionally by industry or type of work. In rural homes, where neither parent has a university degree, youth are less likely than their urban counterparts to expect to attend, let alone complete, university (Andres and Looker, 2001). Alternative paths include travelling or migrating to a different location for work or adventure, postponing career decisions, or seeking challenge and variety rather than career progression (Locke, 2010; Nixon, 2010; Dries, Pepermans, and De Kerpel, 2008; Tang, 2009).

Another factor affecting education and employment choices is the individual desire to remain in one's hometown: "attachment to place." Tang (2009) found that almost half (49 per cent) of rural Newfoundland youths studied were either willing or preferred to out-migrate, mainly for employment or adventure. The rest, however, were committed to staying and taking whatever employment is available locally, even if that meant lower pay, fewer benefits, and casual or otherwise unstable hours. Tang (2009) further reports the most important reasons that Newfoundland and Labrador students choose their home province as their preferred location for their first job after graduation were: living in one's hometown, proximity to family and friends, and "loving this place." As Vodden et al. (Chapter 1) and Fürst (Chapter 4) have high-lighted, it is also important to remember that some people are able to be mobile, while others are not due to family or other reasons (Betz and Partridge, 2012). Thus, despite socio-economic changes and increasing geographical mobility in society in general, cultures of class and place still matter (Mac-Donald and Marsh, 2001; MacDonald, 2008). An irony is that this increased geographic mobility can impede governments' action to help individuals in underperforming areas. If development policies result in increased economic activity in a struggling region, some of the best job opportunities might be taken by skilled workers migrating into the area (Barca et al., 2012). As a result, one policy lever that governments can use is to develop human resources and skills attainment of the local population, so that they are better positioned to benefit from new opportunities that may arise (Betz and Partridge, 2012).

RESEARCH METHODS

This exploratory analysis is based on two separate, but related, studies. The first includes the responses to semi-structured interviews of 27 young adults (aged 18–29) regarding education, employment, and location held in several communities within rural Ireland, Newfoundland, and Ontario between 2009 and 2012. The second study involved interviews and focus groups during 2011 with 113 individuals between the ages of 18 and 25 in six areas of rural Ontario: Guelph/Wellington, Hanover, Huntsville, Niag-ara/Welland, Owen Sound, and Sudbury. The majority of participants in the first study were on an academic track (i.e., were attending, or had attended, a post-secondary institution). Conversely, researchers actively sought more disadvantaged participants in the second study to understand the particular issues facing these young adults.

Individuals in rural Newfoundland were the initial target of attention because of the depth of the perceived lifestyle and opportunity differences that exist between those living in the St. John's capital region versus elsewhere in the province. A decision was made to undertake comparative research to provide the opportunity to search for similarities and differences between rural individuals in multiple locations. Individuals in Ireland were included in the study for three reasons. Similar to their Newfoundland counterparts, there is a commonly known tradition among Irish workers to out-migrate if local employment options are not attractive. Second, there are cultural similarities between individuals in the two jurisdictions, since Newfoundland has a significant proportion of citizens of Irish descent. Third, Ireland's "Celtic Tiger" boom was seen as a model for Newfoundland, although by the time the study started, Newfoundland's economy was strengthening on a relative basis, while Ireland was suffering from the bursting of its housing and credit bubbles, and then was further damaged by the global economic downturn (see also Grydehoj and Hayward, 2014).

Participants from Ontario were included because they have both similarities to and differences from the Newfoundland participants. They are subject to roughly comparable corporate and personal tax regimes, employment insurance rules, and education systems, all of which could shape the employment options in rural and urban communities. On the other hand, there is a different economic mix within the two provinces, with Ontario having a stronger manufacturing base (despite recent declines), whereas Newfoundland's economy is more natural resource-based (e.g., fishing, mining, forestry). Ontario also has a much higher population density, such that the employment and education options available to rural residents were presumed to be potentially richer and more diverse than those in Newfoundland.

This research was guided by Betcherman and Lowe's (1997) analysis of, and predictions for, Canadian employment conditions. In essence, Betcherman and Lowe assess the role of power in the labour market, and suggest that among the factors affecting the degree of power held by individual workers is their level of education, the strength of the local economy, and the employment policies implemented by governments.

FINDINGS AND TYPOLOGY

We present the preliminary findings from each of the two studies first. The findings are then analyzed in relation to Cooke's (2012) typology of young rural workers presented at the start of the chapter.

Study 1: Canadian and Irish Participants

Among the young adults in the first study, about two-thirds are full-time post-secondary school students. As such, they are not in a position to hold full-time, year-round employment. The remaining third held permanent full-time positions, and of those, all but one held university degrees. The others were typically in, or had recently held, full-time jobs of a limited term or casual/on-call nature. The majority had, at some point, moved to another location for work or education. Occupations included manual labourer, customer service representative, health care worker, and manager. That said, the ones currently attending a post-secondary institution typically held this entry-level type of employment merely to facilitate their access to a high-status occupation. Few of the workers were employed with a private firm; most were directly, or indirectly, in a publicly funded position.

Among these participants, most indicated a strong emotional attachment to their hometown community. However, they also felt a need to acquire more skills or education after secondary school, and that meant they might need to leave to pursue career opportunities. Many participants contemplated whether to stay and look for local prospects or to leave for work or education. Several had moved away to pursue better opportunities, and that decision had allowed at least two to subsequently return to an attractive job opportunity within, or near, their original hometown. On the other hand, some of the participants who had moved had either established roots in a new location, or had planned to do so. Thus, from the viewpoint of the original community, when young people move away, there is a distinct risk the move will be permanent. We also noticed a split in opinions. While almost all interviewed participants feel deeply about their hometown, many were contemplating the options available to be able to remain in their home community or temporarily move away with plans to return to home. A minority, though, had already concluded that they will be moving away at some point, to acquire education, work experience, and/ or to seek adventure.

Study 2: Ontario Participants

Jobs held by participants in the second study varied from the food industry to general labour (i.e., garage hand, factory operator, painter), office-related work, and retail/cashier positions. On the whole, and for the reasons discussed in the research methods section, a relatively large proportion of workers in this study had entry-level or secondary-market jobs. Although not many had done so yet, the majority of the participants said they would leave their rural community for a better job to make more money and for better opportunities in the future. Of those who would not leave, the main reasons were family and the love of a smaller community. Family and friends were the main reason cited to bring participants back if they did leave the community. Many respondents realized that they needed to develop some extra skills to reach their desired career. However, lack of awareness of and access to post-secondary education and training was a major issue for youth in rural Ontario. When asked about their ideal job, participants suggested either a career requiring post-secondary education (such as medicine, education, and community work) or local employment that did not (working in the local beer store or on the local works crew). There were clearly two different sets of goals, and different levels of career expectations.

Likewise, it was clear there were two groupings of participants with respect to post-secondary education: those whose parents could afford to send them to post-secondary education away from home, and those claiming that they just could not afford it. Individuals in this latter group did not want to take out a loan to go away to school because they believed the chances of getting a good-paying job in their community upon return was very low. Most respondents indicated the government should be doing more to help workers in rural areas. Lack of sufficient transportation was a recurring theme in many of the groups. Respondents complained that they could not easily get to their jobs with the existing transportation system. The participants also suggested that the government should initiate an action plan for rural youth employment that involved a better communication of

local work and educational opportunities, and that post-secondary education or training should be made more affordable in rural areas, since there
is a lack of high-paying jobs in their areas upon graduation.

Relating the Findings to the Proposed Typology

The findings from the two studies are applied below to Cooke's (2012) typology consisting of three categories: High Fliers, Mid Fliers, and Upstream
Swimmers.

HIGH FLIERS: THE ACADEMIC STREAM

Participants within this group pursued, or are pursuing, post-secondary
education after high school, even though it requires moving to an urban
centre. For example, P#2 currently holds a permanent, full-time professional
job within his rural Newfoundland hometown. While his employment
prospects would be better if he lived in an urban centre, he is delighted to
have been able to return home. After high school, he moved to an urban
centre to attend university to pursue his chosen field in the arts with the
hope of returning home upon graduation. One interesting wrinkle is that
he might have been prepared, after graduation, to return to his hometown
even if work in his chosen field was unavailable. Thus, under different circumstances, P#2 could have wound up in the Mid-Fliers group (see below).

P#7 is a female participant, not yet 20, from rural Ireland, and is following a similar path. She moved to an urban centre to attend university
and hopes to start a professional career after graduation. She comes from a
close-knit family, has many friends in her hometown, and enjoys the social
aspects and pace of life. While she treasures growing up in a rural community,
she has already decided that she will only return if she can find employment comparable to that available in an urban area. She wants the lifestyle,
security, financial rewards, and opportunities that accompany a professional
career in an urban centre. She sees only a slight possibility of returning for
lifestyle reasons at a later stage in life, perhaps if married and starting a
family. Under that scenario, she may try self-employment, if financially
feasible, and if suitable paid employment is not available. However, she said
that she will not settle for work outside her chosen field.

There was also a group of High Fliers targeting post-secondary education in the second study. The factors that differentiated them from the Mid
Fliers are that these individuals are willing, or even keen, to go away to
urban (and deemed more prestigious) universities, and can count on financial support from their families. Generally, these High Fliers had come to
realize that their career plans would uproot them away from their hometown communities. While some stated their desire to return at a later stage,
the likelihood of doing so seems low, especially for those unwilling to sac-
rifice their career progression.

MID FLIERS: THE "IN-BETWEENS"

Among the 27 participants in the first study, this was admittedly the most
diverse subgroup of individuals since they share some of the ambition of
High Fliers, yet have the stronger level of attachment to their community and
are willing to settle on the employment front, like the Upstream Swimmers.
Moreover, the existence of this "in-between" type of rural youth was verified
during the interviews with the two long-term older individuals who regularly
interact with students in a rural post-secondary education institution.

P#14 is a 20-year-old rural Newfoundland female. When interviewed,
she was temporarily employed for the summer in a publicly funded, full-
time tourism job within driving distance of her hometown. She was also a
full-time student at a local college and drives 30 minutes each way between
school and home to be able to live in her hometown while taking courses.
In fact, she chose that institution to avoid having to out-migrate to acquire
post-secondary education. Upon graduation, she intends to seek good-
quality employment in her chosen field in any adjacent community, which
would allow her to remain in her hometown. If necessary she will expand
her search further, but only to the extent that she can live near her hometown. Thus, as with her choice of post-secondary institution and program,
she has chosen location first, and then will search for the best available
employment option while recognizing that this likely involves financial
and career sacrifices. On the other hand, P#8 is choosing to remain in her
hometown and take any available work. She would consider post-secondary
options, but only if available from her hometown location.

As with High Fliers, the second study included Mid Fliers. Some of the participants hope to acquire good-quality local employment, but they also realize that their current set of skills is a barrier. These are the ones who are disappointed that there are few local opportunities to acquire further education and training. Additionally, the cost of post-secondary education and transportation means that it is difficult for these individuals to afford to attend university or college, especially since it probably requires them to move to a different community (thereby eliminating the option to attend while living at home). These individuals are also keen to acquire more and better-quality local employment at a young age to facilitate starting to establish a career. In our view, the main difference between Mid Fliers and High Fliers is that the former are attempting to achieve their ambitions while remaining in, or close to, their hometowns. Moreover, they recognize that their approach probably means making compromises on the career front to be able to remain in the location to which they feel attached.

UPSTREAM SWIMMERS: THE NON-ACADEMIC STREAM

Participants within this category did not pursue post-secondary education. Instead, they sought local employment. The typical outcome was a struggle for good-quality employment within their hometown context. For example, one participant (hereafter referred to as P#3) is male, mid-twenties, and originally from rural Newfoundland. During and after high school, he tried to make a living in his hometown but could only find low-paying, unstable work in the hospitality/tourism sector requiring evening, night, and weekend hours. P#3 reluctantly migrated to seek better employment elsewhere in Canada. He decided to settle in an urban community in Ontario where he found a good job in terms of security, regularity of working hours, and remuneration.

Upstream Swimmers were also found in the second study. These youth were the ones who were less ambitious (e.g., focused on finding local employment, even of a minimum-wage type), or were so attached to their hometown that they explicitly recognize that they might be sacrificing employment opportunities. In our view, and relative to Mid Fliers and High Fliers, Upstream Swimmers prioritize their current living location and lifestyle.

DISCUSSION

Many workers face challenges when trying to acquire good-quality employment, and those challenges are accentuated for young adults in rural locations. However, lifestyle preferences vary, and not all young people are rabidly focused on career progression. Those who are keen to acquire good-quality employment might have to relocate to acquire education and/ or experience. Across the three jurisdictions studied here, there is considerable similarity in the issues facing rural youth in their pursuit of good employment, the acquisition of skills to help obtain that employment, and the decisions regarding staying or leaving one's hometown.

We also detected distinct divisions in the degree of career ambition versus the priority placed on lifestyle and hometown social networks. Thus, while conditions facing rural participants were similar, the individuals' responses differed. That said, the participants' experiences fit within Cooke's (2012) three categories of rural youth: High Fliers, Mid Fliers, and Upstream Swimmers. Some ambitious individuals prioritized career path choice and focused on improving their lives from a career and income-earning perspective. They were not opposed, or perhaps rather resigned, to moving away from their community, although some would ultimately return. Others were determined to stay in their community, mostly due to family and lifestyle reasons. In many cases, their modest career aspirations were for jobs that did not require any post-secondary education or training. Unfortunately, these individuals often faced obstacles in achieving even their more modest employment goals. For instance, low earnings may mean that these individuals have limited access to transportation. We also noticed a third group who would like to have a career/good-quality employment, but they are caught in a bind. These individuals sense that more education/skills upgrading is required, and that moving away might be necessary; yet they also feel a strong attachment to their hometown, and would prefer to stay.

High Fliers are likely to relocate from rural locations to pursue education at urban institutions, and are seemingly destined for occupations that tend to be located in urban labour markets. At the other extreme, Upstream Swimmers are likely to try to remain in their rural hometowns and seek whatever employment options are available for which they are qualified. However, their lack of education, skills, and experience potentially prevents their successful integration into good-quality employment. The Mid Fliers are also ambitious and keen to acquire skills and education like High Fliers, but they seek to do so from their rural location. For them, the local options to pursue that career path tend to be limited in the jurisdictions that we studied.

Consistent with existing literature, many of our participants found it difficult to secure good employment in rural locations, with or without acquiring post-secondary education. However, the pursuit of that education typically led to a need to relocate to an urban location, and only some participants were prepared to make that move, while others sought more local education options or simply searched for work after leaving high school. Although we expected to find a sizable proportion of young participants keen to out-migrate, the people we interviewed generally had a very strong attachment to their rural community. It should be noted that this could be a selection issue, or even the outcome of some methodological bias, if the ones desiring to out-migrate have already done so, and hence were unavailable to be interviewed. Some participants we spoke with, however, were committed to out-migrating for work or school to follow their intended career path, although we found that these individuals tended to be doing so rather reluctantly. These expressions of place attachment suggest the potential for return migration if appropriate career options were available.

CONCLUSION

Acquiring post-secondary education — although sometimes requiring temporary relocation or commuting — is key to the successful pursuit of good employment. Moreover, the decision to acquire this education was intertwined with one's decision to remain in, or leave, one's rural hometown. Being adamant about remaining at home necessarily limited the available education and employment options. Conversely, a willingness to relocate for education or to gain work experience could actually open doors to eventually return to one's rural community to live and work, while also providing opportunities to live and work elsewhere.

We recognize a limitation to our typology because it seemingly implies that those who leave their rural communities for work or education are better off than those who choose to remain in rural places. While that was the case among some of our participants, it does not have to be that way. Indeed, we would support targeted efforts to strengthen rural economies and increase the ability of people in rural places to upgrade their skills locally via post-secondary and/or vocational programs. If these place-based development policies are successful, better local employment opportunities and lower out-migration could result.

We encourage additional research to further clarify the ratio of workers per each of these three types, whether the three types of young workers are replicable, and whether they sufficiently and comprehensively map the typical approaches that the individuals in our studies are taking. We also encourage analyses exploring the movement of rural youth from one category to another. Ideally, additional research would also explore the career paths (and out-migration decisions) of these rural youth as they progress into subsequent stages of life. While we did not find that the degree of "rural-ness" affected one's employment or education decisions, this is certainly worthy of additional attention. Finally, we would also encourage research aimed at assessing the relative effects on mitigating out-migration of direct job creation, infrastructural improvements, economic incentives to local businesses, and/or the expansion of local education options. The goal, of course, would be to allow more targeted place-based development policies available to governments and communities.

ACKNOWLEDGEMENTS

We thank research assistants Deidre Hutchings, Adriana Cordeiro Socha, Kevin Allen, and Mike MacDonald, as well as colleagues Isik Zeytinoglu, Jimmy Donaghey, and James Chowhan. We are grateful for the support of the Social Sciences and Humanities Research Council of Canada and the Ontario Ministry of Agriculture, Food and Rural Affairs.

NOTE

1. Since all interviews were held on the island part of the province, we refer to Newfoundland rather than to Newfoundland and Labrador, the official name of the province.

REFERENCES

Alasia, A. 2003. "Rural and Urban Educational Attainment: An Investigation of Patterns and Trends, 1981–1996." *Rural and Small Town Canada Analysis Bulletin* 4, 5: 1–22. Statistics Canada Catalogue no. 21-006-XIE.

———. 2010. "Population Change across Canadian Communities, 1981 to 2006: The Role of Sector Restructuring, Agglomeration, Diversification and Human Capital." *Rural and Small Town Canada Analysis Bulletin* 8, 4: 1–25. Statistics Canada Catalogue no. 21-006-X.

——— and E. Magnusson. 2005. "Occupational Skill Level: The Divide between Rural and Urban Canada." *Rural and Small Town Canada Analysis Bulletin* 6, 2: 1–28. Statistics Canada Catalogue no. 21-006-XIE.

Andres, L., and E.D. Looker. 2001. "Rurality and Capital: Educational Expectations and Attainments of Rural, Urban/Rural and Metropolitan Youth." *Canadian Journal of Higher Education* 31, 2: 1–46.

Bank of Ireland. 2010. *The Irish Economy: An Overview.* Dublin.

Barca, F., P. McCann, and A. Rodriguez-Pose. 2012. "The Case for Regional Development Intervention: Place-based versus Place-neutral Approaches." *Journal of Regional Science* 52, 1: 134–52.

Bernard, A., R. Finnie, and B. St-Jean. 2008. "Interprovincial Mobility and Earnings." *Perspectives on Labour and Income* 9, 10: 15–25. Statistics Canada Catalogue no. 75-001-X.

Betcherman, G., and G.S. Lowe. 1997. *The Future of Work in Canada: A Synthesis Report.* Ottawa: Canadian Policy Research Networks.

Betz, M.R., and M.D. Partridge. 2012. "Country Road Take Me Home: Migration Patterns in Appalachian America and Place-based Policy." *International Regional Science Review* 36, 3: 267–95.

Boulin, J.-Y., M. Lallement, and F. Michon. 2006. "Decent Working Time in Industrialized Countries: Issues, Scopes, and Paradoxes." In. J.-Y. Boulin, M. Lallement, J. Messenger, and F. Michon, eds., *Decent Working Time: New Trends, New Issues,* 13–40. Geneva, Switzerland: ILO.

Brereton, F., C. Bullock, J.P. Clinch, and M. Scott. 2011. "Rural Change and Individual Well-being: The Case of Ireland and Rural Quality of Life." *European Urban and Regional Studies* 18, 2:203–27.

Bryant, C., and A.E. Joseph. 2001. "Canada's Rural Population: Trends in Space and Implications in Place." *Canadian Geographer* 45, 1: 132–37.

Bullock, C.H., M. Scott, and M. Gkartzios. 2011. "Rural Residential Preferences for House Design and Location: Insights from a Discrete Choice Experiment Applied to Ireland." *Journal of Environmental Planning and Management* 54, 5: 685–706.

Canadian Council on Learning (CCL). 2006. "The Rural–Urban Gap in Education." http://www.ccl-cca.ca/pdfs/LessonsInLearning/10-03_01_06E.pdf.

Cooke, G.B. 2007. "Alternative Work Schedules and Related Issues among Atlantic Canadians." *Workplace Review* 4, 2: 8–15. Sobey School of Business, Saint Mary's University.

———. 2012. "High Fliers versus Upstream Swimmers: Young Rural Workers in Canada and Ireland." In A. Sánchez-Castañeda, L. Serrani, and F. Sperotti, eds., *Youth Unemployment and Joblessness: Causes, Consequences, Responses*, 151–68. Newcastle upon Tyne, UK: Cambridge Scholars Publishing.

Corbett, M. 2009. "Rural Schooling in Mobile Modernity: Returning to the Places I've Been." *Journal of Research in Rural Education* 24, 7: 1–13.

Dries, N., R. Pepermans, and E. De Kerpel. 2008. "Exploring Four Generations' Beliefs about Career: Is 'Satisfied' the New 'Successful'?" *Journal of Managerial Psychology* 23, 8: 907–28.

Felt, L.F. 2003. *Small, Isolated and Successful: Lessons from Small, Isolated Societies of the North Atlantic*. St. John's: Research Paper for the Royal Commission on Renewing and Strengthening Our Place in Canada. www.gov.nl.ca/publicat/royalcomm/research/Felt.pdf.

Fortin, P. 2000. *The Irish Economic Boom: Facts, Causes, and Lessons*. Ottawa: Industry Canada.

Government of Ireland. 2012. Central Statistics Office. www.cso.ie/px/pxeirestat/Staire/SelectVarVal/saveselections.asp.

Government of Newfoundland and Labrador. 2010. *The Economy 2010*. http://www.economics.gov.nl.ca/TheEconomy2010.asp.

Green, A.E., and R.J. White. 2007. *Attachment to Place: Social Networks, Mobility and Prospects of Young People*. York, UK: Joseph Rowntree Foundation.

Grydehoj, A., and P. Hayward. 2014. "Social and Economic Effects of Spatial Distribution in Island Communities: Comparing the Isles of Scilly and Isle of

Wight, UK." *Journal of Marine and Island Cultures* 3, 1: 9–19.

Hango, D., and P. de Broucker. 2007. *Education-to-Labour Market Pathways of Canadian Youth: Findings from the "Youth in Transition" Survey.* Ottawa: Statistics Canada. www.statcan.gc.ca/pub/81-595-m/81-595-m2007054-eng.pdf.

Industry Canada. 2010. *Ontario Economic Overview: February 2010 Update.* Ottawa.

Kelly, U.A. 2009. "Learning to Lose: Rurality, Transience, and Belonging (a companion to Michael Corbett)." *Journal of Research in Rural Education* 24, 11: 1–4.

Lin, J. 2008. "Trends in Employment and Wages, 2002 to 2007." *Perspectives on Labour and Income* 9, 9: 5–15. Statistics Canada Catalogue no. 75-001-X

Locke, A. 2010. "The Social Factors Affecting the Pursuit of Higher Education and Employment for Rural Students." Unpublished report, Memorial University of Newfoundland, MER Program.

Looker, E.D., and G.S. Lowe. 2001. "Post-Secondary Access and Student Financial Aid in Canada: Current Knowledge and Research Gaps." Canadian Policy Research Networks (CPRN).

MacDonald, R. 2008. "Disconnected Youth? Social Exclusion, the 'Underclass' and Economic Marginality." *Social Work and Society* 6, 2: 236–48.

——— and J. Marsh. 2001. "Disconnected Youth?" *Journal of Youth Studies* 4, 4: 373–91.

Matthews, R., R. Pendakur, and N. Young. 2009. "Social Capital, Labour Markets, and Job-finding in Urban and Rural Regions: Comparing Paths to Employment in Prosperous Cities and Stressed Rural Communities in Canada." *Sociological Review* 57, 2: 305–30.

McAleavy, G., K. Collins, and G. Adamson. 2004. "Adult Learning in Northern Ireland: Investigating Further Education Policies for Widening Participation." *Research in Post-Compulsory Education* 9, 1: 83–104.

McGrath, B. 2001. "'A Problem of Resources': Defining Rural Youth Encounters in Education, Work and Housing." *Journal of Rural Studies* 17, 4: 481–95.

Mulcahy, D.M. 2007. "Current Issues in Rural Education in Newfoundland and Labrador." *Education in Rural Australia* 17, 1: 17–39.

Morgenroth, E. 2007. "Trends in the Regional Economic Activity of Ireland: The Role of Productivity." In C. Aylward and R. O'Toole, eds., *Perspectives on Irish Productivity: A Selection of Essays by Irish and International Economists*, 66–83. Dublin: Forfas.

Murphy, A.E. 2000. "The 'Celtic Tiger': An Analysis of Ireland's Economic Growth Performance." EUI Working Papers, Robert Schuman Centre for Advanced Studies, RSC No. 2000/16.

Newfoundland and Labrador Federation of Labour (NLFL), with the Canadian Centre for Policy Alternatives. 2009. "Newfoundland & Labrador: Weathering the Storm?" Discussion Paper. http://www.nlfl.nf.ca/briefs-and-presentations/2009/.

Nixon, A. 2010. "Youth Attitudes and Employment: Is the Emerging Workforce Changing?" Unpublished report, Memorial University of Newfoundland, MER Program.

Organization for Economic Co-operation and Development (OECD). 2005. *From Education to Work: A Difficult Transition for Young Adults with Low Levels of Education*. Paris: OECD.

———. 2006. *Reinventing Rural Policy*. Policy brief. Paris: OECD.

———. 2011. *How Many Students Finish Secondary Education?* Paris: OECD.

Royal Bank of Canada (RBC). 2009. *Provincial Outlook (for Canada), March 2009*. RBC Economics Research. http://www.glennsimoninc.com/images/file/RB-Cprovincialforecast.pdf.

———. 2011. *Provincial Outlook (for Canada), December 2011*. RBC Economics Research. www.rbc.com/economics/market/pdf/provfcst.pdf.

Shucksmith, M., S. Cameron, T. Merridew, and F. Pichler. 2009. "Urban–Rural Differences in Quality of Life across the European Union." *Regional Studies* 43, 10: 1275–89.

Stead, D.R. 2011. "Economic Change in South-West Ireland, 1960–2009." *Rural History* 22, 1: 115–46.

Tang, X. 2009. "Career Choices for Current Post-Secondary Students in Newfoundland and Labrador." Unpublished report, Memorial University of Newfoudnland, MER Program.

Vallée, G. 2005. *Towards Enhancing the Employment Conditions of Vulnerable Workers: A Public Policy Perspective*. Vulnerable Workers Series, No. 2. Mar. Canadian Policy Research Networks. http://www.cprn.ca/documents/35588_en.pdf.

Verma, A., and R.P. Chaykowski. 1999. "Employment and Employment Relations at the Crossroads." In V. Anil and R.P. Chaykowski, eds., *Contract and Commitment: Employment Relations in the New Economy*, 1–20. Kingston, Ont.: IRC Press, Queen's University.

Walsh, B.M. 2006. "Labour Market Adjustment in the Irish Regions, 1998–2005." *Quarterly Economic Commentary* (Autumn): 80–100. Dublin: Economic and Social Research Institute.

PART II: PLACE-BASED DEVELOPMENT IN PRACTICE

CHAPTER 7

"We Live Differently Than the Others": Culture, Islandness, and Alternative Economies on Chiloé and Prince Edward Island

Irene Novaczek

COGNITIVE DISSONANCE: ECONOMIC DEVELOPMENT VERSUS QUALITY OF LIFE

Human beings are infamous for espousing one set of values — for example, concern for community well-being, the environment, or traditional cultures — while concurrently supporting forms of economic development that place these values at risk. Globalized capitalism encourages the accumulation of wealth, conspicuous consumption, and endless growth, while mainstream media and marketing agencies reinforce the idea that this is not only desirable but also good for everyone — the rising tide that floats all boats. There are ample warnings from scientists that various ecological systems that support the industrial model are verging on collapse. The gap between rich and poor is increasing and even the financial systems that prop up the global economy threaten to collapse. The United Nations Development Programme (UNDP, 2011: ii) warns that "remarkable progress in human development over recent decades . . . cannot continue without bold global steps to reduce both environmental risks and inequality," while the World Economic Forum calls for new models of leadership, governance, and partnership because game-changing depletions of water and food, and traumatic climate changes, are imminent (World Economic Forum, 2011,

2012). Yet many people continue to adopt behaviours that place them comfortably within a perceived "normal" paradigm that not only perpetuates such destructive trends but also conflicts with their core values (McKenzie, Mohr, and Smith, 1999) and is not consistent with their long-term quality of life. This leads us to ask: what are the alternatives?

Research indicates that, beyond the point where money purchases a comfortable lifestyle, additional wealth contributes little to happiness, and may even cause stress (Easterlin, 2003; Tang, 2007). Furthermore, a yawning gap between the wealthiest and poorest members of a society promotes unhappiness, ill-health, and social disruption (Chapple et al., 2009; Auger et al., 2011). Modern indices of "quality of life" therefore go beyond measurements of financial status to include factors such as free time, access to services and education, personal health, environmental quality, and sense of community (Sharpe, 2000; Michalski, 2002; McCall, 2005). Indices of regional and national well-being include the United Nations Human Development Index, which reports on factors related to health, education, and living standards. By contrast, gross domestic product, the index employed by most governments and official statistics agencies to measure progress, simply reports on the gross sum of economic transactions, whether or not these result in improved health, education, and living standards. The mountain nation of Bhutan is unique in assessing development against indicators of gross national happiness (NEF, 2010). From the non-governmental sector we have the Happy Planet Index (HPI), whose authors find "mean life satisfaction, life expectancy and HPI scores of small islands to be significantly higher than non-islands — whilst their income levels do not diverge in the same way" (NEF, 2010: 331).

Having access to quality-of-life indices that show what makes people happy has not saved most governments from adopting strategies for economic development that result in damage to valued ecosystems, cultures, and local economies. According to the World Bank (2009) the countries at the bottom of the Human Development Index have no option: they must adopt globalized industrialization, with workers concentrated in urban centres, in order to "progress." This, it is argued, is the inevitable path to wealth, and the paradigm suggests that only the wealthy can afford a healthy environment, heritage conservation, and a vibrant culture.

The one-size-fits-all prescription of urban and industrial development ignores evidence that people find life satisfaction and success (in their own terms) in many other forms of economic activity, pursued at a local level in ways that help them to develop a sense of place and belonging. Stannard (1999) suggests that localism is an inherent human trait, only temporarily effaced by the forces of globalization. Localization of economies within states to establish "a more secure and sustainable balance between trade and local production" is promoted as an avenue for stemming the global loss of biological and cultural biodiversity (Economics of Happiness, n.d.). The Post Carbon Localization Network in the USA (Post Carbon Institute, n.d.), Transition Towns in the UK (Transition Network, n.d.), North American Business Alliance for Local Living Economics (BALLE, n.d.), among others, indicate that, in the twenty-first century, globalized industrial development will be strongly resisted.

Among the alternative modes of development being suggested is the localization of economies built on a foundation of local environmental and cultural resources and developed at a scale appropriate to place. This chapter will focus on islands, because they inherently embody localism, being uncoupled from mainlands and surrounded by water. If the localization, or "islanding," of regional economies is the way of the future, then the successes and failures of island economies, the ways in which islands dare to be different, and how they learn from other islands and mainlands may hold important lessons for future economic development on a rapidly changing planet. We begin with the argument for islands as apt spaces to study the nexus of economic development and quality of life. There follow two case studies focused on islands that are currently entrenched in globalized, industrial-scale development. Chiloé (Chile) and Prince Edward Island (Canada) are examples of small islands experimenting with alternate, human-scaled, ecological modes of economic and social development, based on cultural and natural heritage and a highly developed sense of place. Researchers based at the Institute of Island Studies in Canada have been exploring the nexus of environmental history, environmental health, economic activity, place attachment, and quality of life on these islands over six years. A meta-analysis of the research outputs in the context of the history of the islands' paths of economic development shows that we have much to learn from islands and how they fail or succeed in developing human-scaled, place-based local economies that can provide a rich quality of life with a reduced ecological footprint.

LEARNING FROM SMALL ISLANDS

Small islands (see also Chapter 4) offer manageably scaled social environments for research, where one can quickly gain insight into many levels of society. The susceptibility of small islands to economic, biological, physical, climatic, and human demographic changes is frequently acute, making them canaries in the global development coal mine. Islanders can more easily see the limits of their natural and cultural resources. The values that they attach to culture, environment, and economic status shape the process of development, for better or worse. Being so many and diverse, the small islands of the world comprise a suite of natural experiments for comparing outcomes of various development paths.

Alternatives to industrial-scale exploitation of natural resources that may be successful for small islands include "entrepôt" and "fortress" economies (Warrington and Milne, 2007; Baldacchino, 2011). Each arises from a distinct conceptualization of place. On "entrepôt" islands, people embrace the global economy but reject industrial resource extraction in favour of options such as offshore banking and information technology (IT) services. Successful "fortress" islands use cultural and ecological integrity as resources for varied livelihoods, often related to tourism. The discussion to follow focuses on such islands, where governments must protect natural and cultural heritage as part of a successful development process.

Tourists attracted to "fortress" islands can cause significant damage to ecological and cultural resources in their pursuit of seemingly exotic environmental and cultural experiences (e.g., Robertson, 1995; McKercher and Fu, 2006; Lapping, 2012). Where ecological services, landscape values, and cultural heritage are damaged by development, the possibilities for eco- and cultural tourism are compromised (Serrano and Stefanova, 2011). To conserve the heritage of such islands, limits on the number of tourists allowed to visit sites may have to be imposed, along with other measures including improved leadership, planning, and policies; sustainable enterprise development; locally relevant education and training; and effective conservation programs (Gardener and Grenier, 2011). Yet, even when island residents recognize the threats and make this clear to decision-makers, it may be very difficult to change the "business as usual" practices of government and industry — even on a small island where one might expect direct democracy to be possible (Raymond and Brown, 2007).

On the other hand, where intact Indigenous cultures are found on islands, this can have a positive impact on environmental health and resource management. For example, in Indonesian and South Pacific islands, some community-based traditional management systems have effectively regulated resource use for the long-term well-being of communities (Novaczek et al., 2001, 2005; Techera, 2011). Traditional institutions and cultural knowledge that support environmental management may allow tourism rooted in ecology and culture to drive economic development. Traditional institutions and cultural norms may also shape local business other than tourism (Novaczek and Stuart, 2006), as when rural people "choose to trade-off potential economic business success in order to ensure their family's status is not harmed in any way, and their place in the family, their social identity and their security is not jeopardized" (Cahn, 2008: 8). Thus, the course of development is not a simple linear march to modernity (McMichael, 2009). "Least developed" and remote societies on the planet may be advanced in the pursuit of happiness. Economic activity may be modest but it is scaled to place and attentive to quality of life because of being "interwoven with and embedded in social and cultural aspects of society" (Cahn, 2008: 8). One may well ask whether the "survival of the fittest" is necessarily the "survival of the wealthy." Or, are such small rural islands actually so far behind that they have come out ahead, with natural and cultural resources as well as a deep sense of place attachment more or less intact, and available as a basis for viable, post-industrial development?

CASE STUDY SITES AND METHODS

This chapter focuses on two predominantly rural islands of Canada and Chile, countries that share a history of European colonial occupation and settlement. Both countries rank very high on the Human Development Index (UNDP, 2011). Prince Edward Island and the Isla Grande of Chiloé in the Chiloé archipelago are rather similar in terms of size (5,684 km^2 versus 9,181 km^2, respectively) and population (140,000 versus 170,000), occupy similarly temperate latitudes (46° N versus 42° S), and have (self-identified) Indigenous populations that are outnumbered by European settlers (2 per cent and 17 per cent of the total population). On both islands, the economy is dominated by industrial-scale resource development: government estimates indicate that industrial-scale potato agriculture on Prince Edward Island contributes $2 billion annually in direct and indirect economic benefits (*The Guardian*, 2008); industrial-scale salmon aquaculture in Chiloé in recent decades has contributed up to US$2.4 billion per annum to the economy of the 10th Region, in which the Chiloé archipelago is located (Hayward, 2011).

Qualitative and quantitative data were gathered on Chiloé and Prince Edward Island by researchers based at the University of Prince Edward Island's Institute of Island Studies over the period 2006–12 using a mixed methods approach. On Chiloé a series of four studies explored histories of human–environment relations and economic development on land and sea, paying particular attention to the conservation and application of traditional cultural and ecological knowledge. Researchers used interviews, participatory workshops, and participant observation to explore the relationships among sense of place, economic activities, environmental quality, and perceived quality of life. The theme and methods of data collection employed in each of these studies is presented in Table 1.

Table 1. Research projects conducted by the Institute of Island Studies related to intersections of culture, quality of life, environment, and economic development on Chiloé Island, Chile.

Theme of study and reference	Methods (n = number of participants)
Traditional knowledge of edible and medicinal marine plants as a resource for enterprise development and quality of life (Levangie and Soto Quenti, 2009)	Participant observation; interviews with Williche community leaders, elders (n = 12); Workshop with Williche women, municipal staff, health workers (n = 15)
Ecological and cultural microenterprise and place attachment (D'Ambrogi and Novaczek, 2009)	Participant observation; interviews with small-scale entrepreneurs, government, NGOs (n = 30)
Attachment of youth to the sea and livelihoods based on marine resources (Vazquez and Novaczek, 2010)	Participant observation; interviews with fishing families, students, teachers, community leaders (n = 29); workshop with youth (n = 13)
Use of traditional ecological and cultural knowledge in small-scale agriculture (Rehder, 2012)	Participant observation of elders on subsistence farms; workshops with farmers on biodynamic agriculture (n = approx. 30)

On Prince Edward Island (Table 2) research projects explored similar themes using surveys and key informant interviews, including the use of participatory GIS (geographic information systems) to map social and cultural values attached to geographic space. This provided a concrete image of the place attachment and sense of place that underpins development of place-based and island-scaled livelihoods on this island.

Table 2. Research projects conducted by the Institute of Island Studies related to intersections of culture, quality of life, environment, and economic development on Prince Edward Island.

Theme of study and reference	Methods (n = number of participants)
Factors contributing to quality of life in the rural area of Tyne Valley (Levangie et al., 2009)	Random survey of rural residents (n = 57)
Perceptions of "progress," "development," and environmental change in the Southwest River watershed (Salvo, 2004)	Key informant interviews with elder fishers (n = 6)
Relationship of quality of life, economic development, and environmental health in New London Bay watershed (Novaczek, n.d.)	Random survey of rural residents (n = 29); key informant interviews with community leaders, elders, fishers, farmers (n = 17)
Geographic mapping of social and cultural values in Covehead/Brackley watershed (Novaczek et al., 2011)	Random survey of seasonal and permanent residents, including representatives of all statistical employment categories (n = 60)

Analysis of the suite of research findings in light of published literature documenting the histories of development on Chiloé and PEI allowed an exploration of how sense of place, and the relationships people have with their environmental and cultural heritage, can shape and enrich the diversity of local economies.

RESISTANCE TO INDUSTRIAL SALMON AQUACULTURE IN CHILOÉ, CHILE AND THE RISE OF MICROENTERPRISE

We are people of the island. We live differently than the others. . . .
We live in another rhythm.

Female entrepreneur, Chiloé, 2008

The islands of the Chiloé archipelago in the 10th Region (Los Lagos Region) of southern Chile have long been famous for their distinctive culture, traditions of mutual co-operation, and self-sufficiency based on rich natural resources. In the early twentieth century, Chiloé was a classic "fortress" island where the inhabitants (Chilote) carved out subsistence livelihoods based on mixed farming, inshore fisheries, woodcutting, and the collection of plants and animals from rainforests, sheltered estuaries, and the sea. The distinctive culture and architecture reflect both Indigenous and colonial European influences (Verhasselt Puppinck, 2000).

The fusion of colonial and Indigenous realities was not an easy or equitable process. Indigenous Williche were dispossessed of traditional lands and pushed to the margins — quite literally, to isolated hamlets along the coast. During the Pinochet regime of 1973–90, the suppression of Indigenous knowledge, languages, and cultures was national policy. In the 1990s, traditional chiefs of the Williche people finally regained management control over part of Chiloé's national park, one of the last remnants of their traditional territory not altered beyond recognition. They approach their ongoing struggle to regain their language and cultural traditions with a cosmological perspective, *wekimun*, the conscious fusion of traditional Williche knowledge with the best of what European and other cultures have to offer. This is the way, the chiefs assert, to move through current adversity to a prosperous future (M. Munoz Millalonco, personal communication, 2008).

Explosive growth of industrial salmon aquaculture has been the dominant economic driver in Chiloé since the 1980s, reducing unemployment to less than 4 per cent, enhancing the tax base in many municipalities, and bringing improvements in infrastructure and services. But for the Williche and other rural people, the rapid economic development has been a mixed blessing (Hayward, 2011). Many welcomed increased opportunities for employment, but the migration of rural young people into aquaculture centres decimated the agricultural labour force. Industrial working conditions were often unhealthy, and the wages for poorly educated rural youth were low. Rapid growth of urban populations outstripped infrastructure and service development, leaving many workers with limited access to decent housing, health care, and education. In 2007–08, a disease called infectious salmon anemia ravaged the salmon farms, causing many to go bankrupt and ushering in widespread unemployment (Vazquez and Novaczek, 2010). The salmon farms are now (2012–14) making a comeback, but the long-term impact of the industry in terms of environmental and social well-being is still in question.

Another major industry in Chiloé's economy is forestry. The temperate rainforest has been and continues to be cut at unsustainable levels, mainly to provide domestic firewood (Venegas, 2007). Unlike salmon aquaculture, which mostly benefits international corporate shareholders, forestry benefits almost all Chilote people because the vast majority of homes are heated solely with wood. We did not detect any widespread concern about over-cutting of forests during the various studies conducted in Chiloé.

Microenterprises and small businesses comprise a vibrant and important economic sector. Data available on the small and microenterprise sector of Chile are difficult to interpret because there is no consistent definition of small and microenterprises. Chile may have 83,340 small and microenterprises (SMEs), not including informal enterprises, fishers, or farmers, with the majority (86 per cent) being microenterprises employing fewer than 10 staff each (INE, 2006). In the 10th Region alone, there may be roughly 4,600 formal SMEs employing more than 60,000 workers (INE, 2006). Or, there may be as many as 29,945 microenterprises — 5.1 per cent of the national total (Organización Internacional del Trabajo y Servicio de Cooperación Técnica, 2010). A recent report (Chiloé Cómo Vamos, n.d.) suggests that in Chiloé Province 37 per cent of workers are employed by large corporations (defined on the basis of annual sales); 17 per cent by medium-sized companies; and 46 per cent by small and microenterprises. What is consistently clear is that SMEs are an important part of the economy, and female workers are relatively concentrated in the microenterprise sector. Cultural enterprises are a highly visible component of the sector and form a core attraction for tourism. In 2010, a total of 84,591 tourists visited Chiloé, primarily in the months of January and February (Sernatur, 2010).

A strong counter-movement to industrial development was evident among the small-scale entrepreneurs interviewed in Chiloé. They almost unanimously voiced concerns that their ecological and cultural heritage has been put at risk by the many intensive salmon farms occupying the sheltered interior coast of Chiloé. Their belief that salmon farming causes pollution has been verified in scientific studies (Instituo de Estudios Indigenas, 2003). Another concern was that the salmon farms interfere with the access by artisanal fishers to traditional fishing grounds. Many concerns are summed up in the Chilote song "Señor Salmon," composed by Nelson Torres and Claudio Alvarado, a key verse of which has been translated by Hayward and Garrido (2011):

> And if the sea dies, and the lake becomes barren
> Where can I find the thread? How can I unravel it?
> And if the river becomes so polluted that no one believes
> that it can be restored
> The voltage that powers the economy will be turned off.

Cultural knowledge and skills related to agriculture, fisheries, and handcrafts are also endangered because of the increasingly limited opportunities for rural elders to pass them on to younger generations. Elders deplore the consumer culture, which they see as infecting young people, and worry about the impact this has on community cohesion and identity. Overall, these trends diminish possibilities for developing the authentic touristic products and experiences that Chiloé seems well placed to pursue. As our Chilote respondents noted:

> The majority of foreigners come for tourism, and so they are interested in the exotic, the south of the world, where the world stops, far from everything. . . . When they arrive and see a product that is made by hand, and of really good quality, they will buy it. (Cosmetics entrepreneur, Chiloé, 2008)

> The first thing we have to do is to take care, preserve . . . because we know how to work with the resources we have. (Garlic processor, Chiloé, 2008)

> We are losing things that are our essential traditions. We are seeing this as we produce more, as we have a desire for more money, and in the end that is the result. Lamentably, we live with a society that is very distant and different from our culture. (Construction worker and former fisher, Chiloé, 2008)

> We were confused, not knowing what we could do be-
> cause everyone had gone to the other side — industrial-
> ization, capital, salmon, work. . . . History was calling on
> us to do something. . . . It was not the objective to sell
> culture, but to do something for the culture. My wife
> knew how to knit. I started with potatoes. Some need to
> take care of the woods. Some need to take care of the
> ocean. And if everyone did this, their part of the culture
> would be maintained. (Member of doll-making collec-
> tive, Chiloé, 2009)

A provincial government agency has recently published a document acknowledging the negative impacts of rapid aquaculture development on Chilote culture (SUBDERE, 2010). The agency recommended co-ordinated efforts by public, private, and academic sectors to use both physical resources and territorial identity to support endogenous economic development, and, in particular, emphasized the potential for family microenterprise and community-based development that could be branded using the Chilote sense of identity (SUBDERE, 2010). (See Chapters 8 and 11 for further discussion of branding as a place-based development strategy.)

Chiloé has a history of resistance to large-scale developments that goes beyond the issue of salmon farming. Our attention was drawn to these public controversies because a similar pattern of engagement was evident on Prince Edward Island around the same issues: linkage to the mainland and development of large-scale wind power infrastructure (see below). In 2006, public discourse and street-level graffiti on Chiloé objected to a national government project to build a bridge connecting the island to the mainland. This project was being actively resisted by Indigenous chiefs, university students, and cultural practitioners, among others. For these dissenters, a bridge would bring no significant benefits to local people, but would allow external capitalists to strip the island of its marine and forest resources with greater efficiency. In 2009, a new crop of graffiti was noted, protesting an industrial-scale wind farm proposed for lands in the flight path of migratory birds and next to blue whale habitat (Langman, 2011).

Although cultural enterprise offers an alternative to wage labour in the aquaculture industry, it faces significant challenges: the seasonality of tourism, the lack of access to micro-credit, and limited access to training in business management, marketing, and use of the Internet to reach off-island markets. On the positive side, Indigenous entrepreneurs attest that in recent years they have gained a new level of acceptance and respect. Although their financial prospects are modest, entrepreneurs continue in their businesses because of personally satisfying benefits such as independence, flexibility, and time with family. Cultural entrepreneurship is clearly rooted in a profound sense of place and the desire to manage and conserve the ecological and cultural assets of the archipelago. Despite the challenges, Chiloé already has well-established artisanal food and craft production, and a lively artistic and musical community. The Museo de Arte Moderna in the provincial capital, Castro, is volunteer run and established on municipal land. Cultural, culinary, and eco-tourism are gaining ground. Emerging trends include niche products from organic agriculture; international support for preserving native potato varieties; development of local specialty breeds of sheep; introduction of modern designs into traditional knitting and weaving; organic cosmetics; and various forms of Indigenous enterprise, including medicinal herbal products (Novaczek, personal observations; D'Ambrogi and Novaczek, 2009). The fact that Chiloé retains significant virgin forest lands and has not lost its working landscape of small family farms gives it a degree of inherent resilience in the face of a changing global economy. On Prince Edward Island, by contrast, the land has been much more severely impacted by industrial development, in ways that have eroded inherent resilience to a much greater degree.

FINDING ALTERNATIVES TO INDUSTRIAL AGRICULTURE ON PRINCE EDWARD ISLAND, CANADA

> *You couldn't beat this island to live in.... Anybody who lives here*
> *would never want to leave here, the only thing is that the money*
> *is no good.*
>
> Retired farmer and horse breeder, PEI, 2009

Prince Edward Island, with its population of approximately 140,000 people, was clothed in Acadian forest and inhabited by Aboriginal Mi'kmaq people when European settlers arrived some 400 years ago — first French, then British. Settlers cut timber for shipbuilding and burned away the rest of the dark woods in order to transform the island into a centre of food production. Agricultural settlement peaked in the early 1900s, when field crops occupied more than 550,000 acres of land (MacDonald, 2000). At this point, the Mi'kmaq had been decimated by disease and warfare and relegated to small reserves. Only very recently have they begun to flex some economic muscle, especially with respect to fisheries (Novaczek et al., 2009).

Occupational plurality of nineteenth- and early twentieth-century island households, which pursued diverse production and harvesting activities, did not fit within the twentieth-century push for agribusiness development. From the 1960s on, successive island governments, abetted by federal agencies, forced a shift from small mixed farms and multi-species fisheries to corporate agribusiness and separate, professionalized fisheries and aquaculture. An attempt to veer from this track in the 1970s was short-lived (MacEachern, 2003).

By the turn of the twenty-first century, the ecological damage resulting from these development choices was painfully apparent: species extinction, forest fragmentation, groundwater pollution from agricultural chemicals, fish kills and anoxia in streams and estuaries (Liao, 2008). Standards of living had risen, but per capita income lagged behind the Canadian average, reinforcing the growing recognition that the benefits of industrialization have not matched the costs. The provincial government admitted that "Prince Edward Island farmers have found themselves unable to prosper by competing in these globalized, efficiency-driven commodity markets"

(Government of Prince Edward Island, 2009: 3–4). As had occurred in Chiloé, policy-makers went on to recommend more ecological alternatives, diversification, value-added niche production, creativity, and co-operation (Government of Prince Edward Island, 2009).

The island still grapples with poorly controlled coastal development and the mixed blessings of mass tourism, which brings a million or more visitors to the island every year (Tourism Research Centre, 2010). But in the background, a movement towards more diverse and human-scaled forms of agriculture and tourism is visible. Whether this represents a "new" vision, or a modern reconstruction of traditional livelihood options, is an interesting area for further inquiry. The shift is consistent with the fact that Prince Edward Island has high rates of volunteerism and charitable giving, despite annual per capita incomes that are among the lowest in the country (Statistics Canada, 2006). The depth and breadth of the social economy, made up of co-operatives, non-profits, and charitable organizations that help close the gap between the island's wealthy elites and more marginalized citizens, is impressive (Groome Wynne, 2008). The island has a long history of co-operative enterprise development (Bruce and Cran, 2004).

In the history of Prince Edward Island, as on Chiloé, resistance to various forms of industrial development is recurrent. The island is famous for having once banned automobiles (MacDonald, 2000), and a tug of war between proponents and resisters to the idea of linking the island to the mainland with a bridge went on throughout the twentieth century until the Confederation Bridge, spanning 12.9 kilometres, opened in 1997 (MacDonald, 2007). In the 1980s, the target of public ire was a proposed government subsidy to Litton Industries, a military technology company (MacDonald, 2000). In the twenty-first century, locally owned wind farm development was welcomed by island consumers, who willingly paid a premium price for renewable energy (Stuart, 2006; Liao, 2008); but, for many reasons related to environment, landscape aesthetics, public health, and place attachment, development of large-scale private wind farms and transmission lines designed to export the power off island have sparked resistance (*The Guardian*, 2008).

As Baldacchino explains in Chapter 3 of this volume, forms of informal

sector entrepreneurship can be essential for economic survival in peripheral economies. On Chiloé, the workers resort to subsistence farming,
woodcutting, and/or marine harvesting activities to survive periods of
unemployment or to augment inadequate cash incomes. This was also the
case on Prince Edward Island prior to the advent of federal unemployment
insurance in the 1960s. Now called Employment Insurance, this program
is paid into by workers and their employers to provide an income subsidy
for workers facing periods of unemployment or underemployment. Because
core industries — including fishing, farming, and tourism as well as wage
labour opportunities in building and home construction — are highly seasonal, a classic Prince Edward Island livelihood pattern is seasonal wage
work during the peak summer season, followed by periods of dependence
on employment insurance. Far from being a period of helpless dependence,
the season of "worklessness" is, for many participants, highly productive: a
time to tend to family commitments (especially child and elder care) and
community service, self-education, creative pursuits, and other projects
important to personal health and well-being. Alton MacLean's folksong of
the late twentieth century, collected by Ives (1999), declares:

> Since I have been laid off I'm back home again,
> Each Sunday morning I make church by ten.
> I look up to Heaven, saying "Dear Lord, let it be . . .
> If you find work for someone I sure hope it's not me!"

Contentment with modest levels of cash income and attention to
work–life balance were evident in the results of research conducted in rural
Prince Edward Island in 2006 and 2009 (see Table 2). In the Tyne Valley
area, for example, seasonal fisheries, aquaculture, farming, forestry, construction, and tourism are prevalent. Unemployment rates can be twice as
high and average annual household incomes 10 per cent lower than the
provincial average (Prince Edward Island Community Accounts, n.d.). Yet,
when asked to identify factors that contributed to their quality of life, Tyne
Valley residents rarely mentioned jobs or income. They focused on aspects
of community social well-being such as "safety and security, peacefulness
and calm, the feeling of belonging and attachment, the knowledge that you

can depend on other community members for help, community pride and spirit, and living in a place that has a pleasant and happy atmosphere" (Levangie et al., 2009: 26).

In the New London Bay watershed, where many residents are university-educated and upper middle-class, people prioritized personal well-being while exhibiting a profound sense of place and appreciation for the natural environment. Factors related to community social well-being and positive personal relations also contributed to quality of life, but economic factors were rarely mentioned.

> I guess the first thing about quality of life is a work–life/
> home–life balance . . . it's very much a sense of place. . . .
> We love living here, being on the water, being able to swim
> and boat. . . . This community still has an old fashioned
> sense of community. . . . The lady next door gives us a pie
> when her cows get out on the road and we put them back
> in. (Urban professional living in rural area, PEI, 2009)

> You can smell the lupins. . . . Earlier on you could smell
> the apple blossoms, and later it will be the wild roses. It
> doesn't get much better. . . . Night time here is spectacu-
> lar. When there is no ambient light taking away from the
> sky, the stars are fabulous. In the winter time it's fabu-
> lous. (Retired professional living in rural area, PEI, 2009)

> You really don't need a whole lot of external things when
> you are happy inside. . . . If you can walk an hour and
> never leave your property, think how good that makes
> you feel. And at great sacrifice you keep that, because
> what else is important? (Retired farmer and politician,
> PEI, 2009)

When social and cultural values attached to place were explored in the Covehead and Brackley Bay watersheds (see Table 2), the process of locating these values on a map of the local area elicited written testimonies illustrating intense place attachment. "Hot spots" that were piled high with value markers included rivers, bays, national park beaches and larger forested areas; the local fishing wharf, historic resorts, the golf course, and long-term cottage developments; community halls, churches, and cemeteries (Novaczek et al., 2011).

SMALL-SCALE AND CULTURAL ENTERPRISE ON PEI

As in Chiloé, the small and microenterprise sector on Prince Edward Island is substantial: more than 10,000 enterprises appear to be family- or owner-operated; another 4,500 firms have fewer than 10 employees (Industry Canada, 2011). These include many small-scale fishing, farming, forestry, and tourism enterprises as well as many artists and artisans. Census data report 1,960 cultural workers on Prince Edward Island (Statistics Canada, 2006), but the actual number is at least double that (Williams and Hill, 2010). Musicians and singers are the most numerous in the cultural worker category, followed by artisans and craftspeople, and various writers, composers, and performers. Many hold one or more jobs in addition to their artistic endeavours. They frequently engage in seasonal wage work, often in tourism, and may apply for income assistance from federal employment insurance in winter (Williams and Hill, 2010).

Artisans and craftspeople on PEI express concerns similar to those highlighted by Chilote artisans. They feel that too few young people are being drawn into their industry, and traditional skills are not being passed on to younger generations. Cultural workers on Prince Edward Island also express the need for business skills training and mentorship (Williams and Hill, 2010). On the positive side, the island's cultural community is described as closely knit and supportive. Many practitioners establish alternative lifestyles in rural communities where housing and studio costs are more affordable. They have "resigned themselves to living with less cash flow than their neighbours" in return for "freedom to live their creative lives" (Williams and Hill, 2010: 18).

Emerging trends in the evolving economy of Prince Edward Island include a rapidly growing music industry; culinary, cultural, agricultural, and eco-tourism supported and promoted by government; cultural festivals in rural small halls that cater to both locals and tourists; organic agriculture; and Indigenous enterprise. A vocal movement espouses an "organic island"; a socially active group has identified themselves as "islanders by choice"; an ever increasing number of farmers' markets and community-supported agriculture ventures are evident; and a food security network actively promotes sustainability in agriculture. The Fall Flavours Festival involves an island-wide celebration of local food, and Experience Prince Edward Island offers touristic activities that engage visitors with islanders where they work—on small boats, in artists' studios and potteries, on beaches, and in farm fields. The variety of "experiences" on offer and the success of this style of cultural tourism provide inspiration and encouragement to small islands such as Chiloé, where tourism is less developed.

DISCUSSION: SMALL ISLAND FUTURES IN A CHANGING WORLD

Societies may adopt development options that are destructive to the long-term public good and quality of life. According to social theorists, approval within our intimate social spheres and the examples set by our fellow citizens are powerful motivators (McKenzie et al., 1999). Therefore, direct interaction with persons and organizations that dare to pursue alternative paths is a potential countervailing force to a destructive economic paradigm. As seen on Prince Edward Island and Chiloé, ecological damages — such as pollution of freshwater and inshore marine environments — as well as the social impacts of rural depopulation and the loss of connection to traditional skills and knowledge, show up quickly and are very visible to the residents of small islands. The recognition of such trends can stimulate new modes of development, and these may be adopted and replicated quite rapidly in a small-scale society. Within a circumscribed society such as that of a small island, one can conceive of a social movement being started through positive examples provided by a small number of visible and widely networked actors, and the relatively rapid achievement of a tipping point, beyond which the momentum for change becomes irresistible.

The study of small islands — treating them as if they were end points in a diverse range of natural experiments — shows that being marginalized from the process of globalized industrial activity (either by chance or by design) can have certain benefits. "Fortress" islands that reject industrialization to focus on maintaining cultural and ecological integrity can engage the world from a basis of strength that derives from having landscapes and authentic cultures that the rest of the world is keen to experience. The walls of the fortress that can shield an island against the ravages of inappropriate development are not physical, but cultural. The mortar in the cultural wall is a strong sense of place, often a notable characteristic of small island peoples. As Vodden et al. observe in Chapter 1, sense of place, or belonging, is in effect a resource (Stratford, 2009).

People on Chiloé and Prince Edward Island exhibit strong place attachment, and many are struggling to identify types and scales of economic activity that maintain environmental and cultural values and quality of life. Aboriginal populations of both islands have suffered serious impacts of European colonization, and are therefore in the process of reconstituting and recovering their cultures. The islands seem poised to break open new arenas of possibility, even as collapsing global financial systems and climate change threaten to drastically reduce the potential scope and scale of future economies.

Because of the need to overcome damages to cultures and ecosystems, the path to an alternative economy is not easy or simple; it requires courage, creativity, and hard work. Development of small-scale businesses based on cultural and natural assets often involves forgoing accumulation of wealth in favour of other values such as independence and self-sufficiency, personal and family health, community well-being, and stewardship of culture and the environment. A diverse, sustainable livelihoods approach has been a hallmark of many islands of the developing world, but can also be pursued in relatively wealthy places such as Chiloé and Prince Edward Islands, where place attachment shapes livelihoods and attention to work–life balance can provide a rich quality of life. Many believe that the widespread adoption of this approach is essential to future sustainability on our planet.

Livelihoods that exploit but at the same time conserve and protect cultural and natural resources are human-scaled options that seem especially suited to islands. For example, carefully controlled cultural and eco-tourism can be a successful alternative development path for islands. The island mystique, which in part draws power from the perception that space on small islands is both uniquely endowed and limited and therefore has special value, encourages visitors to pay a premium for a limited-access experience. Because tourism is an economic activity where visitors consume local products on site, it functions as an export industry that does not incur the expense of transporting goods off-island. To maximize this benefit inherent in tourism, the island must grow and manufacture many of the goods that tourists consume. An effective strategy is to focus on products that meet the needs of native islanders as well as visitors and, therefore, to have a year-round market. Optimally, these products would also provide opportunities for locals to conserve and celebrate natural and cultural heritage. When locals participate actively in defining and supporting tourism products, these are more likely to retain the authenticity that tourists seek. Active support from governments, NGOs, and university researchers is generally required to facilitate co-ordination and exchange of information, provide timely training to entrepreneurs, support marketing and branding strategies, offer funding programs, and enforce basic standards.

Culinary tourism is being actively pursued by both Chiloé and Prince Edward Island, with their agricultural heritages and interesting food culture fusions. This option depends on and proudly displays culinary traditions, requires healthy ecosystems to support traditional food production, and is clearly a promising option for small islands that need to retain local food security and avoid over-dependence on costly imports. Artisanal farming and fisheries and cultural enterprises provide more than incomes. Fresh local food, high-quality handcrafted goods, and cultural entertainments serve local needs while also providing the basis of an authentic, high-value touristic experience. Pursuing such development options can strengthen public infrastructure and the supporting environment (forests, rivers and bays, parks, community halls, landscapes), and build social capital, creativity, sense of place, and community cohesion.

Isolation and limited resources encourage mutual assistance on small islands, and both Chiloé and Prince Edward Island are typical in this regard. Prince Edward Island has a long and rich history of co-operative business development, while on Chiloé, informal co-operative activities among neighbours and within extended families are common. It is tempting to argue that the communal forms of enterprise often apparent on small islands are somehow more reflective of humankind's indigenous or natural state. Be that as it may, one can also find social enterprises in modern Western societies. Co-operatives (International Co-operative Alliance, n.d.) hold social, cultural, and ecological sustainability as core values, and other companies may also practice environmental and social responsibility (Segerlund, 2010). The ways in which co-operatives and other forms of socially responsible enterprise may be particularly well suited as drivers of "ecological economic development" on small islands suggest a promising theme for future research.

The dark side of the close-knit, supportive society found on "fortress" islands such as Prince Edward Island and Chiloé can be the exclusion and resentment of outsiders (MacDonald, 2000; Baldacchino, 2006). Yet, as recognized by the Williche people of Chiloé, a willingness to integrate new ways of thinking and being, new people and new technologies, is essential to a vibrant and evolving society and economy. Finding the balance between stubborn adherence to traditional norms and acceptance of the best that the rest of the world has to offer — termed "glocalization" by Robertson (1995) — is a common conundrum that successful island(er)s learn to master.

As Baldacchino (Chapter 3) and others in this volume also point out, evolving information technologies facilitate post-industrial development. They may enable and foster civic participation and co-operation in local governance, community-building, and creative enterprise development. Although there is a risk that information technologies will have a homogenizing influence on human cultures, they can just as readily allow communities to collaborate and learn from one another while maintaining and celebrating cultural distinctiveness.

Openness to learning and change may well be key to future development on "fortress" islands. Greenwood et al. (2011) note that effective social engagement between sectors is critical to innovative economic development on the island of Newfoundland, as well as in the remote rural mainland communities of Labrador. Cross-fertilization among sectors within as well as beyond a community can be surprisingly limited, and a purposeful effort may be required to strike a balance between the bonding characteristic of many small-scale societies and the bridging that opens them up to innovation and external sources of expertise (Woolcock and Narayan, 2000). The Williche concept of *wekimun* exemplifies this fruitful blend of different ways of being and knowing that facilitates social and economic development.

CONCLUSION

The Prince Edward Islanders we interviewed and surveyed over the past six years expressed very clearly that quality of life, imbricated in a deeply felt sense of place, trumped material ambitions. They had made conscious decisions to remain on or return to Prince Edward Island despite the prospects of lower incomes and fewer services than could be enjoyed in many other parts of Canada, just as the small-scale entrepreneurs on Chiloé had rejected the relative safety of wage labour jobs in the salmon industry in favour of various forms of seasonal self-employment. These islanders seek work–life balance, family and community engagement, and a quality of life that is enhanced by connection with a healthy and aesthetically pleasing living environment. Although placing great value on personal independence and self-sufficiency, they also frequently build livelihoods through collective action, and help fill the gaps in community services through volunteerism and charitable giving.

Researchers and activists increasingly speak not simply of post-industrial development, but of post-development. This is not an outright rejection of the development process, but an invitation to forget everything we think we know about what is or is not legitimately "development" and to embrace the variety of paths that people invent to suit their own needs and values, at a local level. These include "a vast array of non-capitalist and alternative capitalist enterprises, unpaid and alternatively paid labour, alternative private and open-access property, non-market and alternative market transactions and alternative and non-market finance" (Gibson-Graham, 2010: 228). In the past, "economists have rendered non-capitalist economic activity non-credible or non-existent" and so have robbed us of human potential that needs to be reclaimed (Gibson-Graham, 2010). Gibson-Graham, like

Dahl (1996), invites us to reintegrate the "eco" into economy by, among other strategies, learning to mimic the resilient dynamics of nature.

This is a path of acceptance where new realities can be envisioned and spoken or acted into existence, without judgment or imposition of constructed hierarchies, in ways that foster creativity and pay attention to place and appropriate scale. On Chiloé, certain female elders are recognized as "Masters of Peace," because they have visions that help guide community decision-making. One such elder spent her life dreaming into being cultural knowledge of medicinal plants that had been forgotten during the decades when the Chilean government suppressed Indigenous cultural practices (Manuel Munoz Millalonco, personal communication, 2010). The people of other rural and remote communities can learn from her example to take strength from their sense of place to open the doors of possibility, dream a new reality (or resurrect and reconstruct an ancient reality), and speak it into being to build alternative, place-based economies that serve not only human beings but also their supporting environments.

REFERENCES

Auger, N., D. Hamel, J. Martinez, and N.A. Ross. 2012. "Mitigating Effect of Immigration on the Relation between Income Inequality and Mortality: A Prospective Study of Two Million Canadians." *Journal of Epidemiology and Community Health* 66, 5. doi: 10.1136/jech.2010.127977.

Baldacchino, G. 2006. *Coming to, and Settling on, Prince Edward Island: Stories and Voices.* A report on a study of recent immigrants to PEI. Charlottetown: Population Secretariat of PEI.

———. 2011. "A Fresh Consideration of Development Strategies for Smaller Island States and Territories." In G. Baldacchino and D. Niles, eds., *Island Futures*, 53–72. Tokyo: Springer.

Bruce, M., and E. Cran. 2004. *Working Together: Two Centuries of Co-operation on Prince Edward Island.* Charlottetown: Island Studies Press.

Cahn, M. 2008. "Indigenous Entrepreneurship, Culture and Micro-enterprise in the Pacific Islands: Case Studies from Samoa." *Entrepreneurship and Regional Development* 20: 1–18.

Chapple, S., M. Forster, and J.P. Martin. 2009. "Inequality and Well-being in OECD Countries: What Do We Know?" Paper presented at the 3rd OECD World

Forum on Statistics, Knowledge and Policy: Charting Progress, Building Visions, Improving Life, Busan, Korea. http://oecd.org?dataoecd/31/53/44109816.pdf.

Chiloé Cómo Vamos. n.d. Primera cuenta publica ciudadana: Chiloé como vamos? Indicadores de calidad de vida de Chiloé: Una radiografia de su desarrollo. Castro, Chile.

Dahl, A.L. 1996. *The Eco Principle: Ecology and Economics in Symbiosis*. London: George Ronald/Zed Books.

D'Ambrogi, K., and I. Novaczek. 2009. *We Are People of the Island: Social and Cultural Microenterprise on Chiloé*. Charlottetown, PEI: Island Studies Press.

Easterlin, R.A. 2003. "Explaining Happiness." *Proceedings of the National Academy of Sciences of the United States of America* 100, 19: 11176–83.

The Economics of Happiness. n.d. *The Economics of Happiness* film trailer. http://www.theeconomicsofhappiness.org.

Gardener, M.R., and C. Grenier. 2011. "Linking Livelihoods and Conservation: Challenges Facing the Galápagos Islands." In G. Baldacchino and D. Niles, eds., *Island Futures*, 73–86. Tokyo: Springer.

Gibson-Graham, J.K. 2010. "Forging Post-development Partnerships: Possibilities for Local and Regional Development." In A. Pike, A. Rodriguez, and J. Tomaney, eds., *Handbook of Local and Regional Development*, 226–36. London: Routledge.

Government of Prince Edward Island. 2009. *Growing the Island Way: The Next Chapter for the Agriculture and Agri-food Economy of Prince Edward Island*. Charlottetown: Commission on the Future of Agriculture and Agri-food on Prince Edward Island.

Greenwood, R., C. Pike, and W.Kearley. 2011. *A Commitment to Place: The Social Innovation in Newfoundland and Labrador*. St John's: Harris Centre, Memorial University of Newfoundland.

Groome Wynne, B. 2008. "Social Capital and the Social Economy in a Sub-national Jurisdiction." In G. Baldacchino and K. Stuart, eds., *Pulling Strings: Policy Insights for Prince Edward Island from Other Sub-national Island Jurisdictions*, 73–106. Charlottetown, PEI: Island Studies Press.

The Guardian (Charlottetown). 2008. "Residents Collect Petition Signatures to Voice Concerns over New Line,"11 Apr.

Hayward, P. 2011. "Salmon Aquaculture, Cuisine and Cultural Disruption in Chiloé." *Locale: The Australasian-Pacific Journal of Regional Food Studies* 1: 87–110. http://localejournal.org/issues/n1/Locale%20n1%20-%2009%20-%20Hayward.pdf.

——— and W. Garrido. 2011. "Chiloé: An Offshore Song Culture." In G. Baldacchino, ed., *Island Songs: A Global Repertoire*, 153–69. Lanham, Md.: Scarecrow Press.

Industry Canada. 2011. "Key Small Business Statistics." www.ic.gc.ca/sbstatistics.

INE. 2006. *Encuesta anual de las pequenas y medianas empresas, ano 2006*. Santiago: Government of Chile, INE. http://www.ine.cl/canales/chile_estadistico/estadisticas_economicas/pymes/pdf/resultadospyme.pdf.

Instituto de Estudios Indigenas. 2003. *Los derechos de los pueblos indigenas en Chile: Informe del programa de derechos indigenas*. http://books.google.ca/books. google.ca/books?=id=v3hiZqrYLV4C&pg=PA221&dg=impacto+ambiental+en+Chiloé#=onepage&q&f=false.

International Co-operative Alliance. n.d. www.ica.coop/coop/principles.html.

Ives, S. 1999. *Drive Dull Care Away: Folksongs from Prince Edward Island as gathered by Edward D. "Sandy" Ives*. Charlottetown, PEI: Island Studies Press.

Langman, J. 2011. "Chilean Wind Farm Faces Turbulence over Whales." *National Geographic News*, 29 Nov. http://news.nationalgeographic.com/news/energy/2011/11/111129-chile-wind-farm-impact-on-the-blue-whale/.

Lapping, M. 2012. "Foreword: Geography at Risk." In G. Baldacchino, ed., *Extreme Heritage Management*, 16–24. Oxford: Berghahn Books in association with Island Studies Press.

LeVangie, D., I. Novaczek, S. Enman, R. MacKay, and K. Clough. 2009. *Quality of Island Life Survey: Tyne Valley & Surrounding Areas 2006*. Charlottetown, PEI: Institute of Island Studies, University of Prince Edward Island.

LeVangie, D., and M. Soto Quenti. 2009. *Medicinal Plants of the Mi'kmaq and Williche*. Charlottetown, PEI: Island Studies Press.

Liao, L.M. 2008. "The Environment as a Resource: Lessons for Prince Edward Island from Other Sub-national Island Jurisdictions." In G. Baldacchino and K. Stuart, eds., *Pulling Strings: Policy Insights for Prince Edward Island from Other Sub-national Island Jurisdictions*, 133–60. Charlottetown, PEI: Island Studies Press.

MacDonald, E. 2000. *If You're Stronghearted: Prince Edward Island in the Twentieth Century*. Charlottetown, PEI: PEI Museum and Heritage Foundation.

———. 2007. "Bridge over Troubled Waters: The Fixed Link Debate on Prince Edward Island, 1885–1997." In G. Baldacchino, ed., *Bridging Islands: The Impact of Fixed Links*, 29–46. Charlottetown, PEI: Acorn Press.

MacEachern, A. 2003. *The Institute of Man and Resources, an Environmental Fable*. Charlottetown, PEI: Island Studies Press.

McCall, S. 2005. "Quality of Life." In A.C. Michalos, ed., *Citation Classics from Social Indicators Research*, 117–36. Dordrecht: Springer. http://www.springerverlag.com/.

McKenzie Mohr, D., and W. Smith. 1999. *Fostering Sustainable Behaviour: An Introduction to Community-based Social Marketing*. Gabriola Island, BC: New Society Publishers.

McKercher, B., and C.D. Fu. 2006. "Living on the Edge." *Annals of Tourism Research* 33, 2: 508–24.

McMichael, P. 2009. *Contesting Development: Critical Struggles for Social Change*. London: Routledge.

Michalski, J. 2002. *Quality of Life in Canada: A Citizen's Report Card*. Background Report. Canadian Policy Research Networks. http://www.cprn.org/.

New Economic Foundation (NEF). 2010. *The (Un)happy Planet Index 2.0: Why Good Lives Don't Have to Cost the Earth*. London: New Economics Foundation. http://www.happyplanetindex.org/public-data/files/happy-planet-index-2-0.pdf.

North American Business Alliance for Local Living Economics [BALLE]. n.d. http://www.livingeconomies.org/.

Novaczek, I. n.d. "Quality of Life and Environment in the New London Bay Watershed." Charlottetown: Institute of Island Studies. Unpublished manuscript.

———, R. Angus, and N. Lewis. 2009. "Evolution of Post-Colonial Indigenous Peoples' Fisheries Management Systems: Fiji and Prince Edward Island." In G. Baldacchino, R. Greenwood, and L. Felt, eds., *Remote Control: Governance Lessons for and from Small, Insular, and Remote Regions*, 208–26. St John's: ISER Books.

———, I. Harkes, J. Sopacua, and M. Tatuhey. 2001. *An Institutional Analysis of Sasi Laut in Maluku*. ICLARM Techical Report 59. Penang, Malaysia: The World Fish Centre.

———, J. MacFadyen, D. Bardati, and K. MacEachern. 2011. "Social and Cultural Values Mapping as a Decision Support Tool for Climate Change Adaptation." Charlottetown, PEI: Institute of Island Studies. http://www.upei.ca/iis/files/iis/SCVM%20REPORT%20Dec%2012%20iis.pdf.

———, J. Mitchell, and J. Veitayaki, eds. 2005. *Pacific Voices: Equity and Sustainability in Pacific Islands Fisheries*. Suva, Fiji: Institute of Pacific Studies, University of the South Pacific.

——— and K. Stuart. 2006. "The Contributions of Women Entrepreneurs to the Local Economy in Small Islands: Seaplant-based Micro-enterprise in Fiji and Vanuatu." *Journal of Small Business & Entrepreneurship* 19, 4: 367–80.

Organización Internacional del Trabajo y Servicio de Cooperación Técnica. 2010. *La situación de la micro y pequeña empresa en Chile*. http://www.oitchile.cl/pdf/peq001.pdf.

Post Carbon Instutute. n.d. http://www.postcarbon.org.

Prince Edward Island Community Accounts. n.d. http://pe.communityaccounts.ca/.

Raymond, C., and G. Brown. 2007. "A Spatial Method for Assessing Resident and Visitor Attitudes toward Tourism Growth and Development." *Journal of Sustainable Tourism* 15, 5: 1–22. http://www.landscapemap2.org/kangaroo/mapviewer2.php.

Rehder, M. 2012. *Under the Moon and Stars: A Journey to the Roots of Williche Agriculture and Biodynamics.* Charlottetown, PEI: Institute of Island Studies, University of Prince Edward Island.

Robertson, R. 1995. "Glocalization: Time-Space and Homogeneity-Heterogeneity." In M. Featherstone, S. Lash, and R. Roberston, eds., *Global Modernities*, 25–44. London: Sage.

Salvo, A. 2004. "Environmental Change in the Southwest River Watershed." Student project, University of Prince Edward Island. Unpublished manuscript.

Segerlund, L. 2010. *Making Corporate Social Responsibility a Global Concern: Norm Construction in a Globalizing World.* Aldershot, UK: Ashgate.

Sernatur. 2010. "Plan de Turismo de Los Lagos (859)." http://www.sernatur.cl/planes-regionales-de-desarrollo-turistico.

Serrano, K., and M. Stefanova. 2011. "Between International Law, Kastom and Sustainable Development: Cultural Heritage in Vanuatu." In G. Baldacchino and D. Niles, eds., *Island Futures*, 19–36. Tokyo: Springer.

Sharpe, A. 2000. "A Survey of Indicators of Economic and Social Wellbeing." Canadian Policy Research Networks. http://www.cprn.org/.

Stannard, K. 1999. "How Many Italies? Process and Scale in the Development of the Italian Space-Economy." *Geography* 84: 308–18.

Stratford, E. 2009. "Belonging as a Resource: The Case of Ralph's Bay, Tasmania, and the Local Politics of Place." *Environment and Planning* 41, 4: 796–810.

Statistics Canada. 2006. "2006 Census Release Topics." http://www12.statcan.ca/census-recensement/2006/rt-td/index-eng.cfm.

Stuart, E.K. 2006. "The Influence of Islandness on Energy Policy and Electricity Supply." Unpublished thesis, University of Prince Edward Island.

SUBDERE. 2010. *Tierra cultural Chiloé.* http://www.subdere.gov.cl/sites/default/files/documentos/articles-81336_archivo_fuente.pdf.

Tang, T.L. 2007. "Income and Quality of Life: Does the Love of Money Make a Difference?" *Journal of Business Ethics* 72: 375–93.

Techera, E.J. 2011. "Ensuring the Viability of Cultural Heritage: The Role of International Heritage Law for the Pacific Island States." In G. Baldacchino and D. Niles, eds., *Island Futures*, 37–52. Tokyo: Springer.

Transition Network. n.d. http://www.transitionnetwork.org/.

Tourism Research Centre, School of Business, University of Prince Edward Island. 2010. "Summary Profile of Overnight Visitors to PEI: Results for the Year July 1, 2007 to June 30, 2008." http://vre2.upei.ca/scholartest/download_ds/ir:9304/OBJ.

United Nations Development Programme (UNDP). 2011. *Sustainability and Equity: A Better Future for All*. Summary Human Development Report 2011. New York: UNDP. http://hdr.undp.org.

Vazquez, A., and I. Novaczek. 2010. *The Heart of Mother Earth: Youth Engagement with the Sea and Marine Resources on Chiloé Island, Chile*. Charlottetown, PEI: Social Economy and Sustainability Research Network and Island Studies Press.

Venegas, S.A. 2007. "Leña, energia local renovable para los Bosques Nativos del Sur de Chile." http://www.bosquenativo.cl/index.php?option=com_k2&view=item&id=552:le%C3%B1a-energ%C3%ADa-renovable-para-la-conservaci%C3%B3n-de-los-bosques-nativos-del-sur-de-chile&Itemid=29.

Verhasselt Puppinck, D., ed. 2000. *Archipiélago Chiloé, el encanto de una isla misteriosa*. Santiago, Chile: Editorial Kactus.

Warrington, E., and D. Milne. 2007. "Governance." In G. Baldacchino, ed., *A World of Islands: An Island Studies Reader*, 379–428. Luqa, Malta and Charlottetown, PEI: Agenda Academic and Institute of Island Studies, University of Prince Edward Island.

Williams, M., and K. Hill. 2010. *Creative Adaptation: Hybrid Careers of Prince Edward Island Artists*. Charlottetown, PEI: Hill Strategies Research for the Prince Edward Island Cultural Human Resources Sector Council. http://www.peiculture.ca/pdfs/Hybrid_careers_Book_final.pdf.

Woolcock, M., and D. Narayan. 2000. "Social Capital: Implications for Development Theory, Research, and Policy." *World Bank Research Observer* 15, 2: 225–50.

World Bank. 2009. *The World Development Report 2009: Reshaping Economic Geography*. Washington: International Bank for Reconstruction and Development/The World Bank.

World Economic Forum. 2011. *Global Risks 2011*, 6th ed. An initiative of the Risk Response Network. Geneva: World Economic Forum. http://www.weforum.org/reports.

———. 2012. World Economic Forum annual meeting 2012, "The Great Transformation: Shaping New Models." Geneva: World Economic Forum. http://www.weforum.org/reports.

CHAPTER 8

The Old Rock's Rockin': A Cultural Anatomy of Shetland

Andrew Jennings

INTRODUCTION

> *For this Shetland is an island, with other small ones, encompassed under the rule of the Scots, stiff with cold and exposed on all sides to storms, to whose inhabitants, as in Iceland, dried and crushed fish serves as meal.*
>
> Camden, 1607: 850

This paper dissects the cultural anatomy of Shetland and, in so doing, presents an example of how a small, idiosyncratic community can use its unique assets and attractions to promote itself and enrich the quality of life for locals and visitors alike. Perhaps the dissection will reveal useful evidence for other communities. The chapter begins with an insular biography describing Shetland, its distinctive geographical position, and its cultural identity. It then considers how this distinctiveness is protected and promoted by Shetland Islands Council and in the work and ambitions of Shetland's cultural bodies: Shetland Arts and the Shetland Amenity Trust. A description of the extraordinary range of cultural events put on throughout the year by this small, yet active community serves as a conclusion.

LOCATION AND LEGACY

In the field of rural development, and insular development in particular, it is often considered a truism that if isolated areas adopt a policy to harness their creativity and unique culture they can successfully develop their economies (see, for example, Fullerton in Chapter 9). If they are islands with ambition they might wish to undergo "Islanding," a process Ronström has shown has been successfully carried out in the case of Gotland, where the production of an identifiable Gotlandic heritage has led to a booming tourist industry on the island (Ronström, 2008). In Jersey, which makes an interesting comparison to Shetland, with its "Cultural Strategy" document approved in 2005 (Riddell, 2007) and its indigenous, charitable National Trust, Johnson (2008) has explored how its minority language, Jèrriais, has been harnessed in culture construction, identity building, and by the heritage industry. Thomas and Thomas (2012) have also shown the positive effect cultural events have had on tourism numbers in Jersey, since the publication of the "Cultural Strategy." "Islanding" — the harnessing of local culture and creativity and the promotion of events — is fundamental to the Shetland experience. The other reason to promote the arts and culture can be to improve quality of life (discussed in Chapter 7 and by other authors in this volume). Research has shown that an abundance of cultural and recreational amenities can lower out-migration rates of the young college-educated (Whisler et al., 2008). The maintenance of a young population is certainly the motivation behind the building of Shetland's excellent sports facilities and swimming pools.

Shetland is the most isolated archipelago in the United Kingdom. It lies in the middle of the North Atlantic, a full 14-hour ferry trip from the city of Aberdeen on the Scottish mainland. Shetland's capital, Lerwick, lies almost equidistant from Aberdeen, Bergen on the Norwegian west coast, and Torshavn, the capital of the Faroe Islands. Shetland straddles the 60th parallel, the same latitude as Cape Chidley in Labrador and Port Burwell in Nunavut, and, in the other direction, Helsinki, Finland. It was known to the Romans as Thule, effectively the uttermost end of the earth (Wolfson, 2008). Shetland is closer to the Arctic Circle than to the English city of Manchester. The Shetland island of Yell is the same distance from London, the capital of the UK, as the cities of Marseille, Salzburg, and Szczecin. It lies farther from Edinburgh — Scotland's capital and the nation's cultural and administrative centre — than from Bergen, with which Shetland historically has had more contact.

Shetland has what many would consider an unappealing oceanic, sub-arctic climate with long but mild winters, short, cool summers, and copious quantities of wind. French photographer Georges Dif described it as "Terre de Vent" (The Land of the Wind) (Dif, 1989). In October and March, the average wind speed is about Force Five. However, gales of Force Eight and more blow on average for about 36 days in autumn and winter, while winds of Force Ten batter Shetland several times each winter, sometimes reaching Hurricane Force Twelve or an unlucky Thirteen. A gust of over 200 mph has been recorded, the fastest wind speed ever recorded in the British Isles. It should come as little surprise that Shetland is effectively treeless.

As one would expect given its geographical position, Shetland is not a fertile place. It is known, and with good reason, as "The Old Rock," having some of the most complex and varied geology in Britain, mainly consisting of ancient rocks that were metamorphosed during the Caledonian mountain-building period. Shetland was part of a Norwegian, Scottish, and East Greenland land mass that long predates the opening of the North Atlantic. It also contains some of Scotland's oldest rocks, including a fragment of deep oceanic crust and a host of unusual minerals.

Clearly Shetland has some difficulties to overcome when trying to entice the tourist. Do visitors want to come to the windiest, most isolated and barren group of islands in the British Isles? Do the locals want to remain living here? Of course, Shetland has never been a holiday destination that promoted itself on its weather, and it did not suffer a downturn in tourist numbers when warmer, drier destinations became available, as happened to Jersey, where package holidays to the Mediterranean became readily available in the 1980s. Jersey's economy is far more reliant than Shetland on its tourist industry, where it still accounts for one-quarter of GDP (Thomas and Thomas, 2012). One has to live with what one's been given, and, luckily for Shetland, wild landscapes and poor weather have their devotees. For example, the geological diversity has led to Shetland being recently designated a European Geopark. These territories are defined as those "which include a particular geological heritage and a sustainable territorial development strategy supported by a European program to promote development. It must have clearly defined boundaries and sufficient surface area for true territorial economic development" (European Geoparks, 2010). By promoting geotourism, Shetland seeks to turn its uncompromising geology into an asset.

Shetland's oceanic position also makes it a prime destination for nature tourism. It is a land of birds and sea mammals. A well-developed sector is devoted to selling the delights of the bird life and cetaceans. A recent BBC Television series, produced by the cameraman Simon King, featured the islands' wildlife. King has since returned to guide tours himself and he enthuses:

> The Shetland Isles are a jewel in the crown of Britain; a true wilderness, with the wildlife to match. From some of the most confiding seabirds in the world, including puffins, to elusive and charismatic creatures like otters and orcas, Shetland offers naturalists the opportunity for some dream encounters. (King, 2011)

Isolation has its merits, not only for birds and orcas. As in the "fortress" island economies described by Baldacchino and Novaczek in Chapters 3 and 7, isolation has also helped Shetlanders to preserve their identity as islanders distinct from the inhabitants of the mainland of Scotland, and to hold on to their rich, living cultural heritage, both tangible and intangible. In 2007, Shetland gained the third equal-highest score in *National Geographic*'s survey of 111 of the world's island destinations. Tourists were attracted particularly by Shetland's "extremely high integrity in all aspects of heritage" (*National Geographic*, 2007). There is a good deal of unique material in Shetland for any process of "Islanding."

The living heritage of the Shetlanders, whose population is just 22,000 people of mixed Scottish and Norwegian descent, as well as a large number of incomers from different parts of the world who embrace a Shetlandic identity quite readily, comprises a rich skein of traditions and cultural activities. The following three examples are perhaps the most iconic. The first is knitting, known in Shetland as *makkin*. Fair Isle patterns are famous worldwide. Until 2010, Shetland was the only Local Authority in Scotland to offer free knitting classes to primary school children. The landscape of Shetland has proved ideal for the raising of sheep and the production of wool. There are over 10 times as many of these creatures as there are people on the islands. The second central cultural icon is the fiddle, which is the Shetland instrument par excellence. It arrived in Shetland during the seventeenth century. Shetland subsequently developed its own distinctive fiddle tradition, with elements from Scotland and Scandinavia. Today, there are literally thousands of Shetland fiddlers, and many, such as Ally Bain and groups like Fiddler's Bid, Fullsceilidh Spelemannslag, and Da Fustra, successfully tour the world folk music circuit. The final part of this triptych of tradition is fishing. In the eighteenth century, the truck system operated whereby crofters had to row into the *Far Haf*, the ocean 40 miles offshore, to fish. As a condition of their tenure, they had to sell their catch to their landlords at under market value (Goodlad, 1971). Today, in happier times, over 1,000 people are employed in all aspects of the fisheries and in 2009 over £67 million of fish were landed (Shetland in Statistics, 2010). The fishing industry, both wild and aquaculture, is a much bigger contributor to GDP than tourism. In the summer, local inshore fishing competitions called the *Eela* are still an important feature of community entertainment. The more general maritime heritage of Shetland is celebrated in a couple of museums and two sixareens have recently been built, which were the type of boats used in the *haaf* fishing during the nineteenth century. One, the *Vaila Mae*, was used to ferry the Olympic torch when it came to Lerwick across Clickimin Loch in 2012.

REVIVAL OF IDENTITY

After a period of neglect, Shetland knitting, wool, and lace-making have seen a recent revival in their fortunes, as their cultural and potential economic importance has been increasingly recognized. In a recent study on Shetland identity, knitting and fiddle playing were both rated as extremely

THE OLD ROCK'S ROCKIN'

important icons for Shetland identity, ahead of Viking heritage and even the Shetland pony (Malcolm, 2012: 5–6). The year 2011 proved to be very important for Shetland wool. The first annual Shetland Wool Week was held to promote local skills and products, and, after a concerted campaign, the unique properties of Shetland wool were officially recognized, receiving the sought-after European Union Protected Designation of Origin (PDO) accreditation, which gives it the same status as Parma ham or champagne.

Like Shetland wool, Shetlandic identity is unique. It can be characterized as Scottish with a clear Nordic twist. Shetlandic folklore has both Scandinavian and Scottish elements (Jennings, 2010). Shetlanders today are essentially culturally Scottish, but there is a historical affinity with Norway, and among the older generation a general non-identification with Scotland, which is regarded as "other." In the local dialect, which is still generally spoken, there are still a number of Scandinavian words taken over from Norn, the extinct Scandinavian language of Shetland. Quite uniquely in a Scottish setting, the dialect can still be heard on local radio. There are also many manifestations of *nordophilia*. This is a predilection that took root in Victorian times and is still a popular attitude. It is most obviously seen in the regular practice of dressing as Vikings at the annual fire festivals, including Lerwick's world famous Up Helly Aa, which occur in most Shetland communities during the winter season.

Despite this strong cultural identity, there is hardly any tradition of Shetland-based nationalism (Nihtinen, 2011). There was a campaign for Shetland Home Rule, led by the Shetland Movement, which in the early 1980s had about 800 members and six councillors on the local council. The Movement took part in the Scottish Constitutional Convention, which developed the framework for Scottish devolution. However, at the general election in 1987, the Shetland Movement in association with the Orkney Movement put forward a joint candidate, John Goodlad, who secured a credible, but ultimately disappointing 14.5 per cent of the vote. The recent interest in Scottish independence sparked some debate and may inspire demands for more Shetlandic autonomy (Cluness, 2011). Recently, the local member of the Scottish Parliament (MSP) and the Council Convenor visited the Isle of Man on a fact-finding trip (Scott, 2012.)

PROMOTE SHETLAND, AND THE SHETLAND BRAND

Despite an apparent lack of political enthusiasm, Shetland's unique identity is recognized within Shetland by the cultural and heritage bodies and by Shetland Islands Council. The Council clearly has a mission to promote Shetland and encourage the Shetlandic identity. In a quite radical move, the Council set up Promote Shetland, a third-party organization funded by Shetland Islands Council Economic Development Unit, to market the islands. It is run by the Shetland Amenity Trust, Shetland's heritage body, discussed further below. The Council was unhappy with the work of Visit Scotland, Scotland's tourism body. They were not convinced that Visit Scotland sufficiently understood Shetland's unique cultural identity. The use of Scottish symbols, such as the thistle and the saltire, was considered inappropriate. It is not uncommon, while touring Shetland, to see the thistle symbol spray-painted out on the signs that indicate sites of special interest. This shows that some locals at least feel strongly about this particular matter of identity. Visit Scotland still has a presence in Shetland because it runs the Lerwick Tourist Office. Both organizations, although independent, seem to have a good working relationship, holding shared meetings. However, Promote Shetland has a far more proactive role. It maintains an excellent website (Promote Shetland, visit.shetland.org, The Official Site for Shetland Tourism 2012), which includes a number of webcams. These provide live views of Shetland 24/7 and include a live broadcast of Up Helly Aa. One of their most innovative creations is a local tourist radio station called 60-North FM, which provides Shetlandic cultural material. It can also be accessed online, on the Promote Shetland website. Ongoing discussions currently are taking place about the feasibility of developing a Shetland TV station.

Promote Shetland also supports the policy of Shetland Islands Council to increase the population of the islands to 25,000 by 2025. Helping to encourage immigration and the welcoming society suggested by Baldacchino in Chapter 3 and illustrated by the example of Gravelbourg provided by Fullerton in Chapter 9, Promote Shetland maintains the website that encourages immigration, providing information to potential immigrants on life in Shetland, Shetland's culture and history, finding work or doing business in

Shetland, and practical information about moving to the islands (Move Shetland.org, 2012a).

Promote Shetland has also supported "The Shetland Brand." The ethos behind this development is eloquently stated as follows:

> **Identity, location, history, heritage, skill, pride, belonging, uniqueness, origin, environment . . . these were the key components and inspirations behind creating the Shetland Brand.** But why create a Shetland Brand? The world is a competitive place and Shetland needed to establish a competitive edge. We needed to tell the world what makes us so unique, so special and different from other places in order to attract customers and market our products and services . . . a brand which focused on the islands' pure environment, strong archaeological heritage, rich, living culture and quality of craft and manufactured products. (MoveShetland.org, 2012b)

Just prior to the Isle of Man branding project, initiated in 2003 and discussed by Wilson in Chapter 11, the idea of a Shetland brand was first suggested in a document called "Shetland 2012" produced by the Shetland Local Economic Forum in 2002. Here it was stated that there was a need to "rethink radically our approach to economic development . . . [so that] . . . Shetland can continue to have a prosperous economic future" (Shetland Local Economic Forum, 2002). The assumption was that oil revenue would soon run out and Shetland would need to develop other means of earning an income, and a recognizable brand highlighting Shetland's manifest cold-island attractions was what was needed (Grydehøj, 2008). A London company called Corporate Edge was employed to develop the branding. Adam Grydehøj (2008) has reviewed the process and is critical of the outcome, suggesting Shetlanders were not enamoured by the generic island branding that was developed, perhaps because that most potent symbol of Shetland, the Viking, was missing. Shetlanders were clearly confused by what was offered and did not necessarily recognize their islands. Also, money spent by the Council in any sphere is always criticized.

The logo that was eventually developed was a fiddle scroll with the slogan "Pride of Place."

Despite its problematical beginning, the brand has stuck, and in 2011 Promote Shetland encouraged Shetlanders to become "ambassadors" for Shetland using branded material. A pack containing a dozen double-sided page inserts was developed to highlight the Shetland brand and the aspects of island life it stands for. Promote Shetland admitted that the idea of branding Shetland — using the "pride of place" slogan and a new logo — had enthused some but confused others. Andy Steven of Promote Shetland said: "We want people who feel pride in this place to stand up for Shetland, to become ambassadors for all that's great about the isles" (Taylor, 2011).

Despite the continued lack of Viking material, the brand appears to be being taken up throughout Shetland. Currently over 30 businesses and organizations have signed up to be supporters and to express their pride in Shetland. These range from Lerwick hotels, organic food providers, Britain's most northerly brewery, and a Fair Isle patterned teddy bear producer to the University of the Highland and Islands Centre for Nordic Studies, with its programs in Orkney and Shetland Studies up to the master's and doctoral levels. The branded material is being disseminated by Shetlanders when away from the islands. However, I am not aware of any quantitative research that measures its success in attracting visitors, and can only comment that in my personal experience it has a positive impact on those who are exposed to it, creating a positive image of Shetland.

Shetland Islands Council has also been intimately involved in supporting cultural activities and cultural bodies within Shetland. The Council partially funds the two charitable organizations, Shetland Arts and the Shetland Amenity Trust.

SHETLAND ARTS

Shetland Arts was founded in 2006, and today it operates from a busy Arts Office in the centre of Lerwick, the Garrison Theatre in Lerwick, and the Bonhoga Gallery in Weisdale Mill. It also rents out an attractive artist's living and working space in Scalloway called The Booth. Shetland Arts promotes a year-round program of music, craft, theatre, literature, visual arts, dance, and film events and provides grants of up to £3,000 for interest-ing projects. It has an annual budget of £1.4 million and over the last two years its new online box office has seen sales of £1million, which seems quite extraordinary for a population of 22,000 people. On its website, it is quite explicit about the value of, and its commitment to, Shetlandic identity:

> Shetland has an international brand that sets it apart from
> many other communities whether they exist in islands,
> towns or cities. The value of this identity cannot be under-
> estimated: it is a gift that we need to nurture and support.
> It is vital to Shetland's future. (Shetland Arts, 2012)

Shetland Arts' mandate is not only to provide performance space for visiting artists, but also to develop the cultural sector in Shetland. It has identified the development of the creative industries as a priority, and although a recent report has suggested that 4 per cent of the present work-ing population of Shetland, about 400 people, already work in the creative industries, providing £25 million to the Shetland economy, this could be increased (Ekos Ltd., 2008). Shetland Arts has taken this on board and is committed to "promote Shetland as a creative place with global recogni-tion of its creative industry sector and the relocation of creative industries to Shetland" (Shetland Arts, 2009).

There is clearly nothing parochial or lacking in ambition about this statement: Shetland is committed to becoming a globally recognized cen-tre for the creative industries. Clearly, this ties in neatly with Shetland Is-lands Council's ambition to increase the population over the coming decades. Only time will tell whether this is a feasible ambition, but there is a plan on how to proceed, first, through the development of education — one can now study for a bachelor's degree in Contemporary Textiles at Ler-wick College, and further degrees are being considered, for example, a master's program in the creative industries — and second, through the building of an ambitious creative industries centre and cinema complex called Mareel. This has been built in the developing cultural quarter of Lerwick. Mareel has a live performance auditorium, two cinema screens, rehearsal rooms, a recording studio, education and training spaces, a digital media production suite, broadcast facilities, and a café bar with free high-speed wi-fi Internet access. A high-speed fibre optic cable being laid from the Faroe Islands, which Shetland Islands Council has paid over £1 million to connect to the islands, will give Shetland its first proper broadband. This should ultimately allow Mareel to stream live opera from London and also broadcast live from Shetland. In addition, Mareel will provide a program of formal and informal education, training, and learning activities. These will include a National Certificate music course delivered in partnership with Shetland College, UHI, evening classes delivered in partnership with the Council (including audio technology, live sound, and film production), and industry certified Pro Tools training (Shetland Arts, 2011).

SHETLAND AMENITY TRUST

The other important cultural agency in Shetland is the Shetland Amenity Trust, which was set up in 1983. This is an exceptional organization within Scotland, and indeed within the British Isles. Only the Isle of Man and Guernsey have similar bodies, and both of these islands are self-governing Crown Dependencies. Shetland is unique in being an integral part of Scotland but having a conservation trust that effectively acts as though Shetland were independent. It has a wide range of responsibilities. Its role is to preserve Shetland's architectural heritage, as well as conserve and enhance the natural beauty and amenity. According to the Heritage Tourism Investment Program 2008–11, adopted by Shetland Islands Council in 2007, and in itself a suitable indicator of the awareness within Shetland of the importance of heritage for Shetland's future, the mandate of the Amenity Trust is as follows:

> It is concerned with the conservation and enhancement of Shetland's heritage, with particular emphasis on the built environment, archaeology, the natural environment, recycling and place name research. (Shetland Islands Council Economic Development Unit, 2008)

Over 100 people are employed by Shetland Amenity Trust, which equates to roughly 1 per cent of the working population. The Trust receives its funding from annual grants from both Shetland Charitable Trust and Shetland Islands Council. This funding, as well as allowing the Trust to provide its services, has also been used successfully to leverage funding from national and international sources. Over the last five years approximately £22 million has been spent on Trust projects and services, of which approximately £8 million was from external sources.

The Shetland Amenity Trust is involved in a number of exciting projects, including: the excavation and interpretation of Old Scatness, in the south Mainland, which is an exceptionally fine example of an Iron Age village and broch (circular stone tower); Viking Unst, where it has supported a number of excavations of Norse settlements and is in the process of constructing a Norse longhouse, where re-enactments will take place and visitors will learn about Viking skills and Shetland's Viking heritage; the Shetland Place-name Project, which suggests a Scandinavian level of interest in onomastic heritage and employs Scotland's only full-time place-name officer, who is collecting Shetland names and mapping them for posterity before they disappear; the £5.4 million Sumburgh Head Light House redevelopment, which will result in a two-storey visitor centre, a shop, and an educational facility, and ultimately will bring the number of lighthouses available for holiday rent under its ownership and management to three; and the aforementioned UNESCO Geopark, Shetland.

Perhaps, the Shetland Amenity Trust's greatest contribution to the cultural life and heritage of Shetland is the new Shetland Museum and Archives, which opened in 2007 at a cost of £11.5 million. It is owned and managed by the Trust and funded by an annual grant from Shetland Islands Council. The Museum is the "must see" destination in Shetland for anyone wishing to know more about Shetland culture, traditions, and archaeology. Even intangible cultural heritage is imaginatively presented. It has attracted over 80,000 people every year since it opened, four times the Shetland population. In 2009, the Museum was nominated for European Museum of the Year Award and was a semifinalist in the UK National Lottery Awards 2009 (best heritage project) (Shetland Amenity Trust, 2009). The Museum is clearly a focus for the appreciation and exploration of Shetlandic identity. Not only are there the collections to be perused, but its lecture theatre is a venue for regular lecture series on Shetland's history and culture, delivered by both local and visiting scholars.

OFFSHORE OIL AND REVENUE

In addition to being partly funded by Shetland Islands Council, both Shetland Arts and the Shetland Amenity Trust are funded by the Shetland Charitable Trust, which was originally established in 1978 as the Shetland Islands Council Charitable Trust. Unlike the example of Newfoundland and Labrador provided by Walsh in Chapter 5, this Trust was set up in the wake of the discovery of oil and the existential angst created in Shetland by the perceived potential damage to Shetland's way of life and the threat of the arrival of large numbers of immigrant oil workers. Its purpose was to manage some of Shetland's oil funds. The funds have their roots in the 1974 Act of Parliament: the Zetland County Council Act 1974 (Great Britain, 1974), which gave the Council the right to the compulsory purchase of land. The Council bought the land where the Sullom Voe oil terminal was to be sited, thus making the Council the landlord. The Council insisted that all the oil companies had to use the same oil terminal and therefore they all had to pay the Council rent. Under a further agreement in 1978, the Council also ran the port and charged for that too. In May 2011, the community's funds stood at around £650 million, including the Council's reserves and pension fund (Riddell, 2011). The Charitable Trust funds currently amount to about £200 million. It would be a mistake to regard the Trust as a philanthropic entity. It is seen in Shetland as a repository of Shetlanders' wealth. There has recently been a good deal of controversy over its management structure (Robertson, 2012). The Council has negotiated similar terms with the French gas company Total, which is building a huge terminal at Sullom Voe. The company will have to pay a rent of £550,000 a year, plus a levy based on the value of the gas produced. It is conservatively estimated that this project will be worth another £200 million to the Council over the next 30 years, In fact, it may be closer to £1 billion (Clark, 2012). The Shetland Charitable Trust is now independent of Shetland Islands Council and employs its own staff (Shetland Charitable Trust, History of Shetland Charitable Trust, 2010). In 2010, the Charitable

Trust spent £1,080,228 on the Shetland Amenity Trust and £773,376 on Shetland Arts (Shetland Charitable Trust, 2011). Thus, money generated by oil extraction off the Shetland coast is directed into supporting the cultural fabric of the islands.

CALENDAR OF EVENTS

A brief look at the calendar of the events that take place throughout the year suggests that Shetland is a dynamic, busy, rockin' place. Events are seen by Shetlanders themselves as important to Shetland identity — Malcolm (2012) discovered that 86 per cent of those interviewed felt the fire festival Up Helly Aa was important or extremely important, while 90 per cent felt the same way about the Folk Festival. Many of these events are organized by Shetland Arts, which is aware of event tourism elsewhere, while others are independent cultural phenomena, although they often benefit from some financial support in the form of grants or marketing. Cultural events promote tourism, stimulate investment, and enrich lives (Yeoman et al., 2004), both in cities like Edinburgh and in island jurisdictions. Jersey has recently successfully developed event-led tourism, focusing on cultural events, which has had a positive effect on tourism visitor numbers (Thomas and Thomas, 2012).

It would be difficult to imagine a place of similar size and population anywhere else with a more vibrant, energetic scene. In this small archipelago, almost every month seems to have its festival. There has been an attempt to put an economic value on this activity. According to a recent report, "Shetland's Events and Festivals are calculated to have a turnover of about £1 million p.a. [per annum] and to have 127,000 attendees and an economic value of £6.2 million p.a. This is a significant part of the Shetland economy but much more can be achieved" (Shetland Economic Development Unit, 2010).

Shetland Arts organizes many festivals, in addition to the program of concerts, theatrical performances, and cinema that it puts on during the year. In August, it stages the energetic Fiddle-Frenzy. This involves a week-long celebration of Shetland's fiddle heritage and encompasses concerts, dances, and a summer school, where students learn the traditional Shetland fiddle style from experts. In September it organizes Wordplay, Shetland's book festival, which in 2010 celebrated its tenth year, and Screenplay, Shetland's film festival, which celebrated its fifth year. Shetland Arts has had success in inviting figures of note to attend. In 2010, Oscar-winner Jim Broadbent headed the list. There is talk of inviting Martin Scorsese in the future after he proclaimed his Shetland origins (Griffiths, 2011). In October and November, Shetland Arts stages the Peerie Willie Guitar Festival, named after Willie Johnson, the highly regarded guitarist who pioneered the jazz-influenced accompaniment style now prevalent in traditional Shetland music.

In addition to these key festivals, many others are not organized by Shetland Arts. For example, in October the Shetland Accordion and Fiddle Club runs a four-day festival of traditional country dance music and traditional Shetland music. The event in 2012 will be the twenty-fifth. The festival is rounded off with a "grand dance" for over 1,000 people at the Clickimin Centre, Lerwick's local sports complex.

The biggest festival in Shetland takes place in May. This is the Folk Festival, which is now in its thirty-second year. This event is unusual in being organized entirely by a dedicated committee of volunteers. Families open their homes to accommodate the festival artists. The first festival was held in 1981, and it has grown steadily to become one of the world's top folk festivals. In 2010, the Folk Festival won the "Event of the Year" award at the Scottish Traditional Music Awards. It originated with a conversation between the late fiddler and Shetland music expert Dr. Tom Anderson and local scholar and folklorist Charlie Simpson, who both felt that Shetland, with its talent and rich musical heritage, should stage such an event. The festival takes place over four days, and mixes local and international music and talent. From the beginning it has not been restricted to Lerwick — concerts are held all over the islands, even on Fair Isle and Unst.

Festivals also cater to other musical tastes. For those who enjoy country music, there is the Thomas Fraser Memorial Festival, which commemorates the memory of Thomas Fraser from Burra Isle, fisherman, crofter, and old-time country singer extraordinaire. Fraser is honoured in Nashville's Country Hall of Fame and was the subject of a BBC2 documentary in 2008 entitled *Shetland Lone Star*. This is held in November. Shetland also has a popular Blues Festival, held in September, and Vunk Fest, for those who enjoy experimental, metal, and rock music, which takes place in July. June 2012 saw the inauguration of Shetland's first Jazz Festival. Performers will include the Nova Scotia Jazz Band.

The most famous Shetland festival is undoubtedly Up Helly Aa, Europe's biggest fire festival, which takes place on the last Tuesday of January in Lerwick. This is definitely a community event and although tourists are most welcome it is not put on for their benefit. It would be enthusiastically put on even if no tourists turned up, as it was throughout the twentieth century, when tourists were few and far between. It is unquestionably a great spectacle, and tourists and locals alike come to watch as a huge torch-lit procession of about 1,000 guizers snakes through the town in the dark following a Viking longship, which they subsequently burn by tossing their blazing torches into its midst. The first galley was burned in Lerwick in 1889. The British media covered the event in 2012 extensively. There was coverage on the BBC and reports appeared in the *Daily Mail* (2012) and *Telegraph* (2012), among others.

Ten other communities in Shetland outside of Lerwick also have their own Up Helly Aa, or Fire Festival, when community members dress as Vikings, burn ships, and party all night. These can be experienced all over Shetland from the second Friday of January, when the series begins in Scalloway, until the third Friday in March, when it ends in Delting. Although none of these events can match Lerwick for sheer size and spectacular im-pression, outside Shetland they would rank as tremendous fire festivals in their own right. Scalloway burned its first Viking galley in 1898 and usually comprises around 200 flaming torches, while Delting can muster up to 300.

Shetland does not merely burn longships or host musical events. Shet-land celebrates its wildlife in the Shetland Nature Festival in July and its unique wool products in the aforementioned Wool Week.

In addition to all the above events and festivals, during the summer Shetland becomes a hive of activity when a huge number of events take place, which enliven life for locals and visitors. Shetland Sunday teas, which boast some extremely fine home-baked goods, are held in community halls throughout Shetland, the proceeds of which go to charity. There are 17 sailing regattas and the yoal regattas, where local teams race six-oared traditional Shetland boats. There are also local festivals like Unst Fest, encouraging people to visit Britain's most northerly isle, and the extraordinary Big Bannock. This odd occasion is held in North Roe and raises thousands of pounds for charity, with events like baking the largest bannock (a Shetlandic version of the soda scone) and churning the most milk in a given time.

DISCUSSION

It is to be hoped that the example of "peerie" (small) Shetland is of interest. Clearly, "isolated" need not mean boring, backward, or moribund. In Shetland there has been a serious attempt at "Islanding." A heritage body has had the imagination and flexibility to develop and interpret Shetland's own heritage without conforming to a central Scottish blueprint. There is a clear pride throughout Shetland in this unique heritage. Malcolm's study (2012) shows that 70 per cent of Shetlanders visit archaeological and heritage sites at least occasionally, and Fair Isle knitting, fiddle music, and Viking heritage are all important icons of identity (Malcolm, 2012).

Promote Shetland, a native tourism body, has been established with local knowledge and a belief that there is a unique story to tell, and that it can be told using all the modern media. Shetland Arts, a native arts development body, clearly believes that the periphery is not peripheral. More generally, there is an awareness of the value of Shetland-based education, both in the creative arts and in the culture and heritage of Shetland. This was made manifest in the establishment of the University of the Highlands and Islands Centre for Nordic Studies, with offices in both Orkney and Shetland, which offers a master's degree in Orkney and Shetland studies, including history, traditional culture, literature, and dialect. Shetlanders can now take a higher degree in their own culture without leaving the islands.

Despite not having much political autonomy, Shetland clearly has money from its generation and management of oil revenue, which vitally has brought independence of action. Shetlanders have seen the value in culture and heritage and have also had the foresight to use some of this wealth to establish their own cultural bodies and develop their own identity. This need not have been the case — not all public bodies have sympathy towards culture or the arts.

However, not everything in the garden is rosy. The system is fragile. Shetland's vibrant cultural scene depends on public subsidy, both from the Council and from funds ultimately derived from oil revenue and administered by the Shetland Amenity Trust and Shetland Arts. Although these are charitable trusts effectively independent of the Council, the Council partially funds them and often still has an extra role as joint funder on important projects. This is beginning to become problematical in stringent financial times (as discussed by O'Keeffe in Chapter 12). Recently, Shetland Islands Council has decided to make some huge cuts to its budget — like all services, heritage and culture are expected to take their share. In October 2012 it was announced that the Council, despite signing a contract, wanted to cut its annual grant to the Lerwick Museum and Archives, which has already suffered a 27 per cent cut in real terms, by an extra 35 per cent, thus reducing annual funding to £681,000. This could mean, according to some estimates, that 20 jobs would be lost and the facility might become no more than a storage space (Gregson, 2012). However, Shetland Amenity Trust, as a defender of Shetland's heritage, has started to campaign against these cuts. Of course, it is problematical that some of the Amenity Trust's own funds actually come directly from the Council itself, so some of the Amenity Trust's staff may also be in line to lose their jobs. Truly independent trusts could provide a bulwark against political short-termism. Nonetheless, the Amenity Trust is doing its best. Public subsidy is a two-edged sword. It can be a problem if it is withdrawn.

How would Shetland fare without Council subsidy? It would still have its trusts, but these would be smaller without Council financial input and many of the events would not take place. The activities of the Museum and other cultural bodies would be severely curtailed. In addition, Promote Shetland would not exist. Employees there are understandably worried about the Council's new priorities.

What would happen in Shetland if there were no trusts? The large civil engineering projects, such as the Museum and Mareel, are very unlikely to have been built. However, cultural life would continue. The two biggest events in the Shetland cultural calendar would still take place. Up Helly Aa and the Folk Festival are effectively self-funding and are run by volunteers. This is surely good news for other areas that cannot boast Shetland's wealth. Both events predate the concept of "Islanding" and branding and yet both embody Shetland's culture and attract tourists. The key to their success is popular engagement. Volunteering is a Shetland way of life, along with fundraising for an endless number of local and national causes. According to official figures, the economic value of formal volunteering in Shetland is estimated at £11.1 million for the year. This represents just over 500 full-time equivalent jobs in Shetland (Voluntary Action Shetland, 2012). A pro-active population is a vital asset for any community.

Shetland is still predominantly a specialist primary sector economy, with tourism, heritage, and the creative industries small compared with the impact of the fishing industry and the Council. Typically for a subnational island jurisdiction, Shetland has a large public sector and investment decisions of the Council have a huge impact on society. Grydehøj (2011) points out that 9.5 per cent of the population is employed by the Council and it produces around 36 per cent of the economy. As noted above, the creative industries are worth about £25 million annually, while in 2006 total visitor expenditure was £16.4 million, a not inconsiderable sum; however, in the same year, the estimated value of fish landed in Shetland was £53.5 million and the turnover from fish processing was £118 million. By last year the numbers had increased to £67 million and £133 million. Fish are far and away the biggest contributor to the Shetland economy. It looks as if, despite the fears expressed, that this will continue to be the case into the future. In addition, Shetland will also see the construction of the huge community-owned Viking Energy windfarm consisting of 103 wind turbines and the oil rig decommissioning yard at Dales Voe. It is estimated that over its 25-year lifetime the windfarm will pump an extra £23 million annually into the Charitable Trust's coffers (Viking Energy, 2012). Shetland will not be economically dependent on its cultural heritage and creative industries for some time to come, and there is still the potential problem of out-migration.

CONCLUDING REMARKS

In an editorial in the magazine *Shetland Life* the young Shetlandic musician and thinker Malachy Talack (2008), echoing the findings of Whisler (Whisler et al., 2008), claimed that for the young to remain in Shetland, opportunities available on the mainland have to be available here as well. Will Mareel and the opportunity to watch 3D movies simultaneous with their release on the mainland persuade potential emigrants that there is no need to leave? Only time will tell; however, Mareel has proved more popular than the naysayers anticipated. The Mareel business plan had an annual target of 39,834 cinema sales, but after only seven weeks there had already been 14,619 cinema sales. The target for the initial seven weeks in the business plan was 5,362 sales, meaning that the venue had exceeded its cinema sales target for this period by an impressive 9,257 (*Shetland News*, 2012). Shetlanders, both young and old, seem to be taking to their new 3D Cinema.

Is there any evidence that Shetland's attempt to develop a creative, branded economy founded on culture and heritage has been successful? The evidence is equivocal. So far, occupancy levels for hotels, guest houses, and bed and breakfasts have remained static since about 1991. Nor is there as yet any evidence of an increase in population towards the desired 25,000. However, there has been a huge increase in the number of cruise ships visiting the islands. This could be seen as a result of successful Shetland branding. In 2001, 42 vessels carrying 11,601 passengers arrived (Shetland in Statistics, 2010); in 2012, the number had risen to 52 vessels carrying 37,572 passengers, a threefold increase. Anecdotally, Shetland was the highlight for many of the North Atlantic cruise passengers.

Finally, it seems fitting to leave the last words to Shetland Islands Council, which, along with Shetland Arts and the Shetland Amenity Trust, is signatory to the Shetland Cultural Strategy. This Strategy presents a vision for cultural life in Shetland, and one hopes that even in these financially troubled times the Council still believes in the aspiration of this document:

> We seek to ensure that Shetland's cultural assets are conserved, developed and supported in order to allow everyone to reach his or her potential, strengthen community

identity, pride and confidence and secure prosperity for the benefit of present and future generations. We intend that Shetland's cultural assets will be recognised as among the richest and most diverse to be found anywhere. We want Shetland to be the most exciting creative and cultural island community in the world. (Shetland Islands Council, 2008: 8)

REFERENCES

Camden, W. 1607. *Brittania*. London

Clark, D. 2012. "A Golden Future?" *Shetland Life* (Jan.): 14–16.

Cluness, S. 2011. "So Whose Oil Is It Anyway?" *Shetland Life* (Sept.): 18–19.

Daily Mail. 2012. "The Vikings Are Back! Winged Helmets and Longboat Hit the Shetlands (but This Time It's for a Knees-up)," 1 Feb. http://www.dailymail.co.uk/news/article-2094863/Marauding-Vikings-descend-Shetland-Isles-re-claim-ancient-lands-Europes-largest-festival.html.

Dif, G. 1989. *Shetland: terre de vent*. Milan: Fournie.

Ekos Ltd. 2008. *Creative Industries in Shetland Today*. http://www.shetlandarts.org/images/2009/07/creative-industries-in-shetland-today-final-summary-report.pdf.

European Geoparks. 2010. http://www.europeangeoparks.org/isite/page/2,1,0.asp?mu=1&cmu=7&thID=0.

Goodlad, C.A. 1971. *Shetland Fishing Saga*. Lerwick: Shetland Times Limited.

Great Britain. 1974. *Zetland County Council Act*. London: H.M. Stationary Office.

Gregson, B. 2012. "Shetland Amenity Trust: Letter to the Editor." *Shetland Times*, 18 Oct.

Griffiths, R. 2011. "Famous Film Director Scorcese Claims Shetland Ancestry." *Shetland Times*, 1 Dec.

Grydehøj, A. 2008. "Branding from Above: Generic Cultural Branding in Shetland and Other Islands." *Island Studies Journal* 3, 2: 175–97.

———. 2011. "Making the Most of Smallness: Economic Policy in Microstates and Subnational Island Jurisdictions." *Space and Polity* 15, 3: 183–96.

Jennings, A. 2010. "The Giantess as Metaphor for Shetland's Cultural History." *Shima: The International Journal of Research into Island Cultures* 4, 1: 1–14.

Johnson, H. 2007. "Constructing Islandness on Jersey: A Study of Language and La

Fête Nouormonde." *Refereed Papers from the 3rd International Small Island Cultures Conference*, 55–65. Charlottetown: Institute of Island Studies, University of Prince Edward Island.

King, S. 2011. "Simon King's Ultimate Shetland Safari." http://www.simonking-wildlife.com/ShetlandItineraryW.pdf.

Lewick Port Authority. 2012. "Cruise Season at Lerwick Ends on New Highs." http://www.lerwick-harbour.co.uk/cruise-season-at- lerwick-ends-on-new-highs.

Malcolm, M. 2012. "Shetland Identity Today: Is There Such a Thing?" MLitt dissertation, Centre for Nordic Studies, University of the Highlands and Islands.

MoveShetland.org. 2012a. "Promote Shetland." http://move.shetland.org/.

———. 2012b. "The Shetland Brand." http://www.shetlandmarketing.org/prideof-place.

National Geographic. 2007. "Island Destinations Rated: North & West Europe." http://traveler.nationalgeographic.com/2007/11/destinations-rated/north-and-west-europe-text/11.

Nihtinen, A. 2011. *Ambivalent Self-Understanding:Change, Language and Boundaries in the Shetland Islands, 1970–Present.* Helsinki: Åbo Akademi University Press.

Riddell, A. 2007. "Jersey: The Development of an Island Cultural Strategy." *Shima: The International Journal of Research into Island Cultures* 1: 72–87.

Riddell, N. 2011. "Oil Wealth Fund Managers Beat the Market but Council Outspends Growth." *Shetland Times*, 27 May. http://www.shetlandtimes.co.uk/2011/05/27/oil-wealth-fund-managers-beat-the-market-but-council-outspends-growth.

Robertson, J. 2012. "Ratter and Wills to Lead Shetland Charitable Trust." *Shetland Times*, 24 May.

Ronström, O. 2008. "A Different Land: Heritage Production in the Island of Gotland." *Shima: The International Journal of Research into Island Cultures* 2: 1–18.

Shetland Amenity Trust. 2009. "Awards and Credentials." http://www.shetland-museum.org.uk/background/awards/.

Shetland Arts. 2009. "Hansel for Art Promises Action Plan 2008–2013." http://www.shetlandarts.org/images/2009/06/hansel-for-art-promises-action-plan-aug-2009.pdf.

———. 2011. "Mareel." http://www.shetlandarts.org/venues/mareel/.

———. 2012. "About Shetland Arts." http://www.shetlandarts.org/about/.

Shetland Charitable Trust. 2010. "History of Shetland Charitable Trust." http://www.shetlandcharitabletrust.co.uk/who-we-are/history-of-shetland-charitable-trust.

———. 2011. "SCT Financial Statement to March 2011." http://www.shetlandcharitabletrust.co.uk/assets/files/accounts/SCT%20Fanancial%20Statements%20 to%2031%20March%202011.pdf.

Shetland Economic Development Unit. 2010. *Shetland's Events and Festivals*. Lerwick: Shetland Islands Council.

Shetland Islands Council. 2008. *On the Cusp . . . Shetland's Cultural Strategy*. Lerwick: Shetland Islands Council.

———. 2010. *Shetland in Statistics*. Lerwick: Shetland Islands Council.

Shetland Islands Council Economic Development Unit. 2008. "Heritage Tourism Investment Program." http://www.shetland.gov.uk/policy/documents/HTIP2008. pdf.

Shetland Local Economic Forum.2002. *Shetland 2012: Economic Development Strategy*. Lerwick: Shetland Local Economic Forum (now part of Highlands and Islands Enterprise).

Shetland News. 2012. "Islanders Like Their Cinema." http://www.shetnews.co.uk/ newsbites/5709-islanders-like-their-cinema.

Talack, M. 2008. "The Emigration Question." *Shetland Life*, 8 July.

Taylor, R. 2011. "People Urged to Become 'Brand' Ambassadors for Shetland." *Shetland Times*, 22 June. http://www.shetlandtimes.co.uk/2011/06/22/peopleurged-to-become-brand-ambassadors-for-shetland.

Scott, T. 2012. "Isle of Man: Tynwald Welcomes Shetland Islands Guests." http:// tavishscott.com/2012/11/isle-of-man-tynwald-welcomes-shetland-islandsguests/.

Telegraph. 2012. "Up Helly Aa in Pictures: Viking Festival in Lerwick, Shetland Islands." Feb. http://www.telegraph.co.uk/news/picturegalleries/uknews/7083166/Up-HellyAa-in-pictures-Viking-festival-in-Lerwick-Shetland-Islands.html.

Thomas, B., and S. Thomas. 2012. "Cultural Events and Tourism in Jersey." *Shima: The International Journal of Research into Island Cultures* 5: 114–31.

Viking Energy. 2012. "The Project Community Benefits." http://www.vikingenergy. co.uk/benefits-community.asp.

Visit.shetland.org: The official site for Shetland tourism. 2012. http://visit.shetland.org/.

Voluntary Action Shetland. n.d. "Annual Review 2011–2012." http://www.shetland-communities.org.uk/Downloads/VAS/VAS%20annual%20review%20 2012.pdf.

Wisler, R.L., B.S. Waldorf, G.F. Mulligan, and D.A. Plane. 2008. "Quality of Life and the Migration of the College-Educated: A Life-Course Approach." *Growth and Change* 39, 1: 58–94.

Wolfson, S. 2008. *Tacitus, Thule and Caledonia: The Achievements of Agricola's Navy in Their True Perspective*. Oxford: British Archaeological Reports.

Yeoman, I., M. Robertson, J. Ali-Knight, S. Drummond, and U. McMahon-Beattie, eds. 2004. *Festival and Events Management: An International Arts and Culture Perspective*. Amsterdam: Elsevier, Butterworth, Heinemann.

CHAPTER 9

Arts, Culture, and Rural Community Economic Development: A Southern Saskatchewan Case Study

Christopher Fullerton

INTRODUCTION

In recent years, rural development scholars throughout the industrialized world have sought to identify effective means of achieving sustainable rural community development. In this regard, a growing consensus has emerged that place-based, grassroots-driven approaches have the greatest potential to bring positive results (Bryant, 2002, 2010; Terluin, 2003; Bridger and Alter, 2008). The first part of this approach, place-based development, "is a holistic and targeted intervention that seeks to reveal, utilize and enhance the unique natural, physical, and/or human capacity endowments present within a particular location for the development of the in-situ community and/or its biophysical environment" (Markey, 2010: 2). That is, place-based development seeks to harness local assets rather than looking to external sources of investment.

This approach differs substantially from the more traditional sector-based approach, whereby rural communities tended to rely on a single, often externally controlled primary or secondary industry as their raison d'être. With global competition having grown to unprecedented levels over the past several decades, the comparative advantage once enjoyed by many rural communities and regions is no longer guaranteed, if it even still exists.

Instead, places everywhere are quite literally competing with places everywhere for development — such as, for example, developed countries vs. developing countries, towns and villages vs. cities and metropolitan regions, or rural communities vs. rural communities. This has led to a greater focus on building competitive advantage, where each place attempts to build up its own unique bundle of assets that will help it stand out from the crowd and, with this, make it an attractive place to live, do business, or visit (Markey, Halseth, and Manson, 2006; Huggins and Thompson, 2011). As rural communities engage in place-based strategies, residential, tourism, recreational, and other forms of development are now just as significant as, if not more important than, the economic activities that have sustained them throughout their histories, such as agriculture, mining, forestry, or fishing (Epps, 2002; Koster and Randall, 2005; Duxbury and Campbell, 2011).

The increasing focus on place competitiveness has heightened the importance of building and maintaining a community's "quality of place" (Bridger and Alter, 2008). Andrews (2001: 201) has defined "quality of place" as "an aggregate measure of the factors in the external environment that contribute to quality-of-life." A review of the literature suggests that, for any given community, the quality of place is influenced by three overarching characteristics: the attractiveness of its built environment, or its aesthetic appeal; the local availability of amenities and services, such as parks, theatres, and health care facilities; and opportunities for social interaction within the community, such as festivals and other events. Together, the resulting quality of place can do much to influence people's sense of place and, with this, their quality-of-life perceptions as they relate to the community. "Sense of place" generally refers to the "feelings evoked among people as a result of the experiences and memories that they associate with that place" (Knox, Marston, and Nash, 2010: 265–66). In the case of someone who has never been to a particular place, they may still feel a "sense of place" about that setting. As Walsh points out in Chapter 5, this connection may occur even for a "non-place" that exists only in the lyrics of a song. In these instances, sense of place can refer to "the character of a place as seen by outsiders — its unique or distinctive physical characteristics or its inhabitants" (Knox et al., 2010: 266). "Quality of life" (see also Chapter 7) can be defined as "a feeling of well-being, fulfillment, or satisfaction on the part of residents of or visitors to that place" (Andrews, 2001: 201). Thus, individual quality of life — along with perceptions regarding the overall quality of life a community offers, more generally — is strongly impacted by people's experiences and interactions in that place (Bridger and Alter, 2008). Accordingly, working to ensure that a strong quality of place and quality of life exist within a rural community is key to building its competitiveness (Ray, 1998; Markey and Reimer, 2008; Huggins and Thompson, 2011). In so doing, places are more likely to retain their current populations and perhaps also to attract newcomers, whether new residents, businesses, or tourists (Benson and O'Reilly, 2009; Halfacree and Rivera, 2010).

As previous authors in this volume have suggested, the topic of governance has also received growing attention in the contemporary rural development dialogue. As part of place-based development, harnessing local human capacity endowments ideally means taking advantage of all the skills and talent available within the community, thus implying that participatory and collaborative development processes are necessary for maximizing a community's ability to achieve its development goals and objectives. In this sense, place-based strategies are highly compatible with another approach to rural development receiving increased attention in recent years: community economic development (CED). Ross and McRobie (1989: 1) define CED as "a process by which communities can initiate and generate their own solutions to their common economic problems and thereby build long-term community capacity and foster the integration of economic, social and environmental objectives." Thus, just as place-based development is much more holistic in its identification and use of local endowments, CED is more holistic than past practices in terms of how development actions are planned and carried out. CED efforts are largely grassroots-based, where local leaders share their power with members of the local community — for example, the business community, service clubs, or individuals. Ultimately, each person or group involved in the process contributes to the development process in their own way, based on their own interests, knowledge, or skill sets. At the same time, volunteerism plays a central role in most local CED initiatives, something that can make this approach more attractive for communities with limited financial resources to carry out development activities.

The preceding discussion leads to a number of ongoing research issues still in need of being more fully addressed. First, as relatively new approaches to rural development, place-based and CED strategies, employed either on their own or in combination with one another, require more study. More specifically, municipalities, development practitioners, and government policy-makers stand to benefit greatly from "best practices" research that might help them to understand issues such as how these processes work, how long they take, and what sort of enabling environment is required to make place-based, grassroots-driven efforts succeed. The need for more research demonstrating the ways in which CED processes unfold is exemplified by the results of a survey of municipalities across rural Ontario conducted by Douglas (2003), who found that only a very small percentage of communities had employed, or were planning to initiate, a CED-based approach to economic development. Instead, most respondents indicated that they intended to use the traditional and much more narrowly focused "smokestack chasing" approach that involves limited community collaboration, or else they had no plans to engage proactively in development activities at all.

The need for further research regarding place-based and community-driven approaches to rural development is particularly great within the context of peripheral regions (see also Chapter 1, this volume). Polèse and Shearmur (2003) define Canada's periphery as those rural parts of the country located beyond a one-hour to one-and-a-half hour drive from a major metropolitan area (population over 500,000); in contrast, they use the term "central area" to describe the remaining rural regions. The more pressing need for research in peripheral contexts stems from the fact that places within these regions typically face more difficult challenges in maintaining their viability than do more central rural places. The latter have the opportunity to harness development opportunities provided by their geographical proximity to urban centres, such as providing a place to which exurbanites can move or a weekend playground for urban and suburban dwellers, and many have prospered and grown significantly in meeting

these urban-centred demands. Peripheral rural communities, generally located too far away from cities for these to represent feasible development
options, must therefore be more realistic in their expectations when it
comes to the conceptualization of revitalization strategies. To be sure, some
peripheral rural communities have done well for themselves despite their
geographical location (Barnes and Hayter, 1992; Markey, Pierce, Vodden,
and Roseland, 2005; Mwansa and Bollman, 2005); however, for most such
places, shrinking in size gracefully or simply slowing down the process of
decline by maintaining the population currently in place may be more rea-
sonable long-term goals than attempting to achieve any sizable economic
or population growth (Polèse and Shearmur, 2003; Slack, Bourne, and
Gertler, 2003; Heald, 2008). This does not imply that there is no scope for
place-based development within such communities. Instead, as Huggins
and Thompson (2011, citing Easterlin, 1974) have argued, "the ultimate
aim of place-based policymaking should [perhaps] be to increase the
well-being of the population residing within these places." In other words,
the quality-of-place, sense-of-place, and quality-of-life concepts are all just
as important in peripheral rural places as in more central rural areas if the
retention of existing residents and businesses is desired.

Research concerning place-based, community-driven development in
peripheral regions can follow any number of avenues. For example, is there
potential for peripheral locations situated in outstanding natural landscapes to tap into the growing flows of amenity migrants that have also
brought new residents and economic growth to more central rural places,
such as Whistler, British Columbia, and Wasaga Beach, Ontario? What
role(s) might tourism play in diversifying the economies of traditionally
resource-dependent peripheral regions? What about value-added manufacturing activities that build on the community's long-standing primary
sector-based economy? And how, if at all, might arts and cultural initiatives contribute to broader place-based development efforts and, thus, to
the long-term sustainability of peripheral communities? It is on this latter
question that the remainder of this chapter will focus.

There is considerable urban-oriented analysis of the ways in which arts
and culture can enhance the local quality of life and deem a place more

livable, much of which stems from the pioneering work of Richard Florida and his colleagues regarding the notion of the creative economy (e.g., Florida, 2002; Florida, Mellander, and Stolarick, 2008). Researchers have only recently begun to consider how Florida's ideas apply within rural settings, but where such investigations have been conducted, emphasis has been placed primarily on rural communities located within the urban field (such as Ontario's Niagara Region and Prince Edward County). Still, the creative economy dialogue has more to do with how the creation of an environment desired by the so-called "creative class" might attract new residents and new businesses to a community. Some attention has been directed at investigating the creative economy's applicability to peripheral rural Canadian settings (e.g., Petrov, 2007, 2008). Conversely, far less attention has focused on the more fundamental question of how the arts and culture can enhance the quality of life of individuals already residing in the community and "community well-being," more generally, as well as how this, in turn, can add a sense of vitality to the community that might then lead to further development benefits, such as population and business retention. The work of Nelson, Duxbury, and Murray (2013: 368) is one exception; however, as they have also noted, "scholarly attention to the intersection of culture and economic regeneration in rural, remote areas . . . has languished in global cultural circuits."

ARTS AND CULTURE IN THE HINTERLAND

The purpose of this chapter is to provide further evidence that the pursuit of arts and cultural initiatives can do much to enhance people's perceptions of the quality of place and quality of life to be found in a rural community and that, furthermore, the generation of a positive sense of place in this regard can contribute a great deal to the revitalization of rural and remote places in Canada and elsewhere. This will take the form primarily of a case study about the experiences of Gravelbourg, Saskatchewan, where, in conjunction with several other CED projects over the past 15 years, local residents have embraced the arts and culture to build a community that many of the research participants feel exudes a very high quality of place. Through this approach, the town has witnessed a plethora of initiatives that celebrate its multicultural heritage. As the many newcomers moving to the community in recent years have further diversified the town's cultural mix, these people and their cultures have also been warmly embraced and celebrated. Finally, the community has gone further in its efforts by bringing in musicians and other cultural acts from places such as Quebec, Cuba, and Mexico, which has further enhanced the quality of place and the popular public sentiment about Gravelbourg. With this has come the building of a very strong and positive sense of place that reflects a relatively vibrant and prosperous community amid what many would consider an otherwise bleak economic landscape. Gravelbourg's experience suggests that there is a very important role for the arts and culture to play in the revitalization of peripheral rural communities.

Before continuing, it is important to define "arts" and "culture" as they are meant in this chapter. "Arts" is "notoriously difficult to define," but it can generally be considered to include all forms of creative expression that fall within the visual, performing, and literary arts (Anwar McHenry, 2011). "Culture," on the other hand, is a much more broadly encompassing term that can include all the components of the arts as defined above, as well as foods, languages, religion, folklore, and natural heritage features (Ray, 1998). When talking about rural revitalization, however, it is also important not to dwell only on *indigenously created* arts and culture. For example, arts and culture activities brought into the community from outside, such as concerts and festivals, can also do much to enhance the vitality of a place, either on their own or in combination with local talent.

Although the volume of literature discussing the impacts of the arts and culture on rural places is limited, the research conducted thus far has identified numerous benefits for both individuals and the community. These extend from social and spiritual to economic in nature. At the individual level, exposure to arts and culture has been shown to contribute greatly to one's physical, social, and mental well-being (Kay, 2000; Matarasso, 2007; Anwar McHenry, 2009, 2011). This can include the building of one's technical skills through participation in the planning and/or execution of cultural events, such as plays or festivals. These might include, for example, script-writing or choreography, set design and construction, or more general project management skills (Matarasso, 2007). Beyond these technical skills, working with others to carry out an event can help one develop his or her social and interpersonal skills, expand his or her social network, and express his or her identity. It may also provide one with a sense of achievement and a heightened level of self-confidence upon completion of a project, something that in turn can enhance an individual's perceptions of his or her quality of life. At a more basic level, of course, it is important to note that taking part in arts and cultural activities can also simply represent an enjoyable way of spending one's leisure time.

Researchers have also drawn attention to the *community-wide* benefits associated with arts and cultural initiatives. In a sense, many of these can be described as the individual benefits outlined above *writ large*. For example, the senses of confidence, belonging, and identity brought about by individuals' participation in such activities can, collectively, build a cohesive and resilient community that is well equipped to address the various forces of change affecting rural places today (Anwar McHenry, 2011; Duxbury and Campbell, 2011). This happens in a number of ways. First, participation in arts and culture events can instill in people a strong sense of camaraderie and place attachment. This, in turn, may lead them to be more committed to helping the community prosper and thrive, such as by volunteering to assist with other development initiatives. Second, efforts to celebrate the local culture — for example, by displaying the work of local artists in public spaces or by providing a venue for local performing artists to share their talents with the community — can have the subsequent impact of strengthening the community identity, that is, how the community understands itself (Duxbury and Campbell, 2011). An added benefit in this regard is how the arts and cultural activities can also facilitate understanding among and across groups (Kay, 2000; Anwar McHenry, 2011).

In examining the role of arts and culture in rural communities, researchers have also identified obstacles and barriers that can prevent such initiatives from being carried out (Anwar McHenry, 2011; Duxbury and Campbell, 2011). The high dependence on volunteers to make things happen in rural communities leaves these places susceptible to the impacts of population aging and decline (Duxbury and Campbell, 2011), both of which have the potential to reduce the number of volunteers able to take part in the planning and delivery of initiatives. Furthermore, potential or current volunteers may shy away from taking part because they fear too much will be asked of them as far as their levels of expertise are concerned or the amount of time that may be required. Moreover, even with a strong volunteer cohort, the cost of holding events or sustaining long-term initiatives can exceed the budgets available to many rural communities.

Although arts and cultural activities clearly will not solve all the complex problems facing rural communities today, early evidence suggests that "culture can play important roles in the process of community adaptation, development and, sometimes, reinvention" (Duxbury and Campbell, 2011: 118). Beyond the direct benefits such activities have been shown to provide to participants, it seems clear that culture and the arts can bring about further positive community development outcomes. Thus, as Kay (2000) argues, arts and culture initiatives should be viewed as being *directly* associated with broader community development projects, not as some unrelated and/or insignificant part of community life. In this regard, the need for more research demonstrating the importance of arts and culture to rural communities is similar to the need for further research regarding the economic benefits of community development efforts highlighted by Mac-Neil (1997). At that time, policy-makers were still somewhat averse to the creation of programs and policies supporting community development due to their long-standing emphasis on sectoral-based development and, with this, their reliance on economic indicators as measures of project success. Since then, researchers have demonstrated quite effectively how seemingly "soft" development activities can bring about positive economic development results for rural places. This has culminated in the growing call for rural communities and regions to engage in place-based development strategies highlighted at the start of this chapter.

METHODOLOGY

The case study presented here is drawn from a larger and ongoing research project that has aimed to explore the dynamics and outcomes of the rural community economic development process. As much as there has been growing support for CED approaches in lieu of more traditional top-down, sector-specific rural development strategies, remarkably little longitudinal research has been conducted that can help rural development researchers, policy-makers, and practitioners better understand how CED approaches might best be carried out and what types of outcomes can ensue from the application of such a development model. Certainly, it is likely that one of the key reasons community-based approaches have been avoided in some rural places has been a lack of understanding of these things. Returning to MacNeil (1997), "there is room within the community development field itself for practitioners to be precise about the development process and systematically demonstrate how it functions." Rural development scholars are ideally positioned to help make this happen, of course, and observations such as this provided the impetus for the research project profiled here.

The primary data collection tool used to conduct this case study has been the key informant interview. Over the course of several visits to Gravelbourg (in 2005, 2007, 2008, and 2010), a total of 31 interviews were conducted with a variety of local actors who, in one way or another, have been involved in community development activities in Gravelbourg since 1998, the year in which the town formally began to engage in the CED process. The interviewees included local politicians and administrators, community and economic development officials, business owners, and active community volunteers. The interviews were conducted in the participants' homes or workplaces, and lasted anywhere from 30 minutes to two hours. Each interview was recorded with the participant's permission, and later transcribed to facilitate the subsequent analysis.

From the outset, the research was designed in such a way that it would give precedence to these local actors in telling the story of what development activities have transpired in Gravelbourg since 1998, At the same time, however, it is important to point out that, as much as the key informants had more extensive knowledge of the CED activities being discussed than most local people, they were being asked to share *their own perceptions* regarding how those events unfolded and how they impacted the community. What follows is a consideration of the comments offered by the key informants within these discussions that related to the community's integration of arts and culture-related initiatives into the broader CED strategy.

GRAVELBOURG, SASKATCHEWAN: CASE STUDY

The town of Gravelbourg (population 1,200) is located in south-central Saskatchewan, over 100 kilometres from the closest city and near the centre of Canada's drought-prone Palliser's Triangle. Accordingly, people travelling the highway from Moose Jaw to Gravelbourg for the first time could easily be forgiven for expecting to find yet another dying prairie town such as the many through which they pass along the way. Upon arriving in the community, however, the visual evidence suggests this not to be the case. A few kilometres east of Gravelbourg, the town's skyline begins to appear. Two of the most obvious landmarks in this skyline are found at the town's extreme southern and northern edges. To the south are the tall spires of the Our Lady of the Assumption Co-Cathedral; to the north is a grain elevator. Together, these two structures serve as tangible evidence of the dual functions that Gravelbourg has served throughout its unique 100-year history — Gravelbourg has been an agricultural service centre, not unlike so many other prairie communities, and an important religious centre for the French-Canadian Roman Catholic Church. Continuing into town on Highway #43, one passes Trailtech, a successful and home-grown custom trailer manufacturing firm that employs over 100 people. Continuing along First Avenue/1ère Avenue (the street signs are bilingual) up to the intersection of First Avenue and Main Street (or "rue Principale"), one passes several stately homes reminiscent of those found in a much older Quebec town. Lush and mature trees abound (a rare sight in this part of Saskatchewan), as do public parks and green spaces. Driving down the ornately decorated Main Street, one passes the nicely landscaped Town Hall, located in the former Court House building, a number of unique businesses stretching block after block, and even the architecturally distinctive Saskatchewan Liquor Board Store. Each of these sights suggests, in its own way, that Gravelbourg's residents are proud of their town and optimistic about its future. Gravelbourg's vibrancy as a community amid an otherwise bleak southern Saskatchewan settlement landscape has much to do with its long-standing place-based and grassroots-driven program of sustainable rural community development. As a key part of this, Gravelbourg's recognition of how the arts and culture — including both those aspects intrinsic to the community and elements imported to the town from elsewhere — can do much to enhance individual and community wellness has played a central role in shaping a place where, according to the key informants who participated in this study, the local quality of life has made the town an attractive place to live and do business, both for long-term residents and newcomers.

Gravelbourg's revitalization process began in earnest in 1998, when a new mayor and six councillors began a new term of office. Several of these individuals had campaigned on a platform that included the need for a more aggressive and proactive approach to economic development. Indeed, in the years leading up to 1998, and in the years since, Gravelbourg has faced the same difficult circumstances as many rural Canadian communities. The agricultural economy was in serious trouble, the on- and off-farm population of neighbouring municipalities was in a long-standing state of decline, and there was also the constant threat of the local railway line and grain elevators being closed. Gravelbourg's downtown was replete with vacant buildings and enrolment was declining in the local schools. Clearly, something had to be done.

The first step in the move towards more formal development planning in Gravelbourg was the hiring of the town's first-ever Economic Development Officer (EDO) in 1998. In the early days of his position, the EDO convinced the municipal council that the CED approach, rather than the more traditional industrial recruitment (or "smokestack chasing") model, was most likely to lead to successful outcomes in Gravelbourg. The early days of the CED program also saw the town commit itself to the use of a "sustainable community development" model, whereby the potential economic, social, and environmental implications of any proposed projects would be given due consideration before moving forward. In looking internally, it quickly became apparent that the town had many cultural and other assets upon which it could build a development strategy. The town's religious heritage and its multicultural composition — in particular, its heavily francophone population, and its (for rural Saskatchewan) unique architectural features — represented features of the community that could help it build its own competitive advantage. Over the next decade and a half, these and other assets have been harnessed to build a strong quality of place in Gravelbourg; in many cases, integration of the arts and culture has been key to mobilizing these assets.

As noted earlier, quality of place is influenced by characteristics of the built environment and aesthetic considerations. One of the most important ways in which the arts and culture have been central to Gravelbourg's revitalization has to do with the many efforts made to enhance the aesthetics of the community's built environment. Over the course of the 1980s and 1990s, as more and more stores were shuttered, torn down, or simply neglected by their owners, much of the town's appearance — and that of the Main Street business district, in particular — did little to inspire a sense of local pride or to attract outside visitors or investors. Since the town began to engage more actively in CED in the late 1990s, however, a number of initiatives have transformed the community into a place that many research participants proclaimed to be much more beautiful than it had been in a long time and whose aesthetic charms have attracted many in-migrants to the community. A number of groups have been involved in these efforts. In most cases, they have worked collaboratively to carry out various projects that highlight the community's cultural heritage and the work of its local artisans. These include: the Save Our Little Elevator Committee (SOLE); the town's beautification group, known as the Keep Gravelbourg Beautiful Committee (or KGB for short); the Touch of Europe Committee; the Gravelbourg and District Chamber of Commerce; and the local municipality itself, the Town of Gravelbourg.

One of the most significant initiatives in which the arts and culture played a significant role involved the beautification of Gravelbourg's downtown core. In this case, the Touch of Europe Committee, the KGB, the Chamber of Commerce, and the town initiated what came to be known as the Main Street Revitalization Project. Through a co-ordinated effort, each group was responsible for one or more components of the project. The Chamber of Commerce was put in charge of replacing the lampposts, the

Touch of Europe Committee spearheaded the sidewalk reconstruction, and the KGB placed flowerpots and cleaned up green spaces along Main Street. Funding for the project came from a number of sources, including a lottery sponsored by the Chamber of Commerce, donations from Main Street merchants and property owners, and contributions of money and labour by the Town of Gravelbourg. Although not all business owners contributed, either because they were reluctant to do so or simply could not afford it, costs were kept to a minimum through the use of as much volunteer labour as possible. New interlocking brick sidewalks were installed on a block-by-block basis as funding became available, with many volunteers spending their evenings and weekends on their hands and knees laying down the bricks. Ornamental lampposts, complete with metallic banners, were installed along the course of the newly constructed sidewalks. The banners were crafted by a local artisan and depicted various aspects of Gravelbourg's heritage, such as the wartime contributions of local residents, the town's agricultural roots, and the community's widely acclaimed folk dance troupe, Les Danseurs de la Rivière la Vieille. Several business owners also incorporated the community's cultural heritage into the enhancement of their building facades. For example, the local accountant gave her office a German architectural look, complete with writing the word "accountant" in German on her sign, while another local entrepreneur opened a new restaurant called Café Paris. The Main Street Revitalization Project also involved the painting of new murals that celebrated the community's heritage, such as a large mural illustrating the town's grain elevators as they existed at the peak of its role as an agricultural service centre.

A further example of how the arts and culture have been integrated into the broader CED effort is provided by yet another beautification effort spearheaded by the KGB. In this case, a litter-strewn and weed-filled vacant lot located beside the busiest building in Gravelbourg, the post office, was turned into Humphrey Park. Named after a local resident, the park's construction was once again primarily a volunteer-based effort, with further assistance provided by town employees. Beyond providing additional green space along Main Street, the park has a sculpture, a fountain, and a mural, all created by local artisans. The KGB engaged in a similar effort when it expanded another Main Street green space, Soucy Park. In this case, a local resident — frustrated by the presence of a vacant, dilapidated house beside the park — bought the building and donated it to the Town of Gravelbourg on condition that it be demolished and replaced with green space. Through the efforts of local volunteers and town employees, Soucy Park was doubled in size and adorned with a fountain, gardens, benches, and a stage. This transformed a little-used public space into a prominent local park and a popular venue for community events, such as those held during the Southern Saskatchewan Summer Solstice Festival (discussed below).

One of the most significant arts and culture-related initiatives completed as part of Gravelbourg's CED efforts has been the revitalization of the Renaissance Gaiety Theatre. Originally built as the town's movie theatre in the 1940s, this building had fallen into disrepair and was taken over by the Town of Gravelbourg in the mid-2000s as a result of the owner having fallen into tax arrears. Upon inspection it was clear that the facility needed much in the way of repairs to keep it in a usable state; however, a key informant noted that the Town Council of the day felt that the facility was an important part of the community's heritage and also that it should continue to play a role in the town's social life. After creating a non-profit Community Arts Board and completing a feasibility study financed by the Saskatchewan Heritage Foundation and the Town of Gravelbourg, a business plan to create the Gravelbourg Community Arts Centre was put into action. In what was described by one interviewee as a "bit of a whirlwind project," the Board of Directors spearheaded a year-long top-to-bottom renovation of the facility, largely co-ordinated by the Town's EDO and completed with the help of over 100 volunteers of all ages. Further funding was provided by the federal government's Gas Tax Fund, which provides financial support for environmentally sustainable infrastructure projects. The Gas Tax funding was used to install energy-efficient windows, a high-efficiency furnace, and other green energy-related upgrades. Thus, as one research participant put it, the project involved promoting the arts and environmental sustainability at the same time, thereby contributing in multiple ways to the town's sustainable community development mandate.

As in Shetland with Lerwick's Mareel creative industries centre (Chapter

8), a central facility dedicated to the arts has played an important role in Gravelbourg. The Gravelbourg Community Arts Centre/Renaissance Gaiety Theatre reopened in March 2010, and by June 2010 the facility had already hosted a plethora of events. These included a performance by the Regina Symphony Orchestra, concerts by Hecho en Cuba (a Cuban band that has visited Gravelbourg on numerous occasions) and other travelling solo performers and groups, and a mentalist show. On Friday and Saturday nights, the theatre is also used regularly for its original purpose, to show Hollywood films. However, rather than as a for-profit venture, movies are shown by non-profit community groups as fundraisers, thus allowing the town to offer the movies without having to pay staff. Instead, each group picks which weeks it would like to run the theatre and which movie it wants to play. They then run that weekend's activities, give the town a set percentage of the revenues to help towards the building upkeep, and keep any remaining profits for their own purposes.

After the opening of the Community Arts Centre several other events were organized by the local Artist-in-Residence, hired by the Town of Gravelbourg through a program administered by the Saskatchewan Arts Board. This individual organized and engaged in a variety of local arts and culture activities throughout her one-year contract period. While some took place in the local schools, the bulk of her activities transpired at the Community Arts Centre. This included a weekly coffee house event — an "open mic" night where people could share their talents — and other events where people could hone their skills in such areas as improv comedy and dramatic acting. One key informant who took part in this research was among those participating. She recounted her experience as follows:

> Researcher: How did you end up becoming involved as an actor at the Community Arts Centre?
> Interviewee: [Laughs] I have no idea! Well, Claire is the town's Artist-in-Residence, and I've always been interested in drama. I like live plays and such on stage. So when she started her theatre nights, it was kind of a drama club. And she had an improv night. It was more for fun that I joined, which it was. It was so much fun. So we'd

go on Thursday nights and do little skit things or whatever she had planned.

The Artist-in-Residence also wrote a play with a plot based loosely on
the community of Gravelbourg and recruited local residents to be the actors
in a public production of the show. The aforementioned key informant offered this summary of what transpired:

> Interviewee: [The Artist-in-Residence] said she was
> writing a play for the town and that she wondered if any
> of us would be interested in being actors. So I said "Oh,
> sure!" not even thinking for a minute that this was on
> stage in front of people. But the more you get into it, the
> more fun it is. And we just did it.
> Researcher: And I hear you sold out a couple of very suc-
> cessful shows. It was very well attended.
> Interviewee: Yeah, very well attended. It was fun.
> Researcher: Were there a lot of other people from town
> who got involved in the acting that were also like you,
> everyday people from the community?
> Interviewee: Yes, and I was very surprised at all the ones
> that were there.

As the participant noted, both shows sold out. With 200 seats in the Renaissance Gaiety Theatre, this was clearly a major local event. In further discussing the play, the Economic Development Officer noted that people had
to be turned away at the door on the second night due to fire code restric-
tions that prevented anyone else from entering the building. Also notable
was the fact that, as mentioned above, many local residents took part in the
production as actors. This included children as young as six years old
through to people in their eighties. A few residents from other nearby
communities also acted in the play, while other visitors from outside the
community also came to watch it.

Since June 2010, when local residents were last interviewed as part of
this study, the Community Arts Centre has been firmly established as the
major local venue for arts and cultural activities. The Community Arts

Board attempts to hold at least one live event per month at the Centre, and the Town of Gravelbourg's Sports, Culture and Recreation Development Officer assists the Board in ensuring that events planned at the Centre do not conflict with those being held by community organizations at other venues, such as the Centre Culturel Maillard, which is operated by local francophone groups. Many of the events held at the Community Arts Centre are funded in part by the Saskatchewan Arts Board, with the Town of Gravelbourg providing financial assistance as well.

The quality-of-place enhancements provided by the incorporation of arts and culture into the physical spaces of Gravelbourg, such as parks and the local theatre, have been complemented by the holding of several events, many of which are now annual affairs. One of these is the International Food Festival, the brainchild of a local resident who wanted the community to better appreciate Gravelbourg's cultural diversity. Her account of how this event first started is provided below:

> I thought, "You know, Gravelbourg is known as a French settlement," but I thought, "You know what, there are so many other people here than just French." And I thought we should emphasize this a little better. So I went to Regina and they have Mosaic (a multicultural festival) there, and I thought, "We can do something like this." Smaller, but, you know, it would be nice. So we started out with eight countries, and it was in the Cultural Centre and it was packed! And people had to go sit outside, there was music, and it was wonderful! I was just overwhelmed! So I thought, next year, we have to go to the curling rink because it's bigger. It drew 500 people — packed! We got fiddlers. We had some entertainment, so people from all over, they come to visit. And it gets known, you know, that we have all this food, and people dressed up, and I had some costumes come in from Holland, you know, so I'm all dressed up in my costume, and wooden shoes. Then, the third year, we went to the big rink. The skating rink. And that was nice. Yeah, we had

about 600 people there, and it was very nice. And now, next year, we're going to have our Centennial, so there will be lots of people there. I expect a thousand people next year for our food festival.

Again, as in other cases presented in this volume, food (see Chapters 3, 7, and 13) and festivals are important aspects of place and culture. The International Food Festival, which by 2012 had grown to showcase the cuisine, clothing, and other cultural artifacts of 20 different cultural groups, has become an annual tradition. It now takes place on the first day of a much larger cultural event, the Southern Saskatchewan Summer Solstice Festival. This event, which also started on a much smaller scale, first took place in 2000 as an early component of Gravelbourg's effort to build a sustainable rural community. Recognizing culture as a critical element of sustainable development, the festival's organizers (led by the town's Economic Development Officer, who had much prior experience in planning cultural events) put together a weekend of book and poetry readings, musical performances, children's entertainment, dances, and other activities that incorporated both local and outside talent. Now a much larger event, with some 1,800 people having taken part in the festivities in 2010, the Southern Saskatchewan Summer Solstice Festival is organized by a nine-person board of directors and put into place by an army of volunteers on the June weekend closest to the date of that year's summer solstice. Events take place in many of the facilities mentioned earlier in this chapter, such as the Renaissance Gaiety Theatre, Soucy Park, the Centre Culturel Maillard, and along Main Street. Many local residents enjoy the event, as do out-of-town visitors from as far away as Moose Jaw, Regina, and Saskatoon, the latter of which is three hours from Gravelbourg by car.

The initiatives discussed in the preceding pages are only a few of the many arts and culture-related initiatives that have made up part of Gravelbourg's broader CED efforts. These examples already show how the arts and culture can serve as important resources for a rural community. The following section considers several ways in which the initiatives profiled here have contributed to improved individual and community wellness, with arguments supported by the input of local residents themselves.

THE BENEFITS OF PARTICIPATION

Research participants noted that they and/or others they knew had benefited from either participating directly in such initiatives (e.g., as organizers or performers) or simply by being involved as audience members. One of the most notable instances of an individual benefiting directly is represented in comments made by one of the founders of the Touch of Europe Committee:

> So, I got to know a friend, and she convinced me that I should take this leadership course. However, I did not think that I was a leader or had any possibilities to do something like that. So, I took this course with a group of people in town. There were about 10 or 12 people. It was a three-day course, held in three different places. And I came out of there and I thought, "Hmm," you know, "what now?" You know, you listen and you learn something but you don't know what. Then, after that, we had another session, and we had to work on a project, they kind of force you to work together on a project. And, so we formed a group, what we called the Touch of Europe Committee, and our first project was just painting a wall. This ugly, concrete, falling-apart wall on Main Street, and we decided, this group, to paint this wall, and that was our first project. And then, slowly, the group went on their own and each decided to do their own little projects. A pie-baking contest or other small things. And then one year, somebody said, "How about a parade?" A Santa Claus Parade. And I remember seeing those parades and it was just like a drunken Santa Claus on a half-ton [pickup truck]. And I thought, "Oh! I think, you know, we can do better than this!" And so, I suggested that maybe the Touch of Europe would like to be involved in the Santa Claus Parade. And so, I started phoning around. You know, I thought, "I can do this. I can do better than this Santa Claus on a half-ton." So, I phoned

around and it ended up as a beautiful parade. And I felt
so good about it and I thought, "Oh, I can do this!"

Another important point drawn from this case study is how arts and culture initiatives (as they were defined earlier in this chapter) can provide a social and creative outlet to those who aren't interested in sports, which traditionally have played a central role in the social and cultural life of many rural communities. When a call was put out for volunteers to serve on the Community Arts Board, the required number of directors was easily achieved. Also, the Board members often volunteer to help out with events held at the Arts Centre, even when they are not required to do so (such as on the weekend movie nights). As one key informant noted, these individuals "are excited to participate because they are excited by the (arts centre) project." The same research participant also noted that many local teenagers have been particularly excited to contribute to the operation of the Community Arts Centre:

> [There are] so many kids in town that, you know, don't
> like hockey, they don't like sports, and this has provided
> them an avenue to experience something new which
> builds that community development, it builds that com-
> munity spirit and that pride in their community. And
> that's where the sustainability of the community can really
> spring from.

In order to take advantage of this enthusiasm, and as an opportunity to contribute to the development of local youth, the Board was considering creating a position for a youth Board member. At the same time, the interviewee who pointed this out noted that they might have to make the candidates compete for the position because so many wanted to be on the Board.

At a broader level, Gravelbourg's experience also appears to provide further evidence of how arts and culture initiatives can promote community wellness. A common point made by the research participants was how events like the Summer Solstice Festival and the International Food Festival have made residents more "worldly" and more understanding of other cultures. As one interviewee stated in 2005:

> Well, I think Summer Solstice has been very good be-
> cause with Gravelbourg, in the past, cultural stuff has
> not been a big thing. I think it's been, you know, we're a
> recreational town, and a lot of things have been done to
> the recreational aspects. So when [we] brought in the
> Summer Solstice with more cultural stuff, it opens our
> eyes to more. . . . I had a friend say once that, you know,
> "Living in Saskatchewan is like living in a cultural void."
> She was from down East, so you have always had that
> access that we have not. So it goes back to that thing that
> if you never had it, you don't miss it. So by bringing in
> this stuff it opens our eyes to all these things that are out
> there, which is a bonus to us.

Another important outcome that goes beyond the topic of wellness has
been the ways in which arts and culture events have provided local groups
with a source of revenue generation. Thus, groups such as sports teams, the
local hospital foundation, the Girl Guides and Boy Scouts, among others,
have secured much-needed funding to maintain their respective activities
by holding events in which the arts and culture are the main attraction. A
further positive outcome often associated with this has been the social
capital generated when groups have worked together to make events happen. The Main Street Revitalization Project provides one such example;
whereby four different groups worked together to collaboratively improve
the appearance of Gravelbourg's shopping district. Several similar partnerships were highlighted by the town's Sports, Culture and Recreation Development Officer in a 2010 interview. The Harvest Ho-Down, an adults-only
dance with a live band and a beer garden held every September, was designed to be a potential fundraiser for interested groups. In 2009 eight
organizations helped in running the event, which over 500 people attended.
In the end, each group garnered $1,000 to put towards its own activities. A
similar arrangement was created to run the Gravelbourg Winter Festival, a
one-day family-oriented event held in early February. In this case, because
it was not a licensed event at which alcohol would be served, local youth
groups were able to participate in running the day's events. As a result,

groups such the Girl Guides and the local karate club helped make the Winter Festival a success in its first two years.

Among the many community benefits of arts and culture initiatives highlighted in the literature have been the enhancement of community pride and heightened sense of community. Some have criticized Gravelbourg's multicultural approach to community development with the argument that the town's francophone heritage is what makes it a distinctive place and, thus, what should be emphasized in its branding and development activities. However, many research participants pointed out that that there is now a widespread appreciation of the town's growing multicultural composition that might otherwise never have come about without the many cultural events having taken place over the past decade.

Many of the events held in Gravelbourg have also been beneficial in that they have "put the community on the map" and enhanced the town's reputation among outsiders. Certainly, many of the aforementioned initiatives have been aimed primarily at a local audience, but they have also attracted people from throughout Gravelbourg's surrounding rural communities and from urban centres further afield. One interview participant quoted a casino manager from Moose Jaw as having said that Gravelbourg had earned the reputation of being innovative and a community that, unlike so many others in Saskatchewan, was not going to "dry up and disappear in a few years." Another participant noted how people in Moose Jaw, Swift Current, and Assiniboia would often make comments to her such as "Oh, Gravelbourg! There's always so much going on there!"

Although it is difficult to attribute causality to any particular factor, there was also a perception among the research participants that Gravelbourg's cultural vitality and culturally inspired aesthetic charm have been responsible for attracting many new residents to the community. Around 2006, local residents began to notice that the many "for sale" signs on homes and businesses in the community were starting to disappear, with many of these properties having previously languished on the market for several years. Over 250 new residents moved to Gravelbourg between 2006 and 2008 alone, according to statistics compiled by the town. The local real estate firm sold 46 properties in 2007, more than double the average year's sales. One key informant noted that he had lived his entire life in Gravelbourg (some 50 years) and realized that he could no longer say he knew everyone in town. Many came from Canadian places of origin, especially (but not exclusively) BC and Alberta, while others had moved to the town from other countries, such as the Philippines, China, Mexico, and the Netherlands. Many interviewees provided anecdotes regarding the reasons why people chose to move to Gravelbourg. Some were retirees looking for an inexpensive place to live that would also provide an escape from big city life, while others were parents of small children seeking a safe non-urban place to raise their families. Others were entrepreneurial members of visible minorities who were looking for a welcoming community in which they could operate a local business, such as a restaurant. However, Gravelbourg's cultural vitality, aesthetic charm, and welcoming personality (including its explicit recognition of the community's multicultural character) were most commonly cited as important deciding factors by many interviewees. As one person noted, "the town sells itself." Further evidence was provided by one newcomer who moved with his wife to Gravelbourg from Victoria, British Columbia:

> I guess Victoria was too busy, and whatever . . . expensive, I guess. So, we thought, "Well, let's maybe look somewhere else." . . . We were looking at southern Alberta and the prices were going up there and everything was disappearing that was nice, so we extended our search, and found the little southwest corner of Saskatchewan had a lot to offer. We made a trip out here and toured around and Gravelbourg just had something about it that attracted us. I don't know what you could describe it as, I don't know. It just was a feeling, I guess. It had the beautiful brick houses, it has some heritage buildings, that kind of thing. It just had something. The friendliness of people, whatever. More than some of the other communities we had looked at. And we found this little house that we could fix up, and we're here. And enjoying it.

Another participant cited the story of a newcomer who had been try-ing for some time to purchase a house in Gravelbourg. Having been fre-quently outbid by other buyers, he gave up on ever being able to move to the community and instead put a deposit to buy a house in another town elsewhere in Saskatchewan. Before he moved there, however, a house came available in Gravelbourg; he subsequently forfeited his deposit on the other property and moved to Gravelbourg. The interviewee finished sharing this anecdote by stating that "this sort of thing is what we hear from people over and over again."

As a further benefit, many of the newcomers have added valuable human capital to the community by themselves becoming volunteers. For example, one newcomer from British Columbia ran successfully for Town Council shortly after his arrival, another from the Netherlands became a board member at the local museum, and a new resident who relocated from Atlantic Canada is an active participant at the community's French-language radio station. The impact of newcomers in the town's vol-unteer sector is also evident on the Community Arts Board, which was composed almost completely of newer residents in 2010. The Southern Saskatchewan Summer Solstice Festival organizing committee is also com-posed largely of relatively new residents.

Gravelbourg's cultural vitality may have contributed to an air of opti-mism within the town's business sector. A notable case involved the con-struction of a new $800,000 Saskatchewan Liquor Board store on Main Street, complete with an Italian Renaissance architectural design in keeping with the town's "Touch of Europe on the Prairies" theme. As one interviewee noted, the provincial government's show of faith in the community's future, particularly after long being viewed by many as having little interest in helping Saskatchewan's rural communities, also instilled a higher level of confidence in other local entrepreneurs and business owners. The provin-cial government's investment of close to a million dollars in a remote rural community, and its willingness to spend more on the construction of a build-ing in order for it to fit nicely into the town's branding strategy, was viewed by many research participants as a critical point in Gravelbourg's commu-nity development process. By subsequently encouraging entrepreneurs and firms to purchase, expand, or renovate a business, or to start a new one, the provincial government's investment in Gravelbourg, in a sense, validated all of the community's "soft" development activities, such as the beautification of Main Street and the holding of arts and culture events, which some people, up to then, had questioned in terms of their economic development impacts. In effect, it also demonstrated the truth of a point made by one of the research participants to a doubtful local resident in the early days of the Main Street Revitalization Project. As he described it:

> I interviewed [a fellow] who had taken over his father's trucking business. He's a young third-generation owner who is aggressive and is building up the business and succeeding against all odds. I ask him what he feels about our economic development efforts. His answer is you won't get much economic development fixing up the main street. I asked him why he spent so much time cleaning his trucks. A simple question. He started to answer, then realized the trap I set. He smiled and I saw how he quickly understood what I was getting at.

Anecdotal evidence provided by many of the interviewees in 2005, 2008, and 2010, along with feature articles in the *Gravelbourg Tribune* newspaper, also show that many local businesses have been bought by newcomers who were drawn to the town by the cultural vitality of the community. Furthermore, several prominent businesses in Gravelbourg were started by a former resident now living in British Columbia. Having already established a successful real estate investment career on Canada's west coast, the gentleman was convinced by family members still residing in Gravelbourg to invest in his hometown. After noting how vibrant the community had become in recent years and how determined the residents were to build a strong future for the town, he bought several local buildings and established new businesses that included a bed-and-breakfast and a dollar store. He also created a new business, called "Styles," in a vacant grocery store on Main Street that sold many everyday goods that had not otherwise been available in the community for many years. The store itself has also become a tourist attraction, with one key informant noting that bus tour groups would often stop there and another sharing an anecdote about three women from northern Alberta who "had come all the way to Gravelbourg to check out this place called Styles that they had heard about." To top it off, they ended up staying in Gravelbourg for three days after seeing all the town had to offer in terms of cultural and other amenities.

DISCUSSION AND CONCLUSION

Through a case study of Gravelbourg, Saskatchewan, this chapter has helped to fill a notable gap in the place-based development research by examining the ways in which the arts and culture can enhance quality of life in peripheral rural regions. The various initiatives implemented by Gravelbourg's municipal government, key personnel (the Economic Development Officer and Artist-in-Residence), and the community's many volunteer committees have created, according to many of those who participated in this study, a highly livable small town that exudes a strong quality of place and a positive sense of place. This, in turn, has helped to retain many residents and businesses and has created an environment where people feel confident enough about the future of the town that they have become willing investors themselves, whether in maintaining the aesthetics of their own properties, the purchase or expansion of existing business, or the starting of a new enterprise. Gravelbourg's strong quality of place has also enhanced its reputation externally, which has led to the in-migration of new residents and the arrival of growing numbers of tourists.

The findings in this case study also demonstrate that, although the arts and culture can do much for a rural community, engaging in such activities is clearly also a time-consuming process that requires a great deal of patience, social capital, and risk-taking on the part of local residents. Rural communities, while quite capable of doing things on their own, still require the help of more senior levels of government, particularly in terms of funding. But most important, perhaps, is this final point: for the arts and culture to have a positive impact in a rural community, two other forms of culture are also required, a *culture of confidence* that breeds a willingness to try new ideas and a *culture of volunteerism* that can take those ideas and put them to good use.

Through its analysis of the positive contributions that the arts and culture can make to rural community life, this case study also demonstrates
the important linkages that exist between the notion of place-based development and the process of community economic development. As noted
earlier in this chapter, place-based development aims to make use of a
community's natural, physical, and human endowments for development
purposes, while community economic development is a holistic, participatory, and collaborative process that depends on the contributions of a
broad cross-section of community members for the successful achievement of economic, social, and environmental objectives. By taking advantage of its numerous place-based assets — such as its theatre, parks, and
other public spaces, its multicultural heritage and diversity, and, perhaps
most importantly, its abundant stock of social and human capital — and by
employing a grassroots-based approach in identifying and harnessing
these resources, Gravelbourg has become a vibrant rural community where
residents enjoy a high quality of life. While it has taken several years to
bring about these positive outcomes, Gravelbourg's experience suggests
that other rural communities ought also to consider adopting a place-
based, grassroots-driven approach to community and economic revitalization. It also suggests that researchers should look for other communities
that have employed such an approach and study those places to determine
whether similar results have been achieved. By completing such studies, a
more robust body of literature that will assist in the formulation of evidence-
based rural development policy can be created.

REFERENCES

Andrews, C.J. 2001. "Analyzing Quality-of-Place." *Environment and Planning B:
Planning and Design* 28, 2: 201–17.

Anwar McHenry, J. 2009. "A Place for the Arts in Rural Revitalization and the Social
Wellbeing of Australian Rural Communities." *Rural Society* 19, 1: 60–70.

———. 2011. "Rural Empowerment through the Arts: The Role of Arts in Civic and
Social Participation in the Mid-West Region of Western Australia." *Journal of
Rural Studies* 27, 3: 245–53.

Barnes, T.J., and R. Hayter 1992. "'The Little Town That Did': Flexible Accumulation and Community Response in Chemainus, British Columbia." *Regional Studies* 26: 647–63.

Benson, M., and K. O'Reilly. 2009. "Migration and the Search for a Better Way of Life: A Critical Exploration of Lifestyle Migration." *Sociological Review* 57, 4: 608–25.

Bridger, J.C., and T.R. Alter. 2008. "An Interactional Approach to Place-based Rural Development." *Community Development* 39, 1: 99–111.

Bryant, C. 2002. "Urban and Rural Interactions and Rural Community Renewal." In I.R. Bowler, C.R. Bryant, and C. Cocklin, eds., *The Sustainability of Rural Systems: Geographical Interpretations*, 247–69. Dordrecht, Germany: Kluwer.

———. 2010. "Co-constructing Rural Communities in the 21st Century: Challenges for Central Governments and the Research Community in Working Effectively with Local and Regional Actors. In G. Halseth, S. Markey, and D. Bruce, eds., *The Next Rural Economies: Constructing Rural Place in Global Economies*, 142–54. Cambridge, Mass.: CABI.

Douglas, D.J.A. 2003. *Towards More Effective Rural Economic Development in Ontario: An Applied Research Project*. Guelph, Ont.: University of Guelph, School of Environmental Design and Rural Development.

———. 2004. "Investing in Capacity Development: An Economic Development Agenda for Rural Ontario." *Municipal World* (Apr.): 31–37.

Duxbury, N., and H. Campbell. 2011. "Developing and Revitalizing Rural Communities through Arts and Culture." *Small Cities Imprint* 3: 111–22.

Easterlin, R.A. 1974. "Does Economic Growth Improve the Human Lot? Some Empirical Evidence." In P.A. David and M.W. Reder, eds., *Nations and Households in Economic Growth*, 89–125. New York: Academic Press.

Epps, R. 2002. "Sustainable Rural Communities and Rural Development." In I.R. Bowler, C.R. Bryant, and C. Cocklin, eds., *The Sustainability of Rural Systems: Geographical Interpretations*, 225–46. Dordrecht, Germany: Kluwer.

Florida, R. 2002. *The Rise of the Creative Class: And How It's Transforming Work, Leisure, Community, and Everyday Life*. New York: Basic Books.

———, C. Mellander, and K.Stolarick. 2008. "Inside the Black Box of Regional Development: Human Capital, the Creative Class and Tolerance." *Journal of Economic Geography* 8, 5: 615–49.

Halfacree, K.H., and M.J. Rivera. 2012. "Moving to the Countryside . . . and Staying: Lives beyond Representations." *Sociologia Ruralis* 52, 1: 92–114.

Heald, S. 2008. "Embracing Marginality: Place-making vs. Development in Gardenton, Manitoba." *Development in Practice* 18, 1: 17–29.

Huggins, R., and P. Thompson. 2011. *Culture and Place-based Economic Development: Perspectives from Wales*. CASS Papers in Economic Geography 01/2011. Cardiff, Wales: School of City and Regional Planning, Cardiff University.

Kay, A. 2000. "Art and Community Development: The Role the Arts Have in Regenerating Communities." *Community Development Journal* 35, 4: 414–24.

Knox, P.L., S.A. Marston, and A.E. Nash. 2010. *Human Geography: Places and Regions in Global Context*, 3rd Canadian ed. Toronto: Pearson Prentice-Hall.

Koster, R., and J. Randall. 2005. "Indicators of Community Economic Development through Mural-based Tourism." *Canadian Geographer* 49, 1: 42–60.

MacNeil, T. 1997. "Assessing the Gap between Community Development Practice and Regional Development Policy." In B. Wharf and M. Clague, eds., *Community Organizing: Canadian Experiences*, 149–63. Toronto: Oxford University Press.

Markey, S. 2010. *Primer on Place-based Development*. http://researchsalons.crcresearch.org/files-crcresearch_v2/ReimerMarkeyRuralPlaceBasedPolicySummary Paper20081107.pdf.

———, G. Halseth, and D. Manson. 2006. "The Struggle to Compete: From Comparative to Competitive Advantage in Northern British Columbia." *International Planning Studies* 11, 1: 19–39.

———, J.T. Pierce, K. Vodden, and M. Roseland. 2005. *Second Growth: Community Economic Development in Rural British Columbia*. Vancouver: University of British Columbia Press.

Matarasso, F. 2007. "Common Ground: Cultural Action as a Route to Community Development." *Community Development Journal* 42: 449–58.

Mwansa, P.B., and R.D. Bollman. 2005. "Community Demographic Trends within Their Regional Context." *Rural and Small Town Canada Analysis Bulletin* 6, 3: 1–36.

Nelson, R., N. Duxbury, and C. Murray. 2013. "Cultural and Creative Economy Strategies for Community Transformation: Four Approaches." In J. Parkins and M. Reed, eds., *Social Transformation in Rural Canada: Community, Cultures and Collective Action*, 368–86. Vancouver: University of British Columbia Press.

Petrov, A.N. 2007. "A Look beyond Metropolis: Exploring Creative Class in the Canadian Periphery." *Canadian Journal of Regional Science* 30, 3: 451–74.

———. 2008. "Talent in the Cold? Creative Capital and the Economic Future of the Canadian North." *Arctic* 61, 2: 162–76.

Polèse, M., and R. Shearmur. 2003. "How Can We Halt the Demise of Canada's Peripheral Regions?" *Policy Options* (May): 47–52.

Ray, C. 1998. "Culture, Intellectual Property and Territorial Rural Development." *Sociologia Ruralis* 38, 1: 3–20.

Reimer, B., and S. Markey. 2008. *Place-based Policy: A Rural Perspective.* Report prepared for Human Resources and Social Development Canada. http://re-searchsalons.crcresearch.org/files-crcresearch_v2/ReimerMarkeyRuralPlace-BasedPolicySummaryPaper20081107.pdf.

Ross, D., and G. McRobie. 1989. *A Feasibility Study for a Centre for Community Economic Development at Simon Fraser University.* Burnaby, BC: Community Economic Development Centre, Simon Fraser University.

Slack, E., L. Bourne, and M. Gertler. 2003. "Small, Rural, and Remote Communities: The Anatomy of Risk." Paper prepared for the Panel on the Role of Government.

Terluin, I.J. 2003. "Differences in Economic Development in Rural Regions of Advanced Countries: An Overview and Critical Analysis of Theories." *Journal of Rural Studies* 19, 3: 327–44.

CHAPTER 10

Poles Apart: Trans-Island Dialogue in Ten Days on the Island

Laurie Brinklow

INTRODUCTION

This story begins in Tasmania, an island that hangs like a dot point off Australia's south coast.[1] In the dying years of the twentieth century, government leaders — not for the first time — were looking for ways to address "the Tasmanian Problem" that identified the island as an "economically dysfunctional, regionally fragmented and demographically declining 'basket case'" (Harwood, 2011: 72). Perceived by both outsiders and insiders as a cultural backwater, mainly because of its peripheral island status that made it expensive and difficult to govern from afar, Tasmania was seen, quite simply, as a problem that needed to be fixed.

Enter, in 1998, newly minted Premier Jim Bacon, who in rather novel fashion considered governance models that looked to culture and cultural industries to reframe Tasmanians' image of themselves, centring on the irrefutable fact that Tasmania was an island (Harwood, 2011). He encouraged Tasmanians to capitalize on the "island mystique" (Bacon, 2001: 41) by looking to other islands for inspiration and models for development. He cited *Baltimore's Mansion* by Newfoundland writer Wayne Johnston — a memoir of growing up on the island of Newfoundland, on the precise opposite side of the globe — as a way of explaining why he believed Tasmania might benefit from the experiences of other islands, rather than always looking to mainland Australia for solutions. Thus, this marriage of culture and islands brought forth, in 2001, the biannual festival that celebrates island cultures: "Ten Days on the Island."[2]

Jim Bacon was not the first to make linkages between Tasmania and Newfoundland. Indeed, explorer James Cook, who surveyed much of Newfoundland's coast between 1763 and 1767 — including the Bay of Islands near Corner Brook in 1767 and whose name appears there, with Cooks Cove and Cooks Brook — may have been the earliest. A decade later he was on the other side of the world: in 1777, he landed his ship, HMS *Adventure*, at Adventure Bay on Tasmania's Bruny Island.

The similarities between these two islands located poles apart do not stop there. They were both colonized by England: Tasmania in 1803 and Newfoundland in 1824. Tasmania gained self-government in 1856 (Boyce, 2010) and Newfoundland won responsible government in 1855 (Cadigan, 2009). Both became sub-national island jurisdictions (with Newfoundland also laying claim to Labrador on the mainland) within a larger federation: Tasmania a state of Australia in 1905, and Newfoundland a province of Canada in 1949. They are fairly similar in land mass (Tasmania, 68,331 km²; the island of Newfoundland, 111,390 km²), population (Tasmania, 510,600 [Australian Bureau of Statistics, 2011]; Newfoundland, 511,722 [Statistics Canada, 2011]), and shortest distance from the mainland (Tasmania, 240 km; Newfoundland, 178 km [to Cape Breton, Nova Scotia]). Both have been viewed as problematic for their colonial rulers and later national administrations. Dependent on natural resources and primarily single industries, both have been characterized as "have-not" areas of their nations, with their island status exacerbating their peripherality — the further from the centre, the higher the cost of maintaining services, with transportation and unemployment being major factors. Over the years Tasmanians have regarded themselves as suffering from "cultural cringe," whereby nothing is ever as good in Tasmania as it is on the mainland; and Newfoundlanders from an inferiority complex (Pocius, 1996; Johnston, 2009: 22–23). Both have carried the stigma of having decimated their original inhabitants and destroyed their cultures: Aboriginals in Tasmania and the Beothuks in Newfoundland. Perhaps because of all this, these "mirror islands" (Polack, 2012) have been referred to as the "psychological sink into which the fears, self-loathings and insecurities of the larger nation are displaced" (Hay, 2006: 27).

Yet, despite the negative portrayal of these two islands, both have experienced cultural renaissances in recent decades (as described by Walsh in Chapter 5 in the case of Newfoundland), capitalizing on their peripherality and pride of place to create rich cultures that are distinctive *because of* that isolation. Indeed, Tasmania's current place in the artistic world led Hobart's daily newspaper, *The Mercury*, to editorialize: "Artistically Tasmania is no longer at the end of the earth but at the centre. It is a conceptual shift of Copernican proportions" (*The Mercury*, 2011: 22). Residents and newcomers alike recognize and celebrate the lifestyle associated with living on these islands. Both fit into the category of "exotic" places to live and visit: not because of the typical sun, sea, and sand tourism associated with warm-water islands, but rather for their rugged natural beauty and pristine shorelines, and their rich cultural heritage.

Popular with outdoor enthusiasts for its easy access to the wilderness, Tasmania is also known for the "stain" of convictism and the wiping out of the Aboriginal population (which the settlers didn't actually do) and the Tasmanian tiger or thylacine (which they did); for Errol Flynn and the Tasmanian devil and "two-headed Tasmanian" incest jokes; and for being the birthplace of the Green Party, born out of disputes over destructive damming and forestry practices. Despite the many "Tasmanias" people might expect when they think of coming to this island, tourism's "Brand Tasmania" has focused on the "clean, green" Tasmania, celebrating its pristine wilderness and clean air, distinctive foods and wines, and culture and heritage: "Tasmania's more relaxed pace of life, lack of pretension, and energetic and connected art scene have attracted writers, artists and performers. While we may have less than three per cent of Australia's population, we are home to nine per cent of its artists." Elsewhere on the Discover Tasmania website, the slogan across a photo of the Port Arthur convict ruins underlines its islandness: "There's a place where you'll arrive curious and walk away enriched — and it's just across the water." Marketers capitalize on an exoticism that mystifies many mainland Australians, a difference made even more striking by having to cross Bass Strait to get there.

Similarly, on the island of Newfoundland,[3] nature is a distinguishing feature, along with its "cultural heritage and traditional way of life" (Overton, 1996: 136). Newfoundland was one of the earliest ports of call for the Vikings (in particular, Lief the Lucky) around the eleventh century and later Europeans (John Cabot) in 1497; and, as happened in Tasmania, the European settlers went on to "eradicate" the Beothuks and their culture in the early nineteenth century (Beothuk and Mi'kmaq, n.d; Polack, 2012). Newfoundland is known for its wild weather, maritime disasters, and the hundreds of soldiers who lost their lives in the First World War; the cod fishery (and its collapse), the sealing industry (and the protests), and, recently, the wealth generated by offshore oil; its distinctive time zone ("a half-hour later in Newfoundland") and the Newfoundland dog; and for being Canada's newest province, only joining Confederation within living memory in 1949.

Although tourists have been enjoying Newfoundland's rugged beauty since the mid-1800s, for many of today's tourists Newfoundland represents a romanticized notion of an earlier, more "primitive" time that eschews modernity (Overton, 1996: 8). The tremendous growth in Newfoundland literature, television, movies, music, and art in the 1970s and 1980s signifies a cultural revival (Overton, 1996: 48) that feeds off a Newfoundland "nationalism" stemming from the narrow victory (52–48 per cent) in the 1948 referendum that led to Newfoundland joining Confederation (Cadigan, 2009: 237). Unlike Shetland, where Jennings, in Chapter 8, notes there is little tradition of nationalism, many Newfoundlanders still believe that the island would have been better off maintaining its status as an independent country. Once the butt of "Newfie jokes" that made fun of backward Newfoundlanders, in recent years Newfoundland is seen by many Canadians as having arguably the most distinctive culture outside of Quebec, bucking the trend towards a culturally homogeneous North America, or indeed, world. As with Tasmania's claim as a thriving cultural destination, Newfoundland and Labrador makes a similar declaration: "St. John's is fast becoming the cultural capital of Canada with one of the highest concentrations of writers, musicians, actors, and comedians on a per capita basis" (Tourism Newfoundland and Labrador, n.d.). Research on St. John's as a "creative city" speaks of "relative size and (dis)connection of St. John's within provincial, national and international networks of places" (Lepawsky, Phan, and Greenwood, 2010: 325) and suggests "there is a dual character to St. John's — as both metropole and margin — that plays a critical role in its ability to attract and retain talent" (Lepawsky et al., 2010: 343). Underlying the message is that Newfoundland is just isolated enough to be real.

But as fast as these attitudes are changing, residents and institutions on both islands are struggling to maintain this distinctiveness in the face of increasing sameness globally. The chapter that follows explores the role of culture — in particular, Ten Days on the Island — in seeking resilience for a place on the periphery. As islands scholar Godfrey Baldacchino has stated, "Constructing place is not done best by statist or nationalist rhetoric; federal political discourse tends towards the patronizing at best, blind and dismissive at worst. If it is meaning that distinguishes space from place, then it is art and culture as meaning makers and markers that offer us hinges to understand better the dynamics of identity and development" (Baldacchino, personal communication, 29 Jan. 2012). Indeed, by looking at the geographies of art that explore place and landscape, experience and emotions, identity and belonging through the lens of phenomenology, we glean a deeper understanding of cultural resistance that can lead to cultural resilience (Hawkins, 2011). At times it is only through the critical distance provided by art — in mirroring ourselves back to ourselves — that we better understand the nuances of our own cultures.

How does a festival showcasing island culture contribute to place attachment and a strengthened island identity? How do the stories of two islands, mediated through the language of theatre, contribute to a healthier sense of self to the extent that island cultures, once deemed to be disadvantaged because of their peripheral island status, are now being celebrated for the very fact that they are *not* mainstream? Drawing from e-mail conversations with the two organizers about how a young people's theatre exchange project came about, and an analysis of the theatrical presentations of youth groups from these islands, as well as on related media and reports, I explore how the language of art — specifically, two groups of young people from Newfoundland and Tasmania who are engaged in telling the stories of their islands — can result in dynamic societies that are writing their own stories, and their own futures, by celebrating the very thing that makes them distinctive: their islandness.

TEN DAYS: SUCCESS STORY?

Islands have long played an important role in history, as sites of evolutionary biology and anthropological exploration, religious symbolism and myth creation, language evolution and cultural distinctiveness, prison cells and paradisaical longings. Because of their unequivocal geographical separation, island space is different from mainland space, geographically, intellectually, emotionally, and spiritually. Writes Pete Hay, "Physical boundedness conduces to psychological distinctiveness, because it promotes clearer, 'bounded' identities" (Hay, 2006: 79). At the same time, islands are connected — traditionally by the sea, but now by the Internet and other twenty-first-century communications technologies — making for a porous boundary that, at its best, contributes to an adaptive and resilient society. Because islands offer a different kind of lifestyle, serving up isolation and individualism on the one hand, and strong community spirit on the other, they are often perceived as attractive places to live in, to belong to, and to visit.

Tasmanian Premier Jim Bacon's vision for an inter-island festival, from his "Welcome" in the 2001 festival *Programme*, demonstrated his grasp of island living: "Island dwellers are different from the masses of continent dwellers. We have skills, characteristics and attributes which set us apart. Islanders have a sense of identity defined by a distinct coastline, not an arbitrary line on a map." Bacon hoped to utilize the idea that sharing island cultures from around the world with Tasmanians, and vice versa, would engender pride in Tasmanians (Harwood, 2011: 166) and help address the problems associated with living on an island that was about as peripheral to the mainstream as you can get.

This first international island cultural festival was purposefully significantly different from most festivals around the world in that it focused on celebrating island cultures. As Bacon wrote in the festival *Programme*, "Unique characteristics dominate the culture of islands. The music, songs and dance; the stories, poetry and drama; the paintings, sculpture and crafts emerging from islands are reflections of distinct qualities not found on greater land masses. It is different because we are different. It is special because we are special." Bacon urged Tasmanians and visitors alike to "celebrate what it means to be an island dweller," and to see their island as the centre of a "world of islands" (Hau'ofa, 1993; Baldacchino, 2007).

Indeed, one travel writer wrote in 2003, "Despite the global village and air fares coming down, there is still something different about living and working on an island and the event allows visitors to reflect on this as they follow the festival trails around the state. What they find is a hive of activity in the arts across all media and disciplines way out of proportion to the state population of 300,000 [sic]" (Britton, 2003).[4]

The Board of Directors hired Artistic Director Robyn Archer, a well-known figure on the festival circuit, having directed arts festivals in Canberra and Adelaide. Sharing a similar vision to Bacon's, she wrote, "It is the quality of this imagination, this learning and this sense of wonder that I believe will be the greatest legacy of Ten Days on the Island — Tasmania unveiling a world of island experiences and thereby enriching the host culture" (40° South, 2001: 9). By bringing culture from islands of all shapes and sizes, and from all corners of the globe, she and subsequent Artistic Director Elizabeth Walsh hoped to benefit all Tasmanians and at the same time share Tasmania's cultural community with the world. Writes Archer, "People have really taken notice of this because it is different. . . . We will inspire Tasmanian artists and they will get the opportunity to do cultural exchanges all over the world. The potential is limitless and it's a potential that is both cultural and spiritual, as well as economic" (40° South, 2001: 9).

In the decade since it began, Ten Days on the Island has not been without its controversies. At the second festival in 2003, major sponsorship from Forestry Tasmania created an uproar from the cultural community protesting clear-cutting and other unsustainable forestry practices. Led by the island's pre-eminent writer, Richard Flanagan, the protest resulted in the cancellation of a planned literary festival and several shortlisted authors (including Peter Carey, Joan London, Tim Winton, and Flanagan himself) withdrawing their books from the Ten Days' flagship $40,000 Tasmania Pacific Fiction Prize, creating a schism between Ten Days and Tasmania's writing community that lasted for years. Indeed, Paul Lennon, who became

Premier after Bacon stepped down in 2004, said in an Australian Broadcasting Corporation (ABC) television broadcast: "Richard Flanagan and his fiction is not welcome in the new Tasmania."

The 2003 controversy demonstrated Tasmania as *contested* island space: how arts and culture, the environment, tourism, politics, and the corporate sector all have a stake in a small island society — but often at cross-purposes. The hostility and ensuing mudslinging among the various stakeholders were part of what many perceived to be "the Tasmanian problem" in the first place. However, by the sixth festival, held 25 March–3 April 2011, fences had mended considerably. A "peace deal" with the forestry industry was in the works, and a major literary festival, "Home Truths: A Feast of Literary Inspiration" — the first such festival since the one planned for 2003 was cancelled — was held in conjunction with Ten Days. Grievous hurts went a long way towards being healed when Premier Lara Giddings awarded the Tasmania Book Prize to Flanagan for his book *Wanting* on 3 April at Hobart Town Hall.

Detractors of Ten Days would say that, 10 years on, the festival has still not delivered on the promise to fix the "Tasmanian problem." There is criticism that the money earmarked for Ten Days could be better used to support the island's own cultural community. There is criticism that it is a "top-down" festival without enough collaboration with local artists and community groups. There is criticism that it is too spread out geographically and that ticket prices are too expensive. And there is criticism that the acts they bring in are too esoteric for Tasmanian audiences — that, unlike, say, MONA FOMA[5] and Taste[6] (which offer mostly free events), the festival does not create the "buzz" that is indicative of success in Tasmania.

Despite the criticisms, the 2011 festival was bigger than ever, boasting a 51.8 per cent increase in ticket sales over the 2009 festival. It hosted 232 events in 111 venues in 62 locations, attracting 150,000 Tasmanians and visitors (Ten Days on the Island, 2011a), reinforcing the idea of the festival as "an arts and culture road trip" (Clarke, 2006). Of the Aus\$3,373,958 received in revenues, 53 per cent of the funding came directly from cabinet; as the current General Manager of Tourism Tasmania, Marcus Barker, noted, "The notion that Ten Days is taking away from arts funding is actually false.

They are two separate pools of money. Even if Ten Days gets less money, it doesn't necessarily mean that Arts Tasmania would get more" (Barker, personal communication, 24 May 2011).

Collaboration with local artists and community groups included Tas-Dance, the Tasmanian Symphony Orchestra, the Tasmanian Writers' Centre, the Makers' Workshop, numerous regional art galleries, museums, and libraries, and even restaurants that featured food and wine from Tasmania. The 62 locations across the island mostly hosted single events: no one was more than an hour's drive from an event. Venues included theatres, streets, pubs, grand houses, historic sites, gardens, town halls, paddocks, mechanics' workshops, and beaches. Artists came from all around the globe, including Canada's Vancouver Island, Cape Breton Island, Prince Edward Island, Newfoundland, and the island of Montreal; from Scotland, Northern Ireland, Singapore, New Zealand, Iceland, the Faroe Islands, Haiti, and mainland Australia, the "island continent." Programming included premieres of theatre productions, music concerts, artists' residencies, dance marathons, and art exhibitions. An open-air light show in the Royal Botanical Gardens was one of the most popular events, attracting over 13,000 visitors alone (Ten Days on the Island, 2011a).

According to the final report, "*Ten Days* generated $24.37 million added value to the Tasmanian economy, representing a nine-fold return on the $2.5 million public sector investment" (Ten Days on the Island, 2011a). With the lion's share of audiences hailing from Tasmania, then, Ten Days on the Island is an example of a cultural event that put islanders first, with tourism spinoffs coming second. Ten Days is a celebration of islandness, by islanders for islanders.

BY ISLANDERS FOR ISLANDERS

An example of islanders making theatre for islanders was the 2011 Launceston-Corner Brook Youth Theatre Island Exchange Project, which connected these two islands on the periphery of their nations during the Ten Days festival — and beyond.

The Project was conceived when Theatre Newfoundland Labrador (TNL)'s play, *Tempting Providence*, was staged as part of Ten Days on the

Island in 2005. Jane Johnson, the director of Mudlark Theatre in Launceston, Tasmania, and Second Story Theatre, its youth theatre company, was so impressed with the show that she travelled to Newfoundland the next year to do a two-month theatre residency. There she met Sarah McDonald-Anderson, director of TNL's youth theatre company, who had been looking for opportunities "to expand [their] horizons and benefit from the experience and talents of other youth theatre groups" (McDonald-Anderson, personal communication, 31 Dec. 2010). They called the meeting "kismet" as they recognized "an immediate kinship between [them] all" (McDonald-Anderson, personal communication, 31 Dec. 2010). They could see so many similarities between their two islands: their islandness, their similar land masses, their populations, their seafaring histories, and the relationship with their mother countries.

"There's an aloneness, a separation, and the need to fend for ourselves that is similar," said McDonald-Anderson (personal communication, 31 Dec. 2010). "We can't take things for granted: getting the soil to grow our food, to deal with the elements — we don't have the luxury of stopping to think about the fact that we live on an island. Islandness is there in our bones."

But the fact that these two islands were poles apart — "as far as you can get from one another and still be on the planet" (Theatre Newfoundland and Labrador, n.d.) — was the clincher for the two theatre groups. Despite the connection to place that Cooke et al. (Chapter 6) describe among young workers in Newfoundland and other locales, one interviewee explained, "The generation now really does not connect with culture and home like generations before did, because of technology and travel. It was exceptional to go anywhere when I grew up. Kids today don't connect with the image of the Newfoundlander. Through this exchange they'll not only learn about Tasmanian culture, but they'll learn about their own" (McDonald-Anderson, personal communication, 31 Dec. 2010).

The Newfoundland contingent was in Launceston from 23 March to 7 April 2011, where they staged a sold-out show in Scottsdale, a small community in Tasmania's northeast, and three sold-out shows in Launceston. That same year, the Launceston youth toured Newfoundland during the first two weeks of August, where they staged the same performances they did in Tasmania: at the Gros Morne Theatre Festival in Gros Morne National Park, the Arts and Culture Centre in Corner Brook, and the LSPU Hall in St. John's. The work they presented included two separate but complementary plays focusing on the culture and heritage of their island homes, *Chasing a Sound Like Rain* before the intermission, and *With Cruel Times in Between* after.

Based on submissions of poetry, writing, and images submitted by young people from around Tasmania, *Chasing a Sound Like Rain* was written by Tasmanian playwright Carrie McLean. With allusions to Tasmania's rich and complex gothic history, the play revolves around seven teenagers who go to the caves at nearby Mole Creek for an end-of-school party; two mysteriously go missing. In talking about what they're going to do after graduation, the students reveal things about themselves and their sense of connection and disconnection to their island, whether they feel free or trapped, and about their own identities as islanders.

Bianca is planning to leave, "crossing to the other side," mainland, civilization, to Sydney. In a moving soliloquy, she rants, "The other side. Typical. Whatever's not Tasmania, seal it up, box it away, throw it in a cupboard and stamp it with 'other side.' It's us or them. It's like Bass Strait is this River Styx or something . . . that by crossing that you enter this other world. Here in this state, this is where you settle down when you're done with life" (Island Youth Theatre Exchange Project video, 2011).

When Jess calls Tasmania a "dumping grounds," where her family has moved to for "a fresh start," another party-goer comes to the island's defence: "You can't see the beauty that's smack-bang in front of your face, Jess. This island . . . where else in the world can you find your own piece of beach except here . . . I'd rather be in touch with mud and sand, with what is real than some mass-marketer's dream . . .The air is so good here . . . it feeds every pore" (Island Youth Theatre Exchange Project video, 2011).

Another girl describes "the convict chains" that tie her to her safe haven, her house. "I'm chained to my own home . . . you can't wait to leave and then spend a lifetime trying to come back" (Island Youth Theatre Exchange Project video, 2011).

Chasing a Sound Like Rain is "a lyrical and frank play that explores the complexities of growing up on an island, young people's search for identity, and people's continual connection to home. It is a very real, contemporary take on being young and living in Tasmania" (Theatre Newfoundland and Labrador, n.d). Their preoccupations, though local to Tasmania, resonate with those of islanders around the world, particularly in Newfoundland, where, for generations, the Newfoundland diaspora has been a way of life.

The Newfoundland contingent's *With Cruel Times in Between* is based on the selected works of Newfoundland poet Al Pittman (1940–2001). Born in St. Leonard's, Placentia Bay, Pittman grew up in Corner Brook, started writing in the mid-1960s, and went on to co-found one of New-foundland's most successful publishing companies, Breakwater Books. The play uses selections from his songs, poems, prose, and plays, which TNL provides as an "example of culture and island life which remains as true to our spirit as the island breeze" (Theatre Newfoundland and Labrador, n.d.). Traditional Newfoundland accents, capturing the island's distinctive dialect and language, are turned off and on as required, making for colourful conversation and stories of outport Newfoundland.

Ten voices form a tableau of interwoven images:

> From here looking north, there's nothing to see but the sea, and in winter, nothing but blue-white ice glowing and flowing from here to the polar oceans. It's a sight to behold. A glance out the window, and you might think you were looking at a blow-up life-size postcard of Ire-land or one of the Spanish provinces. . . . The seasons here are unpredictable, yesterday it was summer, today it's winter all over again.
>
> Them days are gone, gone beyond return. [They sing] "We fished all summer, we fished all fall, and when it was over, we had nothing at all." It's the younger crowd that gives up on the place they was born and raised in, the place the fathers and their grandfathers worked all their lifetime to build up. The old crowd don't care about nothing sure, so why should they care one way or another about the place they belong to. It's a new age, an age of

technology. It used to be. There ain't nothing like it used
to be. There's a time, I tell you . . . It used to be . . . A seafaring people. Fishing boats on water. Garden parties
and weeklong weddings. Home brew and moonshine.
Fiddles and accordions. Seagulls and superstitions. The
stuff novels and poems and plays are made of. She's
changing faster than I could ever come up with . . . It was
like I was saying, sure, it's the times, by, times are changing and things changes with her, and there ain't a bloody
thing in hell a man can do about it. (Island Youth Theatre
Exchange Project video, 2011)

Being part of the writing and production of these plays has taught
these young people about their past and present, and how the two blend.
They learned that their preoccupations with island tropes ring true on both
islands: leaving vs. staying, tradition vs. modernity, feeling cocooned vs.
feeling imprisoned. The groups presented their work in two very different
styles: one a contemporary play set in a series of dark, spirit-filled caves,
reflecting Tasmania's sometimes gothic history; the other a series of linked
images from Newfoundland's oft-romanticized past, with traditional cos-
tumes and music. As they set out to find their way in the world as young
adults, the participants learned through this exchange to better appreciate
their own islandness and their own stories by seeing them through the lens
of others.

As one of the Tasmanian students said, "Performing in an international
context is a precious opportunity that seldom comes along to young performers in isolated, regional communities. This project is challenging me
and what I'm capable of — I don't think I've ever had a chance to test myself
like this before" (Ten Days on the Island, 2011b). It is not a difficult stretch
to say that what these students — "the next generation of theatre-makers
from two islands 'on the edge of the earth'" — have experienced will have
repercussions that will last a lifetime.

That Ten Days on the Island is a cultural phenomenon is undisputed.
As Marcus Barker said, "Is there something which is special to Tasmania,
that only exists here? Could you pick up this model and pop it into Cuba?

We believe that this is a festival that is specific to Tasmania. [It] gives us a point of difference" (Barker, 2011). To his knowledge there is no other festival of this magnitude in the world that is specifically devoted to celebrating island culture.

CONCLUDING THOUGHTS: INGENIOUS "GENUINITY"

When she was hired, Artistic Director Robyn Archer made the case for the festival being a much-needed cultural tourism draw: "So many places in the world are having to turn to tourism when traditional economies are failing and Tasmania has done that really well. It is a beautiful destination — but a lot of people don't want just wilderness. There are many who will go to a place to see the culture of that place. And I am one of them. This could be the turn-around in Tasmania's economy" (Stubbs, 2001: 34).

Although Tourism Tasmania quickly came on board with the festival and has been an integral part of all six, Archer's prediction hasn't necessarily borne out. Current General Manager Marcus Barker noted that Ten Days has a detailed memorandum of understanding with Tourism Tasmania, sharing similar objectives: "to support the activities of Ten Days and Tourism, to bring interstate and international tourism to Tasmania. Currently, 80 per cent of audiences are Tasmanian . . . we can deliver more intra-state tourism" (Barker, 2011).

On tourism websites from both Tasmania and Newfoundland, marketing departments give cultural tourism equal billing alongside nature, offering a transformational experience that comes from experiencing a distinctive culture: words such as "a world apart," "magical," "real and genuine," and "One of the top 10 friendliest cultures in the world" pepper the sites. But tourism planners know that to create an island tourism product that satisfies tourists as well as locals is a challenge. To describe a tourism experience or product as "real" or "authentic" can be dangerous (see also Chapters 2 and 4, this volume). Too often the label is a result of a top-down tourism marketing strategy that fulfills a certain vision or story created to appeal to visitors; but, according to the people who live there, what is served up may or may not be the truth. If it strays too far, tempers of "locals" may fray, resulting in reactions ranging from good-natured barbs to satire, cynicism, or downright hostility towards tourists and tourism in general. Indeed, who wants to feel like they are attempting to live someone else's life (MacCannell, 1973: 601)?

That the "authentic" experience serves to satisfy a "longing" or "craving" for "the immediate, non-commercialized, brute natural world" is in strong reaction to "a strong technologically mediatized, commercialized and socially constructed reality" (Knudsen and Waade, 2010: 1). Experiencing the "authentic" often allows people to connect on an emotional level — what Davidson et al. (2005) call "emotional geographies," satisfying a tourist's hunger for "the real thing," with an "ability to affect, touch and transform him/her" (Knudsen and Waade, 2010: 7). This often allows visitors to feel like they belong there, too, experiencing "empathetic insideness" (Relph, 1976: 51), whereby persons consciously engage and commune with a place in order to understand it.

The organizers of Ten Days on the Island have created a festival that is first and foremost for islanders to celebrate their culture and to see it through the lenses of other similar island cultures; whatever benefits accrue from interstate and international tourism or for the arts and culture sector, both during and between Ten Days events, are a bonus. That it was conceived and created by islanders is hardly surprising given the often cutting-edge art created at the edge, or the fact that nearly everyone has something to say about living on an island. Islands are different. Islands are exotic. Islands are parochial. Islands are a safe haven. Islands get forgotten (as when they get left off maps). Islands are the centres of their residents' worlds. You have to make a conscious decision to get to an island, including the fact that it's typically more expensive to get to, or to leave, and that crossing to and from an island represents something very basic — an in-between time when you can just be. And if you go to one of the 334 islands off Tasmania, say Bruny Island, Tasmania becomes the mainland, leading to a possibly schizophrenic existence. People come to Tasmania for a holiday — and that was 20 years ago. When asked why they stayed, they said the weather, the clean air, the lifestyle, the sheer beauty; or they said it's because it's far enough away from the mainland to be easily reached. Or they said they can't explain it — it was a feeling: they just knew they were home.

As Tasmanian Pete Hay writes, "As the global economy becomes more and more tightly controlled from the centre — it may be that it is only at the fringes that the necessary 'critical distance' will be found. . . . The task of island art, the political task, is to construct from such complexity an island-ness . . . rich in cultural dynamism" (Hay, 2002: 82). A manifesto written by delegates attending Islands of the World V conference in Mauritius in 1998 could have been the seeds for Ten Days on the Island: "That islanders speak, and others hear, of the unique and positive cultural experiences of island living through literature and other forms of creative expression" (Hay, 2002: 79).

Aspects of Ten Days on the Island may represent commodification of culture and identity, or may be seen by some as inauthentic, but the festival and related events build on and help to create a sense of island place and, indeed, of place itself — to the benefit of both Tasmania and Newfound-land. Given the history of governing from afar on both islands, the trans-island dialogue generated by Ten Days on the Island — by islanders and for islanders — is not inconsequential in creating self-reliant and empowered societies that are dynamic and resilient. By using the language of art as a form of cultural resistance, and effecting change at a deep emotional and psychological level — and celebrating the shared stories that emplace them — Tasmanians and Newfoundlanders are re-visioning their futures, making the shift from cultural cringe to cultural resilience. In the process they have placed their small and remote islands precisely at the centre.

NOTES

1. An earlier version of this paper was presented at the seventh annual Small Island Cultures Research Initiative (SICRI) Conference in Airlie Beach, Queensland, Australia, June 2011.
2. For a more detailed account and analysis of events leading up to the creation of Ten Days, see Harwood (2011).
3. For the purposes of this study, I focus on the island portion of the Canadian province of Newfoundland and Labrador, which has traditionally been called Newfoundland.
4. Tasmania's population, as of 31 March 2003, was 476,199 (Tasmania's Population, 2003).

5.   The Museum of Old and New Art's Festival of Music and Art (MONA FOMA) is a privately run festival held for two weeks in January, with most of the impetus and funding coming from philanthropist David Walsh (mofo.net.au).

6.   Held for a week over New Year's, the Taste Festival showcases the best of Tasmania's food and beverages, and is produced and presented by Hobart City Council (tastefestival.com.au).

REFERENCES

Archer, R. 2001. "Arts for Everyone." *40° South* 20: 8–9.

Australian Bureau of Statistics. 2011. http://www.abs.gov.au/ausstats/abs@.nsf/Lookup/by+Subject/1367.0~2011~Main+Features~Estimated+Resident+Population~7.1.

Bacon, J. 2001. "Unique Characteristics." *Island* 87: 39–41.

Baldacchino, G., ed. 2007. *A World of Islands: An Island Studies Reader*. Charlottetown, PEI and Luqa, Malta: Institute of Island Studies, University of Prince Edward Island and Agenda Academic.

Beothuk and Mi'kmaq. n.d. http://www2.swgc.mun.ca/nfld_history/nfld_history_beothuk.htm.

Boyce, J. 2010. *Van Diemen's Land*. Melbourne: Black Inc.

Britton, S. 2003. "Ten Days on the Island." *Artlink* 23, 2.http://www.artlink.com.au/articles/2417/ten-days-on-the-island/.

Cadigan, S.T. 2009. *Newfoundland and Labrador: A History*. Toronto: University of Toronto Press.

Clarke, G. 2006. "Ten Days on the Island." *Travel*, 6 July. http://travel.ninemsn.com.au/domesticbasic/tas/654374/ten-days-on-the-island.

Davidson, J., L. Bondi, and M. Smith, eds. 2007. *Emotional Geographies*. Aldershot: Ashgate.

Department of Treasury and Finance. 2003. "Tasmania's Population 2003: An Information Paper on Recent Trends and State Government Policies." Hobart, Tasmania: Department of Treasury and Finance. http://www.treasury.tas.gov.au/domino/dtf/dtf.nsf/LookupFiles/Tasmania_Population_Paper-final.pdf/$-file/Tasmania_Population_Paper-final.pdf.

Discover Tasmania. n.d. http://www.discovertasmania.com/activities__and__attractions/popular_attractions.

Harwood, A. 2011. "The Political Constitution of Islandness: The 'Tasmanian Problem' and Ten Days on the Island." Doctoral dissertation, University of Tasmania.

Hau'ofa, E. 1993. "Our Sea of Islands." In E. Hau'ofa, V. Naidu, and E. Waddell, eds., *A New Oceania: Rediscovering Our Sea of Islands*, 2–16. Suva, Fiji: University of the South Pacific, in association with Beake House.

Hawkins, H. 2011. "Dialogues and Doings: Sketching the Relationships between Geography and Art." *Geography Compass* 5, 7: 464–78.

Hay, P. 2002. *Vandiemonian Essays*. Hobart, Tasmania: Walleah Press.

———. 2006. "A Phenomenology of Islands." *Island Studies Journal* 1, 1: 19–42.

Island Youth Theatre Exchange Project video. 2011. Videotaped 1 Apr. Launceston, Tasmania.

Johnston, W. 1999. *Baltimore's Mansion*. Toronto: Knopf Canada.

———. 2009. *The Old Lost Land of Newfoundland: Family, Memory, Fiction, and Myth*. Edmonton: NeWest Press.

Knudsen, B.T., and A.M. Waade, eds. 2010. *Re-investing Authenticity: Tourism, Place and Emotions*. Toronto: Channel View Publications.

Lepawsky, J., C. Phan, and R. Greenwood. 2010. "Metropolis on the Margins: Talent Attraction and Retention to the St. John's City-Region." *Canadian Geographer* 54, 3: 324–46.

MacCannell, D. 1973. "Staged Authenticity: Arrangements of Social Space in Tourist Settings." *American Journal of Sociology* 79, 3: 589–603.

The Mercury (Hobart, Tasmania). 2011. "Editorial: Descend into the Chamber." 22 Jan. http://www.themercury.com.au/article/2011/01/22/33155_editorial.html.

Norman, J. 2003. "Ten Days That Shook the Literary World." *Sydney Morning Herald*, 14 Mar. http://www.smh.com.au/articles/2003/03/13/1047431149291.html.

Overton, J. 1996. *Making a World of Difference: Essays on Tourism, Culture and Development in Newfoundland*. St. John's: ISER Books.

Pocius, G.L. 1996. "Folklore and the Creation of National Identities: A North American Perspective." *Journal of the Baltic Institute of Folklore*. http://www.folklore.ee/rl/pubte/ee/bif/bif1/sisu.html.

Polack, F. 2012. "Mirror islands: The Colonial Pasts of Newfoundland and Tasmania." Public lecture, Marine Institute, St. John's, NL, 25 Feb.

Relph, E. 1976. *Place and Placelessness*. London: Pion.

Statistics Canada. 2011. "Quarterly Demographic Estimate." http://www.statcan.gc.ca/bsolc/olc-cel/olc-cel?catno=91-002-X&lang=eng.

Stubbs, B. 2001. "Bullseye for Archer." *The Mercury* (Hobart, Tasmania), 31 Mar., 34, 36.

Ten Days on the Island. 2011a. "Ten Days 2011 Statement of Activity." http://tendaysontheisland.com/.

———. 2011b. "Youth Theatre Island Exchange Project Program." http://tendayson-theisland.org/ten-days-2011-program/the-youth-theatre-island-exchange-project.

Theatre Newfoundland and Labrador. n.d. http://www.theatrenewfoundland.com.

———. n.d. "Youth Theatre Island Exchange Project." http://www.theatrenewfound-land.com/exchange.html.

Tourism Newfoundland and Labrador. n.d. "People and Culture." http://www.new-foundlandlabrador.com/AboutThisPlace/PeopleCulture.

CHAPTER 11

Branding Small Islands: A Case Study of the Isle of Man

Gary N. Wilson

INTRODUCTION

Happy Jack wasn't old, but he was a man
He lived in the sand at the Isle of Man
The kids would all sing, he would take the wrong key
So they rode on his head in their furry donkey

"Happy Jack," The Who

When the British group The Who released the song "Happy Jack" in 1966, the dominant image of the Isle of Man was as a tourist destination for the industrial working classes of the British Isles. As the song suggests, sand (along with sea and sometimes sun) and donkey rides were part of the allure of this small and picturesque island in the Irish Sea. Within the space of two decades, however, this image would change. The onset of budget air travel and low-cost holidays in the Mediterranean, coupled with high transportation costs from the mainland to the island and declining and uncompetitive infrastructure, would deal a serious blow to the tourist industry in the Isle of Man (Winterbottom, 2000). In the 1970s, the island government responded to this decline by taking advantage of its political autonomy as a Dependency of the British Crown and instituting a series of laws that would transform the island into a platform for the international financial services industry

(Kermode, 2000). Indeed, "the dramatic decline in the tourist industry in the 1980s, together with the dwindling contribution of the manufacturing, agriculture and fishing sectors, would have meant economic disaster if the financial sector had not come to the rescue" (Winterbottom, 2000: 272).

The economic transformation of the Isle of Man in the 1970s and 1980s has had a profound effect on all aspects of island life. Nowhere is this more evident than in the area of culture. The exposure of the island to the highly competitive and lucrative financial services industry has enriched its economy, and provided the state with the resources to fund much needed infrastructure and cultural development programs (Wilson, 2008). Rising living standards and access to state-funded educational programs and social services have, in turn, created a generation of islanders who are cognizant and proud of their island heritage, and more supportive of state programs to promote this heritage (Wilson, 2011). On the other hand, the transformation has also changed the Isle of Man's demographic balance, in ways that some islanders feel are detrimental to the island's heritage and future sustainability. An influx of newcomers, most of whom work in the financial services sector, has raised concerns among those who feel that the Isle of Man's ethnic and cultural heritage may be in jeopardy now that less than half of the population was born on the island.

In response to these changes, the Isle of Man government has recently embarked on an ambitious place-branding exercise. The aim of this exercise is to articulate the common values that represent the island and its population and to promote the island in an increasingly competitive and global economy. Although branding has traditionally centred on products and industry, place branding is becoming more common as countries, regions, cities, and other jurisdictions engage in economic competition. And while much of the literature on place branding focuses on the efforts of large countries in this area, scholars are increasingly recognizing that:

> [t]he most urgent problems are faced by small, new nations . . . little known except by their immediate neighbours. . . . These are the nations who most need to develop and then project a clear identity which can differentiate them from the competition. (Olins, 1999: 20)

An important (and understudied) aspect of contemporary place-branding exercises involves the role and place of culture in the brand image (Anholt, 2002). Whereas earlier attempts at place branding focused on the benefits of infrastructural amenities such as housing and transportation, culture has now become a key element of the brand message (Kotler and Gertner, 2002). Given the rich and unique cultural attributes of island societies, and their efforts in the area of place branding, it is not surprising that island studies scholars have made a meaningful contribution to this debate. Some studies have focused on the branding of products, services, and circumstances as a means of promoting the distinct and beneficial features of particular islands and island life (Royle, 2001; Askegaard and Kjeldgaard, 2007; Khamis, 2011; Pigman, 2012), while others have adopted a broader perspective that examines the role that branding plays in positioning small islands, politically and economically, in a global context. For example, in their study of place branding on the island of Funen in Denmark, Askegaard and Kjeldgaard (2007: 145) conclude that branding can serve not only as a means of promoting local cultural sustainability, but also as "an effective tool for local economies to secure a position in a globalizing world."

One of the most contentious issues raised by these scholars is the disconnect between culture, which is often grounded in the past, and branding, which usually involves a vision of the future, or at least a response to some kind of contemporary issue or set of challenges. For example, in his work on place branding in the Shetland Islands, Grydehøj (2008: 183) has criticized branding consultants for offering a generic brand image that "fails completely to touch the souls of Shetlanders" (see also Jennings, Chapter 8). Such concerns have been noted in other island jurisdictions and are certainly part of a much wider debate on questions of identity, heritage, and culture in a world undergoing dynamic change.

With these issues in mind, this chapter will examine the Isle of Man's recent "Freedom to Flourish" branding campaign. Focusing specifically on the role that culture has played in the branding initiative, it will argue that the developers of the Freedom to Flourish brand have struck a balance, not only between cultural recognition and the needs of the island's post-industrial economy, but also between promoting the historical inheritance of the island

and recognizing its current (and changing) demographic and social characteristics. Although the promotional materials associated with the Freedom to Flourish brand are generic in nature, and could apply to other
small, autonomous island jurisdictions, they constitute a representative
and fair image of the island, both to internal and external audiences. In this
context, culture has played an important supporting role in terms of articulating the uniqueness of the island in an increasingly competitive and
global economic environment.

The research for this chapter draws on interviews with public and private sector officials who were involved in the development and delivery of
the branding campaign. It also uses primary sources such as government
documents and parliamentary debate proceedings, as well as secondary
source materials. The first part examines various aspects of place branding,
as well as the critiques of this emerging area of marketing. The second part
explores the role of culture in place branding, and particularly the relationship between culture and branding in small island jurisdictions. The third
section assesses the Isle of Man's recent branding initiative in light of the
criticisms levelled at branding exercises in the literatures on place branding
and branding in other small islands, while the fourth part looks specifically
at the role of culture in the Isle of Man campaign.

WHAT IS PLACE BRANDING?

As a sub-discipline of marketing, place branding draws heavily on the experience of industries and companies and their efforts to promote products and services. Rather than promoting a product or service, place
branding applies marketing strategies to a particular geographical location
or jurisdiction (Fan, 2006). As Olins has pointed out in his comparative
work on place branding at the national scale and product branding:

> While a national branding plan is more complex and in-
> volves more coordination than a commercial identity
> programme, the essentials are the same. Both commer-
> cial and national brand-building are concerned with the
> creation of clear, simple, differentiating propositions

often built around emotional qualities expressing some kind of superiority, which can be readily symbolized both verbally and visually. These propositions must be easy to understand and sufficiently flexible to operate in a wide variety of situations with a large number of audiences. (Olins, 1999: 25)

The recent surge in place-branding initiatives has been driven primarily by globalization and global competition for scarce economic resources. Whereas "old branding projects were aimed at internal audiences — to persuade citizens to pay taxes and fight wars — the new projects are aimed at an external audience — to promote investment, tourism and exports" (Olins, 1999: 11). Indeed, destination branding, especially for small islands that offer the ubiquitous "three S's" (sun, sand, and sea), is a well-trodden area of research and practice (Govers, Go, and Kumar, 2007). To an external audience, therefore, place branding is a marketing tool that attempts to present the historical and contemporary attributes of a particular place in a positive light in order to encourage interest (and investment) in that place. It is often a reaction to (real or perceived) negative stereotypes, and represents an attempt to present "the most compelling strategic vision for the country and ensure that this vision is supported, reinforced and enriched by every act of communication between the country and the rest of the world" (Fan, 2006).

While place-branding practitioners have focused their attention on external markets and audiences, the academic literature suggests that a place brand can also play an important internal role in terms of articulating a common national or regional image and reinforcing a sense of national or regional solidarity (O'Shaughnessy and O'Shaughnessy, 2000). Broadly defined, such identity-building exercises (or perhaps identity re-engineering) have a long pedigree. As an area of study, however, the internal dimension of place branding remains insufficiently researched (Anholt, 2002). Moreover, as Grydehøj (2008: 176) has pointed out, place-branding initiatives "run the risk of focusing too much on the perceived desires of consumers [external audiences and markets], thereby losing sight of the actual places being branded."

Although the terms "place branding" and "nation branding" are often used interchangeably, even in the specialized literature on place branding and public diplomacy, it is important to note that they refer to two distinct, albeit related, concepts. As the name suggests, place branding focuses on the attributes of a specific place or territory. Nation branding, on the other hand, is concerned with the identity of a particular group of people who share certain common characteristics (and may or may not live in a particular place or territory). The overlap between these two terms is reinforced when examining the role of culture in branding because cultural features such as language, art, and heritage can apply to concepts of both place and nation. This study uses the term "place branding" because the Isle of Man's Freedom to Flourish branding campaign is primarily centred on the island's place-based attributes (political, economic, cultural, etc). In this sense, the message is aimed at an external audience, which the brand campaign is trying to attract to the island. At the same time, however, the brand campaign attempts to appeal to an internal audience by articulating a sense of identity based on generic concepts that appeal to the varied members of the Manx civic nation.

THE ROLE OF CULTURE IN BRANDING

Scholars have noted that the relationship between culture and cultural attributes (such as language) and the brand image of a particular place constitutes a significant lacuna in the academic literature on place branding (Anholt, 2002). Part of the reason for this may have to do with long-standing barriers between the disciplines that study these topics and the broader constituencies that they represent within society. For example, cultural scholars might argue that combining culture with the type of "crass" commercial activity of branding and marketing is akin to mixing oil and water. They are naturally skeptical of any commercial activity that seeks to "sell" culture because they tend to view culture as a priceless inheritance rather than as a marketing tool or tourism product. Conversely, while many people who study commerce see the value of culture and partake in cultural activities, there is a perception among the broader commercial class that the "cultural attainments of a country . . . do not sell — or provide return on investment — in the same way that inward investment, brands or tourism do" (Anholt, 2002: 235).

Such perceptions and prejudices, however, are changing. As Kotler and Gertner (2002: 258) have noted, culture has become a key "attractant" for business and investment. In the case of small islands, whose cultures are distinct from mainland societies, culture has become an effective tool for establishing and distinguishing oneself in a highly competitive, global economy (Wilson, 2008). Culture, therefore, could be perceived as the "the rich harmonic accompaniment to the simple, accessible, easily memorable melody of commercial, competitive advantage" (Anholt, 2002: 235). The academic literature on place branding is also recognizing this change. While the dominant sub-field for place-branding publications is still technical and economic in orientation (marketing, management, and tourism), other sub-fields focusing on political and cultural approaches to place branding are establishing themselves within the discipline (Kaneva, 2011). In contrast to the technical-economic and political approaches, cultural approaches tend to be critical of nation branding, viewing the whole process as "contrary to the principles of diversity and plurality" and targeted mainly at an external audience (Kaneva, 2011). As this chapter argues, however, the place-branding initiative in the Isle of Man addressed such concerns by defining common characteristics and values that represented the diversity of the island and by establishing programs that focused on both internal and external audiences.

Categories aside, it is important to recognize the symbiotic and mutually dependent relationship between culture and the economy. A robust and flourishing culture not only helps to market a particular place, it can also make a direct contribution to the national or regional economy (as illustrated by Walsh in Chapter 5, Brinklow in Chapter 10, and others in this volume). Likewise, a healthy and strong economy can provide valuable public (state) and private support for cultural activities. In his work on the Shetland Islands, Grydehøj (2008: 179) has pointed out that "[f]ar from destroying Shetland's traditional culture, the sudden economic boom brought about by the oil era has preserved it better than any gradual transition into wealth could have." Wilson (2008, 2009) has noted the same trend in the Isle of Man, where expanding revenues from the thriving, finance-driven economy have provided the island's government with the resources to invest in cultural development and heritage. The importance of a sound economy to the development of culture on the island has been echoed by Stephen Harrison, the former Director of Manx National Heritage, an organization responsible for promoting and preserving the cultural heritage of the Isle of Man (Harrison, 2002).

Observers of branding initiatives in small island jurisdictions have argued that brand messages developed by corporate branding agencies are often generic in nature and fail to represent the cultural characteristics of the island's population (Grydehøj, 2008). Moreover, they are targeted primarily at an external audience, or, as Baldacchino (2009: 1) has quipped, are "tailored for alien consumption" rather than for the island population. Most industry consultants are aware of these dilemmas. Anholt (2002: 230) has identified the internal dimension of branding or "how to get the populace behind it and make them 'live the brand'" as an important, yet understudied, topic in the discipline. Indeed, one of the key differences between product and place branding is that product branding is directed primarily and almost exclusively at an external market (the consumer). Place branding, on the other hand, serves two masters who may have different motivations. This may explain why branding propositions are often so generic; they seek the lowest common denominator between external and internal audiences and, in doing so, often fail to fully meet the expectations of either group.

The use of culture in a place brand message is made even more difficult because culture is such a subjective, ephemeral, and often personal topic; one person's perception of what it means to be Manx or a Shetlander depends on a variety of factors and may be different from another person's perception of cultural identity. Furthermore, while branding exercises are aimed primarily at changing external perceptions for the purpose of encouraging outside interest, the brand message should also project an honest and objective view of the "product" on offer. Of course, when it comes to marketing, complete frankness is not always the best policy. For example, no product or place-branding exercise would ever choose to emphasize shortcomings or negative attributes. In this sense, therefore, the divide between

marketing subjectivity and critical academic inquiry appears to be un-
bridgeable.

In sum, such considerations highlight the importance of the internal
(as opposed to the external) dimension of any branding exercise, as well as
the difficulties of creating a brand proposition that meets the varied and
often entrenched expectations and perceptions of different groups of people. They also invoke the fear that branding seeks to dilute, boil down, or
even jettison the cultural heritage of a particular place because it does not
fit with the current and future aspirations of that place. Given that identities are multiple and changing, as discussed in earlier chapters of this volume, Stern and Hall (2010) raise the concern that place branding can limit
the future development and evolution of a particular locale by reinforcing
particular place identities.

As noted above, there is a growing literature on branding in small island
jurisdictions. In part, this is a response to the fact that many small islands
have recently undergone branding exercises. Like other small mainland
jurisdictions, small islands are struggling to be recognized (and to reap the
benefits of such recognition) on an increasingly competitive world stage
(Olins, 2002). Small islands also struggle with the issue of representing culture within a brand message. Having evolved in greater isolation from
mainland societies, small island cultures tend to have unique and well-
entrenched characteristics that do not necessarily fit with the image that
the government and their consultants wish to project through the brand.
Baldacchino (2009: 4) has observed that:

> if an island is already deeply wedded to an existing iconic
> image typically connected to some locally available spe-
> cies, craft or material with high levels of local input . . .
> how does it connect with a more contemporary, dynamic,
> technologically oriented symbolism without forfeiting
> its existing baggage, when the latter is likely to have per-
> sisting and long term benefits of reputation, customer
> loyalty and international recognition? Is it too ambitious
> to have one's cake and eat it too?

In the struggle to develop a brand image, therefore, the divide between tradition and modernity can become a key battleground, as can the issue of whether the brand message is meant for external or internal consumption. This is especially true in small island jurisdictions where cultural issues are very sensitive and can generate a great deal of controversy.

FREEDOM TO FLOURISH: THE ISLE OF MAN BRANDING PROJECT

The Isle of Man is a small island located in the Irish Sea, equidistant from England, Scotland, Wales, and Ireland. For much of its history, the island has been subject to outside control and domination. In spite of this control, it has managed to maintain its unique indigenous language (Manx Gaelic) and culture. Its current status as a Dependency of the British Crown provides the island with considerable political and economic autonomy. Although the Isle of Man has long-standing and close political links to the United Kingdom (UK), it is not part of the UK or the European Union, nor does it rely on the UK for economic support (Wilson, 2005). During the post-war period, the Isle of Man's autonomy has been gradually strengthened, and in recent years it has actively used this autonomy to transform its economy and protect and enhance its language and culture (Wilson, 2008).

Using the Isle of Man's branding campaign as a case study, the purpose of this section is to discuss and assess some of the tensions, challenges, and opportunities raised in the literature on place branding and to develop some general conclusions about how these factors influence branding exercises in small island jurisdictions. Specifically, it will explore the role that culture and cultural considerations have played in the development and dissemination of the Isle of Man brand.

The idea of a branding initiative for the Isle of Man was initially conceived by a group of businesspeople on the island who felt that the island could be doing more to promote itself, both externally and internally. The result was the Isle of Man Branding Project, which was initiated in late 2003 and managed by a cross-sectoral, volunteer steering committee comprised of representatives from business, government, and non-profit organizations on the island (Isle of Man Government, 2006).

In June 2004, Tynwald, the Manx parliament, approved an investment of £500,000 ($800,000 CDN) to develop a vision and implementation strategy for a brand. An important part of this process was a research study designed to survey "existing and potential customers on awareness of and attitudes towards the [Isle of Man], plus future needs" (Isle of Man Government, 2006: 3). According to one consultant connected with the project, which was conducted by HPI, a market research company, and Acanchi, a marketing consultancy firm that specializes in country branding, this initial study "was probably, certainly pro-rata and possibly the most comprehensive conducted for a country brand." The research program "involved many interviews, workshops and formal market research surveys of hundreds of people, both on and off the IOM" (Isle of Man Government, 2006: 9).

The result of this program of research was a recommended brand proposition entitled Freedom to Flourish. The basic philosophy behind the Freedom to Flourish brand was:

> The Isle of Man is a land of possibility where people and businesses can reach their full potential. It has been self-governing for over 1,000 years, which has created a secure yet stimulating environment. This gives people and businesses the freedom to flourish, providing foundations for a dynamic economy and unrivalled quality of life. (Isle of Man Government, 2006: 3)

This message was later refined and shortened to read: "The Isle of Man is a land of possibility where people and business will find the right environment in which to reach their full potential, whatever they feel that might be" (Isle of Man Government, 2006: 3). As such, the Freedom to Flourish brand proposition was seen as inclusive and all-embracing concept, directed at both external and internal audiences.

An implementation phase began in 2006, following the development of the brand proposition. The implementation strategy was spearheaded by Alistair Audsley, a marketing consultant who was recruited to work with the private sector and non-profit organizations, and Carol Hunter, who at the time was the Director of External Relations in the Isle of Man government and is currently Head of Communications in the Chief Secretary's Office.

She was responsible for working with public sector organizations, including government departments. Although they worked with different organizations, often with different mandates and agendas, Audsley observed that:

> The irony in all this, of course, is that Carol has found it very useful to bring me along to engage with the public sector because it helps to make them realize that there is a lot of private sector support for this. So it's not just [one government official] talking to other people from government. And similarly, I've found it very useful and valuable to bring Carol along to the private sector to make them realize that government is behind this.

While there is always a sense of general skepticism with campaigns of this nature, Audsley developed creative ways to package his message. Instead of beginning with a discussion of the brand proposition, he talked about three basic and interconnected goals: raising awareness of the island's advantages in order to improve investment; protecting identity, culture, language, and heritage; and working together to improve social cohesion. The brand proposition was presented simply as a vehicle or tool with which to achieve these goals. Audsley also created the Isle of Man Champion scheme to encourage individuals and organizations to promote the Freedom to Flourish campaign. The scheme began in 2007, and within the first six months he had signed up 31 organizations representing an employment base of about 6,000 people — a significant number if one notes that the total employment base of the island is about 27,000.

The campaign to promote Freedom to Flourish has been strengthened by the creation of supporting materials and programs. One of these is the *Positive National Identity Guide*, which is targeted at "Isle of Man residents who want to communicate the Island's advantages more effectively to the outside world." By articulating the positive national characteristics identified in the consultations around the Freedom to Flourish exercise and providing advice on how islanders can communicate these characteristics to an external audience, this guide combines the internal and external dimensions of place branding. Other initiatives connected with the Freedom to Flourish project have focused on socio-economic development on the island. The "Bridging the Gap" scheme, for example, worked in conjunction with the charity Age Concern to retrain and upgrade the skills of older workers.

THE ROLE AND PLACE OF CULTURE IN THE FREEDOM TO FLOURISH CAMPAIGN

Although the Isle of Man has recently undergone a significant process of cultural revitalization (similar to Newfoundland and Tasmania, as described in the previous chapter), it is important to note that its indigenous culture and language underwent a significant decline in the nineteenth and twentieth centuries. This decline was largely the result of political decisions made by the British government, demographic changes related to emigration and immigration, and changes in the island's economy (Wilson, 2008). As a result of this decline, the island's language and culture became the subjects of derision, even among native islanders. It has been largely through the efforts of grassroots activists and the island's government that the Manx culture and language have once again become embraced and celebrated on the island.

Given its location at the geographical centre of the British Isles, the cultural heritage of the Isle of Man has been influenced by successive waves of newcomers and immigrants for over a thousand years (Wilson, 2005). The indigenous culture of the island has its roots in ancient Celtic and Norse traditions; the Manx Gaelic language and Tynwald, the island's parliament, are two of the better-known examples. But it is also the case that over the last several hundred years, the island has been exposed to cultural influences from the British Isles and Europe, and, more recently, influences brought by immigrants from around the world. Whereas some feel that the national identity of the Isle of Man is firmly rooted in indigenous and ethnic Manx traditions, others have argued that:

> [t]he modern Manx national identity is also based on civic loyalties and attachments. The demographic reality in the Isle of Man is that less than 50% of the current population was born on the island, although among some newcomers

> there may be an urge to rediscover or even construct a
> sense of Manx national identity. Overall, for a growing
> number of people, the common Manx identity is based
> more on civic criteria or loyalty to the political institu-
> tions of the state rather than on ethnic factors, even more
> so because the Manx language and culture are so little
> understood and used. It is this aspect of Manx society, the
> balancing of the ethnic and civic dimensions of the evolv-
> ing Manx national identity, which currently present the
> most challenges. (Wilson, 2005: 134)

When thinking about the role of culture in branding the Isle of Man, therefore, it is important to recognize the cultural heterogeneity of the island, as
well as the fact that culture and identity are contested concepts. In other
words, one person's definition of culture (and expectations about the representation of culture in something like a place brand) is likely to be different
from that of another person. Moreover, culture is not a static concept. It is
constantly shifting and evolving in response to new influences.

In order to explore the role that culture plays in branding small islands
and to address some of the concerns raised by the literature on branding in
small island jurisdictions, the following section briefly examines the *Isle of
Man Brand Book* and the *Freedom the Flourish* video, two items used to
promote the brand campaign, focusing in particular on their cultural content and messages. It will then reflect upon observations and criticisms
about the Freedom to Flourish branding campaign made by academics and
members of the public, and draw some general conclusions about the role
of culture in branding small island jurisdictions.

The Isle of Man Brand Book

This book is a glossy and visually enticing publication that explains the
basic principles behind the Freedom to Flourish brand. It begins by introducing the project, explaining the reasons why it was undertaken, and out-
lining the benefits of having a "well defined brand." It then summarizes the
various aspects of the branding, including: the brand proposition (Freedom to Flourish); the brand positioning (the factors that make "the Isle of

Man different and able to stand out from its competitors"); the brand values (independent thinking, resilience, resourcefulness, and community loyalty); and finally, the brand personality ("what sort of character do we project at our best"). The text in the rest of the book explains the brand message, discusses some of the challenges raised in the literature on branding (such as the issue of communicating with different audiences), and talks in greater detail about the background to the project.

The book is illustrated with images and photographs of the island, which range from national symbols such as the "Three Legs of Man," the four-horned Loaghtan sheep, and a motorcyclist in the famous TT (Tourist Trophy) race to images of the island's beautiful countryside and urban streets and businesses. The book also attempts to combine historical images (the Great Water Wheel at Laxey and an example of Archibald Knox's artwork) with more modern images (a space rocket — the Isle of Man Business School has an International Institute of Space Commerce, and a young student sitting in front of a computer). Consequently, the book tries to strike a balance between emphasizing the island's past and its future. While the ideas embodied in the brand values and personality tend to be generic and are probably applicable to other small island jurisdictions, the authors of the book do make a concerted effort to acknowledge the challenges of place branding, as identified in the academic literature.

From a cultural perspective, what is probably most striking about the book, especially for an outsider or someone with little knowledge of the island, is that it is completely bilingual. The Manx language has an equally prominent place alongside English, despite the fact that very few people speak Manx fluently and there are no unilingual Manx speakers. Whereas some might argue that this is an inappropriate use of the language, the authors are clearly sending the message that the Isle of Man is unique and that Manx culture is an important part of distinguishing the island from other places in the British Isles or from competitors in the global economy.

The Freedom to Flourish Video

Like the *Isle of Man Brand Book*, the *Freedom to Flourish* video (http://www. gov.im/cso/flourish/) offers a general introduction to the island that is aimed primarily at an external audience. The dominant message is that the island has a dynamic, successful, and diverse economy and is a good place to do business and invest. The video also highlights the high quality of life that newcomers and residents alike can enjoy on the island. Arts and culture are presented as aspects of this quality of life, and the video focuses on more contemporary aspects of the cultural scene. Aside from some images of historical sites and traditional Manx dancers, and a (somewhat errone-ous) reference to the fact that the island has been self-governing for the past thousand years, images of the island's indigenous culture do not figure prominently in the video.

Instead, the video emphasizes the natural landscape, which is some-thing that everyone can appreciate, whether ethnic Manx or not. The Manx language is not nearly as prominent as in the *Brand Book*. The video does feature a short segment (in Manx) in which Adrian Cain, the Manx Lan-guage Officer, talks about the language and the Bunscoil Ghaelgagh, the Manx immersion primary school. Occasionally, the Manx translation of "Freedom to Flourish" (*Seyrynys dy vishaghtey*) floats across the screen. The predominant images, however, are related to the dynamic and active nature of the island, rather than activities associated with history and traditional culture. In many respects, this reflects the challenges of using historical and traditional images to convey a sense of modern dynamism. Certainly, such images would work if the island was trying to develop its cultural tourism industry, but they do not necessarily work for the financial ser-vices, e-gaming, and the aerospace industries. That said, the introduction to the video does stress the Isle of Man's political autonomy and makes a distinct link between this autonomy and the economic freedom, prosperity, and opportunity available on the island.

What is also apparent is that the video is a far cry from the type of generic image that branding agencies have been accused of creating in other island jurisdictions (e.g., Grydehøj, 2008). In comparison to the *Brand Book*, the video actually provides more specific and useful informa-tion about the island, its economy, and the local society. It conveys a sense that the island is unique and special and that its quality of life and economy are attractive, something that will appeal to an external audience and also to people living on the island. As such, it bridges the divide between external and internal audiences that has been the downfall of branding exercises in other small island jurisdictions.

Assessing the Freedom to Flourish Branding Project

In his critique of the branding initiative in Shetland, Grydehøj took issue with marketing specialists for developing brands that are overly generic and inaccurate. He argues that these brands follow a "cookie cutter" approach that fails to express the special or unique characteristics of a particular place. In the case of Shetland, the brand ignored key aspects of the islands' cultural heritage in order to emphasize more modern and dynamic characteristics of the Shetlands' economy and society.

Do such criticisms apply to the Isle of Man's Freedom to Flourish campaign? Susan Lewis (2008) has observed that:

> In order to listen to stakeholders, you first have to speak with them. Focus groups and surveys, both of which contribute vital information to cultural and market analysis, should be complemented by ethnographic fieldwork, time consuming though it may be.

Simply speaking with the local community may not, however, be sufficient: Lewis argues, with respect to the Isle of Man's "Freedom to Flourish" branding campaign, that the brand developers undertook many qualitative interviews; yet they still produced a brand that many of the interviewees feel is a poor reflection of Man and Manx culture.

As noted above, the question of what constitutes the culture of the Isle of Man is contested and muddied by the changing demographic and social characteristics of the island. The Freedom to Flourish campaign was an attempt to capture the diversity of the island by creating a brand message that could appeal broadly to islanders, as well as to an external audience of people who probably know very little if anything about the island. Granted, the idea of freedom is not unique to the Isle of Man, and is certainly a message that has been used in other branding campaigns, in other jurisdictions; but this should not in any way diminish the idea that freedom, in the form of political, economic, and social autonomy, is a fundamentally important part of the Isle of Man's national heritage. It is obviously appealing to outsiders, many of whom are seeking the financial benefits of low taxation rates on the island or just a change in lifestyle. However, the idea of freedom (especially from outside intervention) has also always been a cherished ideal of islanders, even though the political history of the Isle of Man suggests that they have not had many opportunities to fully experience it.

In his work on Prince Edward Island, Baldacchino (2009: 13) has noted that:

> we must remember that one cannot *become* a Prince Edward Islander. Island residents are loath to encourage newcomers to come, settle and take over their own characteristics. . . . Islanders the world over get nervous when those who "come from away" ["come overs" in Manx parlance] don't just come for a visit, but overstay.

If we accept that this type of division is a general characteristic of island societies, then in the case of the Isle of Man, the concept of freedom perhaps represents a common ideal linking these two solitudes. For those with a long-standing connection to the island, the concept of freedom might represent a historical struggle for autonomy. For more recent arrivals, freedom means economic opportunity and quality of life.

It also demonstrates the difficulties facing place branders when they are trying to create an image that broadly reflects a particular society or place. Many island brand messages are generic in nature precisely because the demographic realities of islands are often very complex. This was certainly the case in the Freedom to Flourish campaign. Indeed, if the brand campaign had focused solely on the historical and cultural inheritance of the island, its depiction of the Isle of Man at the beginning of the twenty-first century would have been misleading to say the least. As one member of the House of Keys (the lower chamber of the island's parliament) put it:

> What we have to recognize, I believe, is that the world is so diverse, our neighbours are becoming so diverse socially, we as an island are becoming more and more

diverse socially. I think if we have a concept that all these different aspects of life can get behind and get underneath and support, then we can all support the Freedom to Flourish [campaign] in our different ways. So we have a job to do if we want to be recognized, not just commercially, but as a place, as a country. All these things mean different things to different people, because there are a lot of people in the Isle of Man who do not think of us as a country. We who are Manx, who were born here, think that way, but half of our population was born somewhere else but they have a high regard for the Island. We need, with this type of concept, to bring everybody together, and I think it is an opportunity. (Tynwald Court, 2006: 1224)

Another important divide identified in the literature on branding is that between internal and external audiences. Due to its foundation in the field of marketing, the natural focus of place branding has been external audiences and, more specifically, businesses and investment. Marketing specialists and other academics, however, have acknowledged that the internal dimension needs to be an important consideration in any branding exercise (Anholt, 2002; Grydehøj, 2008). Given the importance of culture (however it is defined) to islanders, or any place-based community for that matter, one would think that it would play a prominent role in "selling" a brand to an internal audience.

While it is fair to say that the Freedom to Flourish campaign was directed specifically at an external audience, internal perceptions did factor into the rationale behind and the development of the brand. According to the Branding Project Report (Isle of Man, 2006: 3), "[o]ur research showed overwhelming support among residents for promoting a clear identity and image for the [Isle of Man] — 93% thought that it was a good idea. The research also indicated, however, that 68% of our potential customers knew little or nothing about the island."

What is particularly interesting about the various publications and materials produced in the Freedom to Flourish campaign is the surprisingly prominent place of Manx culture and language, especially in light of the fact that Manx Gaelic is spoken by so few people. Even though some would argue that the language and culture should be more prominent, the very fact that they are included represents a significant positive shift in the attitudes of the government and islanders in general. Such an emphasis would not have been possible three or four decades ago because the language and culture were held in such low esteem. That being said, it is important to recognize that subsequent publications connected with the Freedom to Flourish campaign have not included as much text in Manx or on culture. One official who was involved in the project suggested that this is:

> partly because a lot of what's enacted through the Freedom to Flourish project is around business. It's about bringing new investors into the island and raising our identity internationally. So, there is less emphasis on the Manx language now than there was when the project was first launched.

In branding, the importance of the external audience cannot be understated. Places undertake branding campaigns mainly to attract outsiders to their particular jurisdiction. In the case of small island jurisdictions, such as the Isle of Man, the economy (including the cultural heritage industry) depends considerably on outside investment and there is a great deal of competition among island jurisdictions for such investment. A recent survey of business leaders in the Isle of Man painted a rather stark picture of the island's economic prospects if it were forced (by the European Union or other international organizations) to dismantle its favourable corporate tax regime:

> Jobs would leave the Island and go to rival jurisdictions if the Isle of Man introduced corporate tax.... The people surveyed felt that the British Virgin Islands would be the main beneficiary if the Isle of Man lost businesses. But they also predicted that Bermuda, Singapore, Hong Kong, Malta and Jersey would steal business from the island. (*Isle of Man Today*, 2010)

If the Isle of Man economy deteriorated or even collapsed in the wake of changes to its current tax regime, the ability of the public and private sectors to support cultural activities could be severely compromised. Indeed, it is no coincidence that the recent revival of Manx culture and language has occurred at the same time as the economic transformation of the island's economy (Wilson, 2011). The link between economic growth and support for culture is clear and has been noted in other island jurisdictions (Grydehøj, 2008) (see Chapter 8 for the example of the Shetland Islands).

In such a highly competitive global environment for financial services, small islands specializing in such activities need to use a variety of tools to distinguish themselves from competitors (many of which, it is interesting to note, seem to be other small island jurisdictions). Place branding is one (but not the only one) of these tools. As the Isle of Man's Freedom to Flourish branding initiative indicates, culture (however this is defined) can play an important supporting role in marketing small islands. But place branding involves more than selling a jurisdiction to the outside world. It is about depicting a society and its characteristics and values. While the cultural purists may disagree, in the Isle of Man the idea of freedom is a value that not only bridges the divide between ethnic and civic definitions of the Manx nation, but also speaks to both internal and external audiences.

CONCLUSION

Place branding is becoming more common as countries, regions, cities, and other jurisdictions compete with each other in the global marketplace. This approach is especially true in the case of small island jurisdictions where globalization and technology are breaking down the traditional geographical barriers of insularity. This chapter examined place branding in the case of the Isle of Man using the island's Freedom to Flourish branding project as a case study to test some of the assumptions developed in the literature on the role of culture in place branding. The research suggests that the message and the materials associated with the Freedom to Flourish brand struck a balance between recognizing the Isle of Man's indigenous culture and heritage and the needs of its dynamic, post-industrial economy and changing demographic profile. Although the concept of freedom is probably applicable to other island jurisdictions, in the case of the Isle of Man it serves as a common ideal for the different audiences targeted by the brand. Inhabitants of the island view freedom as the embodiment of the historical and contemporary political autonomy of the Isle of Man and the benefits that this brings to the island. Outsiders are largely attracted by the financial freedom and material benefits offered by the island's favourable tax regime and/or the lifestyle benefits that come with island living.

Culture has played an important supporting role in terms of reinforcing the ideals of freedom and autonomy. Although the clear focus of the branding project is business and investment, the indigenous language, culture, and heritage of the island are incorporated into the brand message at various points to reinforce the notion that the Isle of Man is different and that its autonomy and freedom are grounded in the traditions of the past, as well as in the regulations of the present. In many respects, branding and the economic investment and growth it tries to encourage have a symbiotic relationship with culture. Culture supports the quality of life that is one of a number of "attractants" for investment and human capital; investment and economic growth support culture. While the Isle of Man remains vulnerable to the winds of change in the global economy, this symbiotic relationship ultimately provides the foundation for a sustainable economic, social, and cultural prosperity on the island.

ACKNOWLEDGEMENT

The author would like to thank Chantal Carriere for her research assistance.

REFERENCES

Anholt, S. 2002. "Foreword" to special issue on place branding. *Journal of Brand Management* 9, 4 and 5: 229–39.

Askegaard, S, and D. Kjeldgaard. 2007. "Here, There, and Everywhere: Place Branding and Gastronomical Globalization in a Macromarketing Perspective." *Journal of Macromarketing* 27, 2: 138–47.

Baldacchino, G. 2009. "Island Brands and 'The Island' as a Brand: Insights from Immigrant Entrepreneurs on Prince Edward Island." *International Journal of Entrepreneurship and Small Business* 9, 4: 1–17.

Fan, Y. 2006. "Branding the Nation: What Is Being Branded?" *Journal of Vacation Marketing* 12, 1: 5–14.

Freedom to Flourish. n.d. *The Isle of Man Brand Book* and *Freedom to Flourish* video. Douglas: Isle of Man Government. Accessed 1 Sept. 2010. http://www.gov.im/cso/flourish/.

Go, F.M., and R. Govers. 2009. *Place Branding: Glocal, Virtual and Physical Identities, Constructed, Imagined and Experienced.* Basingstoke: Palgrave Macmillan.

Govers, R., F.M. Go, and K. Kumar. 2007. "Promoting Tourism Destination Image." *Journal of Travel Research* 46, 1: 15–23.

Grydehøj, A. 2008. "Branding from Above: Generic Cultural Branding in Shetland and Other Islands." *Island Studies Journal* 3, 2: 175–98.

Harrison, S. 2002. "Culture, Tourism and Local Community: The Heritage Identity of the Isle of Man." *Brand Management* 9, 4 and 5: 355–71.

Isle of Man Government. n.d. *Positive National Identity Guide: Isle of Man, Giving You Freedom to Flourish.* http://www.gov.im/lib/docs/cso/flourish/positiveidentity.pdf.

———. 2006. *Economic and Social Development through the Enhancement of the National Identity of the Isle of Man.* The Branding Project Report. Douglas: Isle of Man Government.

Isle of Man Today. 2010. "Survey Paints Bleak Outlook for Future," 9 Aug. Accessed 28 Dec. 2013. http://www.iomtoday.co.im/news/business/survey-paints-bleak-outlook-for-future-1-1747995.

Kaneva, N. 2011. "Nation Branding: Toward an Agenda for Critical Research." *International Journal of Communication* 5: 117–41.

Kermode, D.G. 2001. *Offshore Island Politics. The Constitutional and Political Development of the Isle of Man in the 21st Century.* Liverpool: Liverpool University Press.

Khamis, S. 2011. "Lundy's Hard Work: Branding, Biodiversity and a Unique Island Experience." *Shima: The International Journal of Research into Island Cultures* 5, 1: 1–23.

Kotler, P., and D. Gertner. 2002. "Country as Brand, Product and Beyond: A Place Marketing and Brand Management Perspective." *Brand Management* 9, 4 and 5: 249–61.

Lewis, S. 2008. "A Land of Possibility? Manx Cultural Identity and the Campaign for a Commonwealth in the Isle of Man." Paper presented at the annual meeting of the American Folklore Society. Louisville, Kentucky.

Olins, W. 1999. *Trading Identities: Why Countries and Companies Are Taking on Each Other's Roles.* London: Foreign Policy Centre.

————. 2002. "Branding the Nation — The Historical Context." *Brand Management* 9, 4 and 5: 241–48.

O'Shaughnessy, J., and N.J. O'Shaughnessy. 2002. "Treating the Nation as a Brand: Some Neglected Issues." *Journal of Macromarketing* 20, 1: 56–64.

Pigman, G.A. 2012. "Public Diplomacy, Place Branding and Investment Promotion in Ambiguous Sovereignty Situations: The Cook Islands as a Best Practice Case." *Place Branding and Public Diplomacy* 8, 1: 17–29.

Royle, S.A. 2001. *A Geography of Islands: Small Island Insularity.* London: Routledge.

Stern, P., and P. Hall. 2010. "Historical Limits: Narrowing Possibilities in Ontario's Most 'Historic Town.'" *Canadian Geographer* 54, 2: 209–27.

Tynwald Court Official Report Proceedings (Hansard), Isle of Man, 17 May 2006. 123(18). Accessed 6 Jan 2012. http://www.tynwald.org.im/business/hansard/20002020/th17052006.pdf.

Wilson, G.N. 2005. "Between Independence and Integration: The Isle of Man's Path to Self-Determination." *Canadian Review of Studies in Nationalism* 32, 1 and 2: 133–44.

————. 2008. "The Revitalization of the Manx Language and Culture in an Era of Global Change." *Refereed Papers from the 3rd Annual International Small Island Cultures Conference,* 74–81. Charlottetown: Institute of Island Studies, University of Prince Edward Island.

————. 2009. "But the Language Has Got Children Now: Language Revitalization and Education Planning in the Isle of Man." *Shima: The International Journal of Research into Island Cultures* 3, 2: 15–31.

————. 2011. "Social Change and Language Revitalization in the Isle of Man: A Post-Materialist Perspective." In J. Sallabank, ed., *Language Documentation and Description,* vol. 9, 58–74. London: School of Oriental and African Studies.

Winterbottom, D. 2000. "Economic History, 1830–1996." In J. Belchem, ed., *A New History of the Isle of Man, vol. 5, The Modern Period, 1830–1999,* 207–78. Liverpool: Liverpool University Press.

CHAPTER 12

Communities, Collaboration, Cohesion, and Centralization: Contemporary Insights from Rural Ireland

Brendan O'Keeffe

INTRODUCTION AND CONTEXT

The Republic of Ireland's recent experience of profound economic, social, cultural, and political change and its remarkable journey from relative poverty to boom and then bust have been well documented (see, for example, Chapter 6 in this volume). While much of the commentary on contemporary Ireland's development trajectory focuses on national actors and institutions — the celebrated and the maligned — insufficient attention has been paid to development efforts and experiences at the local level. This chapter looks at the model and dynamics of rural development that have emerged in contemporary Ireland. It considers the changing institutional, resource, and political contexts in which rural development operates. It looks in particular at the interfaces between local bodies, the state, and the EU, and it assesses the current opportunities and challenges facing rural development actors in Ireland.

Much of the substantial economic, social, and infrastructural change that Ireland has witnessed over recent decades can be attributed to the country's membership in the European Union. EU interventions and influences have modernized agriculture and opened up new markets for industry and services. The completion of the Single European Market, the dilution of interstate boundaries, intergovernmentalism, and EU support for inter-regional collaboration all have contributed to the Peace Process and the normalization of relations between Ireland and Britain. EU membership has enabled a cultural transformation, as Irish people travel more and interact to a greater extent with other European peoples and cultures, and the country is no longer perceived as an appendage of Britain but as a distinct entity (Hourigan, 2004; Fitzgerald, 2005). EU co-financing of National Development Plans since the 1980s provided guidance to aspects of public policy and introduced an emphasis on multi-annual and multi-sectoral planning. EU influences have impacted the way in which the Irish state and its institutions relate to citizens (Adshead and Tonge, 2009; Rees and Connaughton, 2009).

Rees and Connaughton (2009) use the term "Europeanization" to describe EU-influenced political change at all tiers of government. Europeanization encompasses institutional adaptation to take account of participation in decision-making by non-governmental actors, more sophisticated mechanisms of sub-national governance, and increased networking in political processes. At the local/district level, EU requirements for multi-stakeholder partnerships and an emphasis on bottom-up approaches to development have led to the formalization of interfaces between the state and civil society. Partnership initiatives such as LEADER[1] (the EU initiative for rural development) have empowered community and voluntary groups and conferred decision-making competencies and responsibilities on non-governmental actors (Cawley, 2009; Quinn, 2009). Douglas and O'Keeffe (2009) have documented how the regional tier of government was established in Ireland at the insistence of the EU, although they note that regional authorities have been conferred with few responsibilities, as central government has endeavoured to retain key competencies in spatial planning and territorial development. Marshall (2007) outlines how processes of Europeanization have manifested themselves on the governance landscape of the Dublin metropolitan region, in the form of partnership, holistic regeneration initiatives, participatory planning, and proactive approaches by local inhabitants — all made possible by EU investment in Dublin's environment, its pump-priming of renewal projects, and its insistence on collaborative governance. However, Marshall's research questions the extent to which institutions in Dublin and the Irish state have really embraced Europeanization and governance changes, and he is critical of persistent ad hoc approaches in the Irish system and the absence of mechanisms to promote "joined-up urban institutional arrangements" (2007: 178). Similarly, Quinn (2009: 118) claims that "without Brussels' insistence on sub-national partnerships, partnership as a *modus operandi* would not have been implemented at sub-national level."

A series of EU initiatives since the late 1980s have transformed the local development landscape in Ireland. EU-funded anti-poverty programs provided resources directly to civil society groups in mainly urban locations to promote employability and social inclusion. This European support for endogenous bodies, which bypassed the Irish state with respect to the disbursal of funds, laid the foundations for area-based approaches to development that involve a range of stakeholders (Harvey, 1994). Similarly, reforms of the Common Agricultural Policy and the establishment of LEADER as a dedicated funding stream for rural development partnerships were embraced by civil society organizations in rural Ireland. Thus, there is clear evidence of Europeanization in that community development processes and structures have morphed from being highly localized, exclusively bottom-up, and poorly resourced to being more networked, cross-sectoral, and multi-stakeholder (Walsh and Meldon, 2004). Over the past 25 years, agents involved in rural development — LEADER Local Action Groups among them — have generally come to reflect and enact the principles of participative democracy, collaborative governance, and sustainable territorial development. Thus, rural Ireland has gained an attuned and proactive set of institutions with the capacity to devise strategies and implement development programs. Local government has been obliged to adapt and respond to the increased vibrancy and assertiveness of local development organizations; but county and city councils continue to operate in reference to a geography institutionalized in the 1890s and their raison d'être has been characterized as "local administration rather than local government" (Lee, 1989; Callanan and Keoghan, 2003; Breathnach, 2013). Clear differences of emphasis and methodological gaps have emerged between local development and local government actors that add complexity to the governance landscape in Ireland. Central government has on occasions celebrated the successes of what the OECD (Turok, 2000) described as Ireland's "dynamic and innovative" local development partnerships; but it has more generally tended to delimit their functions and autonomy and has attempted — both covertly and overtly — to subject them to local government controls. Significant gaps and some tensions have emerged between local development partnerships, which had come to see themselves as quasi-autonomous development agencies, and the state bureaucracy, as evidenced by an increased raft of regulations emanating from Dublin.

This chapter notes how rural development in Ireland evolved in the context of weak local government and was spurred on by civil society leaders who advocated the need for community self-reliance and independent endogenous action. While Ireland remained a significant beneficiary of EU funding up to 1999, there was a notable Europeanization of the governance landscape, and Irish approaches to rural development were advocated by the European Commission as offering a blueprint for those countries that joined the EU in 2004 and 2007. Furthermore, the Commission pushed for a substantial increase in the level of funding for rural development for the period 2007–13, although its efforts were somewhat tempered by members of the European Parliament, who voted in favour of retaining funding for farm subsidies over rural development. Growing Europe-wide recognition and increased levels of funding appeared to put Ireland's rural development partnerships on a strong footing in 2007 and engendered optimism among rural communities. However, as this chapter describes, such optimism was short-lived, as organizational restructuring, bureaucratic regulations, ministerial changes, and government advocacy of an increased role for government at the expense of governance caused a weakening of local partnership, a re-emergence of uniform exogenous planning, and a consolidation of centralization. Indeed, there is considerable evidence of a reassertion of Victorian-era geographies and institutional behaviours on the Irish landscape as the state has become increasingly bureaucratic, inflexible, and authoritative in its supervision of rural development. This chapter contends that in the context of responses to economic contraction, worrying gaps have emerged between the local and the national, between the volunteer and the bureaucrat, between civil society and state institutions, and between rural development partnerships and national government in respect of policy priorities, mechanisms for delivery, and a vision for rural society. Thus, while central government focuses on reducing the state's debt and budget deficit as quickly as possible, it risks dismantling the sub-national governance infrastructure required to promote territorial competitiveness and sustainable rural development.

DYNAMICS OF THE IRISH MODEL OF RURAL DEVELOPMENT

Greece, Ireland, and Portugal have the shared distinction of being the first EU member states ever to require an IMF (International Monetary Fund) sponsored intervention. The so-called "bailout programs" to which these three countries have been subjected have caused them to lose political sovereignty, as the IMF, EU, and ECB (European Central Bank) stipulate aspects of their economic policies in return for long-term loans at rates of interest that are lower than those available from financial markets. Of the three member states, Greece is being subjected to the greatest degree of external control as its funders exert demands for extensive political and institutional reform, and that country has experienced considerable social trauma as its political leaders seek to impose unpopular economic policies. Portugal, like Greece, has experienced considerable political agitation and popular protests against austerity. However, its leaders have been more successful than their Greek counterparts in reducing the government deficit and introducing public sector reforms. Similarly, Ireland has been required to make considerable and painful fiscal adjustments and to provide for more consistent revenue-raising mechanisms. In response, the Irish government has moved to introduce household charges and a property tax to provide for the funding of local government, which heretofore has relied heavily on the national exchequer to fund its staffing and operations. The introduction of new taxes has ignited a debate — albeit a muted one — about the role of local authorities and the high degree of centralization that characterizes the Irish state. Indeed, it is perhaps no coincidence that a

2006 ESPON (European Spatial Planning Observatory Network) report identified Ireland, Greece, and Portugal as the most centralized states in the EU. These states' adherence to centralization distinguishes them from other small European states, which have been taking steps to promote regional autonomy and subsidiarity at district and municipal levels.

The centralized nature of the Irish state, the absence of a strong regional authority tier, and shortcomings in local government were among the drivers of local agitation and the emergence of self-assured and independent-minded community development organizations in many parts of rural Ireland (McDonagh, 2001; McDonagh et al., 2009). The inabilities of exclusively top-down distributive strategies such as "growth poles" and industrial relocation incentives to arrest rural decline brought about an interest in complementary bottom-up policies in the 1980s (discussed further in the Canadian context in Chapter 13). Cuddy (1992: 75) argued that the "main focus of bottom-up policies must be to increase the efficiency of the development process" through promoting local participation in discharging those responsibilities it is competent to carry out. This perspective, which recognizes the development potential of the local area and the merits of area-based and territorially differentiated approaches, is articulated in the 1988 European White Paper on the *Future of Rural Society*, the recommendations of which have since been taken up by the European Commission. In 1991, the EU Commissioner for Agriculture (and Irishman) Ray McSharry oversaw the creation of a "second pillar" of the Common Agricultural Policy with a dedicated funding stream for rural development. The pillar, which has provided support for diversification of the rural economy, environmental initiatives, and some social interventions (early retirement for older farmers and training for new entrants into agriculture), as well as LEADER, is significant in that it establishes rural development as a core policy objective of the EU. LEADER has evolved in tandem with "the European Model of Agriculture," which emphasizes the multifunctional nature of the countryside and advocates incentivizing and enabling farmers to protect and promote "the rural landscape, biodiversity, and countryside access" (Feehan and O'Connor, 2009: 126). However, some notable criticisms of the pillar emerged, with many observers (O'Hara and

Commins, 1998) contending that it is overly influenced by agricultural concerns, while others, especially the environmental lobby (Ward and Lowe, 2006; Mantino, 2011), claim that it is under-resourced relative to Pillar One (farm subsidies). Throughout Europe, the dominant farm lobby has continued to object to the transfer of resources to rural development (Papadopoulos and Liarikos, 2007), and as Europe prepares for the program period 2014–2020, this old chestnut has surfaced again.

The advent of Pillar Two and the emergence of LEADER were welcomed by the Irish government, which moved to facilitate the formation of 16 Local Action Groups (LAGs) — area-based partnership organizations responsible for the implementation of LEADER I (1991–94) (NESC, 1994). The LAGs were generally driven from the bottom, with civil society organizations being the main protagonists. Statutory bodies, the social partners, and in some cases local government representatives also sat on the LAG boards to provide specialist knowledge, technical support, and match-funding. The independent evaluation of the program in Ireland (Kearney et al., 1995) noted the significance of LEADER in consolidating the establishment of LAGs, and in providing rural areas with a tool for promoting long-term and integrated local development. O'Hara and Commins (1998: 271) noted that LEADER marked "a significant reversal of the situation when local projects operated with virtually no state support (indeed almost in spite of the state), to one where there is now a widespread acceptance and appreciation of the value of voluntarism in local development." The successes of LEADER I led to the roll-out of LEADER II (1995–99), LEADER+ (2000–06), and the mainstreaming of LEADER across the EU in 2007. Since 1995, LEADER has covered almost all of the territory of the Irish state, with the exception of the five main cities.[2] In 2006, the regional gateways and hub towns[3] were excluded from the catchment territories of LEADER LAGs.

Successive iterations of LEADER in Ireland have been implemented exclusively by LAGs. Since 2008, LAGs have been legally obliged to include local government representatives on their boards of directors in the personages of the county manager (or his/her nominee) and a number of elected county councillors. The multi-stakeholder composition of LAGs, their strong association with civil society, and their relative autonomy in decision-making up to 2006 distinguished LEADER in Ireland, Finland, and Spain from the arrangements in some other EU member states, where LEADER tended to be more aligned with local government, although in more recent years the dominant trend across Europe is towards LAGs that are driven by civil society. In their study of rural development organizations in Newfoundland and Labrador and in Ireland, Douglas and O'Keeffe (2009: 89) note that "both jurisdictions have gravitated towards a more local, endogenous, or bottom-up approach over time, with one (Ireland) subscribing more explicitly to the principles of subsidiarity. Successive evaluations of LEADER (Esparcia et al., 2000; ÖIR, 2004, 2010; RuDI, 2010) have lauded the "specific features"[4] of LEADER as offering the optimum governance model for rural areas. The OECD records that "LEADER has demonstrated the benefits that a bottom-up, integrated approach to rural development can bring with relatively little resources, and its success stands in contradiction to and highlights the limits of the sectoral approach to rural areas" (2006: 91). In a similar vein, the Carnegie UK Trust observes that "LEADER is judged to be one of the most successful initiatives ever to come to Europe" (2010: 3).

The transition from LEADER I to LEADER II in the mid-1990s was marked by an expansion of the number of LAGs from 16 to 34 and a corresponding increase in size of the LEADER national envelope (from €43.6 million to €119.2 million). By 1996, the majority of LAGs had also assumed responsibility for the delivery of complementary development initiatives, the most notable among them being the Local Development Program (LDP). Established by the EU and partly co-financed by the Irish exchequer, the LDP sought to promote social inclusion and local economic development. While LEADER was open to any individual or collective body with an eligible idea or project, LDP resources had to be targeted towards the most disadvantaged in society, with the priority being those affected by long-term unemployment. The LDP had a similar overall budget to LEADER II (€112.5), but was more targeted at urban than rural areas; and where it was not delivered by a LAG, the LDP was the responsibility of a designated Area Partnership Company or Community Partnership. Its

implementation was co-ordinated at national level by an independent in-
termediary organization — ADM (Area Development Management) —
rather than by the Irish civil service. ADM included on its Board of Directors representatives of the partnerships involved in the delivery of the LDP,
nominees of government, the social partners, and social advocacy groups.
Its incarnation and the establishment of a LDP Monitoring Committee
represented a very significant Europeanization of Ireland's governance
landscape, as a multi-stakeholder partnership assumed a role that would
have traditionally been the exclusive preserve of a government department
(ministry). Most LEADER LAGs partnerships, particularly those in the
west of Ireland, embraced Europeanization: they assumed responsibility
for the LDP and tendered for the delivery of a range of other EU and
national programs (such as LIFE, Rural Transport Initiative, and Social
Economy Program) on the basis that their mandate was multi-sectoral and
that an integrated approach to rural development was essential (O'Keeffe,
2009). A minority of LAGs, however, were less comfortable with the notion
of taking on responsibilities other than LEADER, and at times there were
tensions at national LEADER Network meetings between the more holistic,
multi-sectoral partnerships and those who described themselves as "pure"
LEADER groups. The decision by some LAGs not to engage in broader
local and rural development contributed to the establishment of parallel
partnership organizations — many with structures and territories that
came within, coincided with, or overlapped LEADER territories — thus
increasing institutional complexity and creating a perception of agency
duplication.

The spawning of local partnership structures between 1995 and 1999
and the ensuing allegation propagated by some politicians and media commentators that a plethora of agencies was operating at cross-purposes
exacerbated what had already been an uneasy relationship between local
development and local government in Ireland. The achievements of the
local development sector — the targets for LEADER II and the LDP were
exceeded nationally — and partnerships' abilities to fund community
projects prompted many politicians to call publicly for local development
functions and budgets to come under the control of local authorities. This

view was supported by the County Managers' Association, which lobbied for change. The external evaluation of LEADER and the ESF (European Social Fund) review of the LDP noted the need to tidy the institutional landscape at the local level, although the ESF report observed that:

> charges of proliferation and overcrowding on the local development scene are not new, nor are they, in our experience unwarranted. However, what is unwarranted is any charge leveled against any of the organizations themselves. Partnership companies, LEADER Companies, ADM-Funded Community Groups, Enterprise Boards and others did not invent themselves. They are all creations of central planners, both at national and EU level and in that respect where there is over-crowding, that over-crowding is the fault of those central planners and of a fund driven rather than objective driven mentality. (European Social Fund Evaluation Unit, 1999: 201)

The failure of the local development sector itself and of national government to grasp this nettle in 1999–2000 meant that, although basking in the successes of significant development outputs, LAGs and other partnerships faced then, as they still do, uncertainty regarding their institutional futures and their interfacing with local government.

THE EVOLVING ROLE OF THE STATE

Although Ireland is the most rural country in Western Europe,[5] it was not until 1999 that the government adopted a White Paper on Rural Development. Until then, a number of commentators had equated Irish policy to "shopping for EU subsidies" (McDonagh, 2001; Dillon, 2010). Douglas and O'Keeffe (2009) observe how the White Paper was influenced by the European agenda to promote multi-functional agriculture and vibrant and sustainable communities. They also note that the government's commitment to rural development has been evident in subsequent National Development Plans and in spatial planning policy. The roll-out of measures contained in the White Paper has seen LEADER Partnerships — now known as Integrated Local Development Companies (ILDCs) — assume an extensive range of development roles, as the state has outsourced to them the delivery of a range of schemes and services. Consequently, ILDCs now operate between six and 10 programs in addition to LEADER; are involved in rural transport provision, conservation initiatives, and community business; and are exclusively responsible for the delivery of two state-sponsored labour market schemes[6] (Maye et al., 2010: 18). Thus, the state has enabled an expansion and consolidation of ILDCs, as they become more involved in the mainstream delivery of public goods. Therefore, the trend identified by O'Keeffe and Douglas (2009: 107) whereby rural development had become "more integrated and multi-faceted or holistic" has been manifest, although its continuation is by no means guaranteed.

The expansion in their role that LAGs experienced up to the mid-2000s and the change in the official nomenclature from either LEADER LAGs or Area/Community Partnerships to ILDCs are associated with what came to be called the "Cohesion Process." Maye et al. (2010: 10) eloquently distinguish this uniquely Irish cohesion process from the better-known "cohesion" that underpins EU regional development policy and territorial solidarity. The drive towards cohesion in Ireland was spearheaded by the Ministry of Community, Rural and Gaeltacht Affairs. The ministry was established in 2002, and included in its mandate the agencies responsible for the development of Gaeltacht (Irish-speaking) areas, the promotion of Irish, community development projects and schemes, as well as rural development, including LEADER. ADM and its programs also came under the ministry, which, at the time of its establishment, was one of only two rural development ministries in the EU. The creation of this ministry meant that all the partnership organizations involved in delivering both LEADER and ADM-sponsored programs were reporting, for the first time, to a single ministry.[7] Having achieved the integration of programs at the level of the national government, the minister and his officials then set about realizing a mirrored integration at the local level, whereby LEADER partnerships and organizations delivering local development (and/or other social inclusion measures) were expected to fuse into integrated structures (Humphreys, 2011). This process of local-level integration known as

"Cohesion" had as its ultimate objective the creation of one partnership structure per county: an ILDC; although, as the process evolved, some flexibility was permitted such that larger counties such as Cork, Kerry, Mayo, Donegal, and the then minister's home county of Galway were permitted to have more than one ILDC.

The process of Cohesion can be seen as giving effect to the LEADER principles of multi-sectorality and integration. Evidence already existed of the synergies that could accrue from joint-delivery of LEADER and the Local Development Program (O'Keeffe, 2009). However, the top-down formula and timetable for Cohesion alienated a number of bodies, particularly the smaller Community Partnerships, who feared their ethos and their specific focus on social inclusion would be lost if they were to be subsumed into a larger organization. There were also fears of job losses and personality clashes in some counties. Consequently, progress on the Cohesion agenda was slow, and it was most problematic in counties Cavan and Monaghan, where directors of the LEADER group there, which had been in existence for almost 20 years, objected to the breakup of their organization so as to come within two new county structures. Indeed, the Cavan–Monaghan LAG explored legal avenues to try to stall Cohesion. The process chugged along between 2006 and 2008, but was brought to a head when the ministry inserted a "compliance with governance measure" in the selection criteria issued to potential LEADER applicants. Thus, only fused entities — ILDCs — could tender to administer LEADER and the Local and Community Development Program for the period to 2014.[8] When it eventually concluded, Cohesion had resulted in a reduction in the number of local development partnerships from 94 to 52.

This expansionary phase in respect of increased responsibilities (up to 2008), albeit camouflaged and somewhat stifled by the protracted cohesion experience, contrasts with what many in the ILDCs currently perceive as the state's stifling of local development through excessive and restrictive bureaucracy, much of which is associated with the fact that, since 2008, LEADER is no longer a stand-alone program, but has become mainstreamed as part of Axes 3 and 4 of the European Agricultural Fund for Rural Development. A survey of ILDCs in 2010 noted that "the current operating rules are proving very 'challenging' and 'restrictive'" (Maye et al., 2010: 20). The survey findings also state that there is clear concern that the LEADER ethos of bottom-up rural development is, in the new main-streamed program, being replaced by a much more top-down approach and that "the principles of innovative, area-based local development strategies that guide the LEADER program . . . (as articulated in the Cork Declaration in 1996), which make a clear statement in support of the philosophy of bottom-up rural regeneration, are, for some, in danger of being lost" (Maye et al., 2010: 24). The RuDI (2010) scoping study of rural development across several EU states reported that agricultural ministries remain the strongest single institutional influence on rural development policy. This perspective is shared among LEADER stakeholders in Ireland, who also point to the growing influence of the Ministry of Environment[9] (the ministry responsible for local government). LEADER staff report that, up to 2008, they had positive working relationships with government inspectors, who gave advice in addition to monitoring projects. Since mainstreaming, however, relations between development officers and the inspectorate have become less collaborative, and interfaces between LAGs and government officials sometimes have been testy. One development officer observed: "The Department Inspectorate is becoming increasingly involved in individual projects," while a LEADER CEO remarked, "We have gone from bottom-up to top-down, due to having to comply with agriculture-type regulations. We need to be removed from being one of the four axes, so that our ethos is not further diluted" (discussion forum).

RURAL DEVELOPMENT AND INSTITUTIONAL INTERFACES

The unease among partnership organizations and their questioning of successive governments' attitudes to them has been heightened by temporal gaps between LEADER programs (one year between LEADER II and LEADER+ and almost two years between LEADER+ and its successor in 2007–08). The establishment of county and city development boards (CBDs) in 2000 and the exogenous approach to the "'Cohesion Process" in 2007 and 2008 — both of which were steered by national government — also raised the ire of many LEADER stakeholders. CBDs were established as part of an ongoing, although protracted, process of local government reform. The CDBs were seen by government as a mechanism to promote interfacing and create synergies between representative and participative democracy (Ó Riordáin, 2010), and their multi-stakeholder composition — involving representatives of civil society, the social partners and statutory sector — somewhat mirrored that of LEADER LAGs/ILDCs. Key distinguishing features of the CDBs, however, include that elected councillors outnumber each of the other sectors, the chair must be a local authority member, and staff are employed by the city/county council. Thus, they are very firmly an arm of local government, and have been charged with responsibility for co-coordinating a city/county development strategy. The boards have been subjected to external evaluation, and have been credited with enabling inter-agency synergies, but they lack a formal mechanism to ensure that national and government bodies give due weighting to local priorities (Indecon, 2008: viii). Many in rural development contend that they provide local government with the necessary partnership-like structure[10] that would qualify county and city councils to assume LEADER and local development functions, and could "with the stroke of a minister's pen be dressed-up in LEADER's clothes for 2014" (interview, LAG chair).

ILDCs' fears of local authorities (CDBs) assuming a supervisory or delivery role in rural development from 2014 have been primed by the fact that they have been required by government (since 2003) to have their annual work programs endorsed (i.e., sanctioned) by the CDBs — an obligation not placed on any other publicly funded organizations. Statements in the government Green Paper on Local Government (2008), which described local authorities as "leaders in the local community" (2008: 89) and commitments in the Program for Government to "move many of the functions currently being performed by agencies — such as community employment and enterprise supports — back to local government" (Fine Gael and Labour, 2011: 27) added to concerns among those involved in rural and local development. Indeed, a number of LEADER representatives reported being taken aback by comments made by a senior government official who, in response to a query about the diminution of local government functions over recent decades,[11] replied, "we have to find something for them to do" (interviews).

The road map for local authorities also is being influenced by a steering group, which was established by the Minister for Environment, Community and Local Government to consider, among other things, how to enhance the role of local authorities in the delivery of local and community development programs and functions. It recommended (March 2012) more joined-up planning under the governance of the local authority and stated that local/rural development territories should be aligned with those of county (and city) councils. If pursued, the latter would have significant consequences in the more rural and peripheral west of Ireland, as along the western seaboard more than one ILDC operates within each county.[12] The west's adherence to flexible and locally delineated sub-county structures may indeed be geographically appropriate given western counties' larger scale, dispersed settlement patterns, and poorer socio-economic profiles. Indeed, the emergence of locally defined geographies of development is hardly surprising: county boundaries, which were delineated by the British colonial regime, have not changed since the seventeenth century (Parker, 2009: 290). Empirical research by Creamer et al. (2009) suggests that social, economic, and cultural connections have distinct geographies that frequently transcend current county boundaries, including in many cases the boundary between the Republic of Ireland and Northern Ireland. Furthermore, the work of Breathnach (2012) and of AIRO (the All-Island Research Observatory[13]) in mapping the catchment areas of towns and functional territories across the island of Ireland exposes the increasing inappropriateness of county boundaries in respect of delineating service catchments, administrative areas, and development territories.

The ongoing debate about the spatial boundaries of rural development partnerships and their relationship with local government has revealed a considerable chasm between the local and the national and between the local and the county. Divergent perspectives have pitched community-based volunteers and practitioners against the county and state officials, while political representatives at all levels have transmitted mixed messages on the prospect of an expanded rural development role for county councils. Many councillors, including those who lead community groups and those who sit on the boards of ILDCs, are supportive of subsidiarity, while others are reluctant to depart from stated party positions. The European Union has taken a jaundiced view of Ireland's attempts to direct its local authorities towards assuming local development functions, while the state is simultaneously pursuing centralization by transferring functions from local government to central government and statutory agencies. A European Court of Auditors Report (2010) reaffirms the EU's commitment to the bottom-up and multi-agency partnership approach, and it cautions against the institutionalization of local partnerships. With reference to the Irish context, the Court of Auditors states: "one of the key features of the LEADER approach is that decisions should be made not by public authorities but by a wider local partnership, where the local government is included but does not have a majority vote" (2010: 18).

As a result of such affirmations from Europe, many rural development actors currently perceive they have more friends in Brussels than in Dublin. As some ILDC managers have commented, "We have been knocked three steps backwards. Fear is all over the place from the board down." "The Department has lost the plot . . . In Europe, other DGs [Directorates General][14] are taking on board the LEADER approach, but our own government is killing it" (discussion forum). However, Ireland's economic growth during the 1990s and early 2000s and the accession to the EU of 12 states in Central and Eastern Europe in 2004 and 2007 mean that the country is no longer a first-tier priority for European Regional and Cohesion Funds. Therefore, the EU's ability to influence the operations of sub-national governance in Ireland is limited, as is the degree of leverage available to ILDCs in responding to state-led centralization.

LEGACY OF THE CELTIC TIGER

During the heydays of the so-called "Celtic Tiger," rural development in Ireland appeared to enjoy something of a renaissance. A White Paper provided policy direction, while a dedicated ministry (Department of Community, Rural, and Gaeltacht Affairs), in particular the personality and drive of Minister Eamonn Ó Cuiv, ensured leadership and a strong rural voice in government circles. At the local level, LAGs matured into ILDCs and moved from delivering a single program (LEADER) to assuming responsibility for a range of government-sponsored schemes, as the state recognized that ILDCs represented a service delivery model characterized by flexibility, innovation, and accessibility to local communities. As their responsibilities expanded, so did the budgets and human resources available to ILDCs; and there was considerable optimism among rural development actors that the Rural Development Programme (2007–13) would be "our most straightforward and innovative" (ILDC manager). The Celtic Tiger economy provided government departments, and by extension the ILDCs — as deliverers of local development and services — with reliable funding streams, while local communities benefited from increased access to supports. Thus, while the ILDCs were increasingly recognized as enablers of development at the local level, their dependence on central government increased, and more energy was devoted to delivering schemes than to policy development or the promotion of better governance; a restructuring of ADM (the name of which was changed to Pobal) resulted in its Board of Directors ceasing to include ILDC and other endogenous representatives, as all directors came to be appointed directly by the Minister for Community, Rural and Gaeltacht Affairs. Consequently, ILDCs lost direct access to a national policy-making body, while Pobal itself has become more oriented towards the administration of local development funding than to the promotion of best development practice, an original core function of ADM. Furthermore, relations between ILDCs and central government were ruptured by a government decentralization[15] program, which saw personnel in the civil service who had rural development experience move to other sections and ministries. In addition, the difficulties with the Cohesion Process, and the subsequent two-year delay to the commencement of the RDP (begun in 2009 instead of 2007) deflated the spirits of many of those involved in ILDCs and caused a loss of some experienced personnel, as a still artificially buoyant national economy offered alternative sources of employment.

In post-Celtic Tiger Ireland ILDCs are challenged to manage public expectations and maintain the level of activities to which they had become accustomed. Their influence on national policy has been reduced and government guidelines prohibit ILDCs using public monies to fund research, evaluation, the production of annual reports, or the training of board members. The increased bureaucratization associated with new personnel in the ministry and mainstreaming at the EU level have led to significant administrative backlogs in program delivery. The Mid-Term Independent Review of the Rural Development Programme[16] noted that in the first three years (2007–10), expenditure on Axes 3 and 4 (LEADER) lagged considerably behind Axes 1 and 2. While the evaluation (Indecon, 2010) acknowledged the need for a lead-in time to animate projects — a view shared by the OECD (2010) — officials in the ministry saw a need to intervene to prevent any possible under-expenditure in Axes 3 and 4. Since 2011 government officials have been much more active in the management of LEADER funds; all projects involving a grant in excess of €100,000 require prior approval from the ministry, while the budgeting of LEADER is now done on an annual rather than a multi-annual basis, as had been the case since LEADER I. The annualization of the funding has allowed the Irish government to reduce its contribution to rural development since 2011, such that the total value of LEADER and the core budget of most ILDCs have been reduced by 25 per cent. Thus, the rural development experience of post-Celtic Tiger Ireland has come to be characterized by cutbacks, centralization, and governance disconnects as the centre and the local become increasingly estranged.

A change of government following national parliamentary elections in February 2011 has done little if anything to arrest the decline in the status of rural development. Indeed, rural communities and actors feel further marginalized by severe austerity, as Ireland seeks to meet the terms of its international bailout and return to the financial markets in 2014. This policy approach has resulted in the closure of police stations, reductions in postal services, and threats to the future of rural hospitals and elementary schools. Austerity is also the primary driver behind rationalization of local government and the amalgamations of several authorities. In October 2012 Phil Hogan, the Minister for Environment, Community and Local Government, announced a reform package for local government that includes proposals directly affecting rural development. The minister's proposals (Department of Environment, Community and Local Government, 2012a: 28, 30) state that "the current enterprise development remits of the local development companies (including LEADER) should be aligned with the functions of the local authority to avoid confusion and duplication" and that "local government will have a more central role in the oversight and planning of local and community development programming." The reform package also provides for the creation of an SEC (Socio-Economic Committee) in each local authority area, with responsibility for decision-making on EU and nationally funded programs and interventions, and with oversight and responsibility for the management and disbursal of local and community development program funds. The reform proposals have been met with strong opposition from ILDCs, who claim that the establishment of an SEC would duplicate and usurp roles currently performed by their boards of directors (ILDN, 2013). Civil society organizations, predominantly in the west of Ireland, have mobilized to oppose the minister's blueprint; local action committees have been formed and several public meetings have been held to enable citizens to voice their concerns and to rally support for LEADER and endogenous approaches to rural development.

The Irish government's current attempts to rationalize local governance are not without international precedent. Douglas (2005) describes how municipality amalgamations in rural Ontario were characterized by a devaluing of local and experiential knowledge. Caldwell (2010: 113) makes similar observations in a wider Canadian context and also claims that efforts to strengthen upper-tier governments can compromise the fabric of rural communities. Such sentiments have also been expressed by civil society representatives in Ireland (Moore, 2013). DeVries (2013) has described attempts by the Dutch government to reduce the number of municipalities in the Netherlands as "blind up-scaling," and he has cautioned that the proposals currently being advocated by the Irish government may prove to be costly. The financial implications of up-scaling have also been subject to analysis by Callanan et al. (2013: 13), who contend that "policy-makers need to tread carefully in this area . . . the savings involved can be secured by alternatives to costly amalgamation exercises, such as through inter-local authority cooperation, shared services and outsourcing."

While up-scaling of local authorities is not unique to Ireland, and the international evidence cautions against such a trajectory, the dismantling of local governance mechanisms, and specifically ILDCs, would set Ireland apart. The European Commission (2011: 1) has held to its view that "Over the past 20 years, the LEADER approach to community-led local development (CLLD) — has proven an effective and efficient tool in the delivery of development policies." The Commission's insistence that non-public sector representatives comprise at least 50 per cent of the membership of a LEADER board of directors is strongly supported by the Metis GmbH evaluation (2010: 20) of LEADER in Europe. The evaluation also claims that:

> more autonomous LAGs show better results in awakening dormant skills and potentials, in strategic thinking and in monitoring the development of their area in a structured way. Autonomy or the decision making power of Local Action Groups should be further developed. Decision making power makes sense if the LAG is willing to exert it, if it is capable to master it and if it is allowed to do so by the managing authority and the programme administration.

The merits of multi-stakeholder partnerships and territorial approaches continue to be advanced by the OECD (2012), which advocates formal and informal institutions facilitating negotiation among actors in order to mobilize and integrate them into the development process. These sentiments echo the views of Greenwood (2010), who notes that the current challenges of rural planning, environmental conservation, and amelioration of climate change require integration across policy silos, a valorization of rural resources, and purposive decision-making that involves local communities and citizens.

CONCLUSIONS

The Irish model of rural development, which was for many years lauded as being among the best in Europe now finds itself in a critical position. From the late 1980s to the mid-2000s locally based partnership bodies (initially LAGs and more laterally ILDCs) expanded in terms of personnel, budgets, policy influence, development functions, and decision-making responsibilities. They also mobilized growing numbers of citizens and communities and gave effect to participative governance and direct democracy in a state that has been characterized by centralization and the absence of formal municipal institutions. ILDCs represent one of the most tangible elements of Europeanization in the governance landscape of Ireland. However, as EU influences and concerns for citizen inputs into decision-making processes have become sidelined in the drive to consolidate traditional exogenous state institutions, Ireland is unravelling key elements of sub-national governance, and risks dismantling an infrastructure with learned experiences, established networks, and a demonstrable track record. Such a trajectory may serve to ensure greater uniformity in the administration of development initiatives and the delivery of services, but it comes at the cost of reducing innovation, disempowering citizens, excluding local voices, and further marginalizing peripheral and disadvantaged communities.

The rural development expansion over two decades paralleled the growth of the national economy and was accompanied by a recognition by Irish and EU authorities of the capacity of area-based partnerships to deliver local development and implement national policies and programs. This expansionary phase also saw increased formalization of development structures and governance arrangements as ILDCs incorporated local government representatives and were subjected to more frequent interfaces with local authorities (county and city councils) and controls from central government. Increased state involvement in the regulation of rural development is associated with standardization and bureaucratization and has resulted in a slow-down in rural development delivery and heightened tensions between the local and the centre. The current proposals by central government to align ILDCs with county and city/county boundaries and to subject them to oversight by a Socio-Economic Committee are representative of clear attempts to clawback to the centre powers that had been acquired by civil society. While government has referred to economic arguments in favour of centralization, it has not published the budgets associated with the establishment of SECs. Indeed, the overwhelming international evidence suggests that any benefits will be overtaken by the costs in the medium to long term.

Following its ascendance and expansion, albeit to some extent in the shadow of the state, rural development in Ireland is now facing the prospect of severe contraction. While central government has been willing to out-source service delivery functions to endogenous bodies, the state's attitude and its actions in the form of financial cutbacks — despite growing local needs, increased bureaucratization, centralization, and attempts to sideline collaborative governance — suggest that it is less comfortable with sharing power and devolving decision-making competencies to partnerships. Indeed, the current scenario brings into question the state's attitude to participative democracy. Ireland's rural development experience has come to mirror that portrayed by Marshall (2007) in respect of the Dublin metropolitan region, where the intransigence of exogenous institutions stifled a durable transition to collaborative local governance and regional planning. The rural development narrative at the local level also reflects the patterns identified by Quinn (2009) at the regional level, which were characterized by a lack of commitment by central government to any meaningful form of devolution and, in fact, showed concerted efforts to preserve the hierarchical. The Irish experience currently manifests characteristics that Douglas and Annis (2010: 301) associate with responses to exogenous forces — reactive adaption, periodic inertia, and degrees of residual dependency. However, the current challenges are also injecting a new radicalism, vocalism, and vibrancy into rural communities, as civil society mobilizes itself in ways it has not done since the 1980s to stand up to the centre and to assert itself as having the ability to drive development initiatives. Now, unlike in the 1980s, communities can point to their 25 years of LEADER experience and consequent knowledge capital as evidence of their capability and commitment.

NOTES

1. *Liaison Entre Actions de Développement de l'Economie Rurale* (Links between Actions for the Development of the Rural Economy).
2. Dublin, Cork, Limerick, Galway, and Waterford.
3. The National Spatial Strategy (2002–20) identified nine regional gateways (Dublin, Cork, Limerick-Shannon, Waterford, Galway, Sligo, Dundalk, Tullamore-Mullingar-Athlone, and Derry-Letterkenny) as drivers of regional accessibility

and growth. A further 11 "hub-towns" were identified as regional service centres.

4. The specific features of LEADER are: an area-based approach, collaboration and networking, innovation, multi-sectorality, partnership, decentralized financing, and a bottom-up approach (AEIDL, 2000; Carnegie UK Trust, 2010).

5. Results of the 2011 census show that 36 per cent of the population reside in what the CSO (Central Statistics Office) defines as rural areas, i.e., the open countryside and settlements with a population of under 1,500.

6. The two schemes are the Rural Social Scheme, which provides part-time employment for smallholder farmers (or their spouses) in delivering community services and improving local infrastructure, and TÚS, which commenced in 2010 and provides training and work experience placements for the long-term unemployed.

7. Heretofore LEADER LAGs reported to the Department of Agriculture, while ADM was under the aegis of the Department of An Taoiseach (prime minister).

8. The Local and Community Development Program builds on previous local development and social inclusion programs that had been supported by ADM. It provides ILDCs with resources to promote community development, training, education initiatives, and youth and family supports.

9. After the 2011 general election, the Ministry of Community, Rural and Gaeltacht Affairs was broken up and its functions reallocated to other ministries, with responsibility for LEADER transferring to the Ministry for the Environment, Community and Local Government.

10. EU guidelines specify that a LAG has to draw at least 50 per cent of its membership from outside the statutory sector.

11. Local authorities have ceded competencies to central government in a number of policy areas such as health, agriculture, traffic, education grants, and the marine (Barrington, 2012; Breathnach, 2013).

12. The number of local development partnerships in counties along the west coast is as follows: Donegal 3, Mayo 3, Galway 4, Kerry 4, and Cork 5. In addition, offshore islands have their own federation partnership.

13. Mapping outputs from the All-Island Research Observatory can be studied on www.airo.ie. The observatory is based in the National Institute for Regional and Spatial Analysis (NIRSA) at NUI Maynooth, www.nuim.ie/nirsa.

14. Directorates General are the cabinet-like policy areas of the European Commission.

15. The term "decentralization" is frequently misused in Irish discourse. While "decentralization," which is synonymous with "devolution," means transferring

decision-making power from central to regional and local authorities, the word has come to be used in Ireland to refer to relocating government offices and personnel from Dublin to locations elsewhere in the country. This misnomer has been uttered repeatedly in Ireland, such that a program to relocate 10,000 civil and public servants announced by the Minister for Finance in 2003 is more often than not referred to as "decentralization." Indeed, the minister himself, Charlie McCreevy, used the term. In practice, the program announced by McCreevy failed to gather much momentum, did not adhere to the geography set out in the National Spatial Strategy, and was formally abandoned by government in 2011. The partial implementation of the program had led to the establishment of an office of the Department of Community, Rural and Gaeltacht Affairs in Tubbercurry, Co. Sligo, and the transfer to that office of personnel from Dublin.

16. The Rural Development Programme is structured according to the following national and community priority areas, which are implemented under Axes 1, 2, and 3:

> Axis 1: Improvement of the competitiveness of agriculture by supporting restructuring, innovation, and development.
>
> Axis 2: Improving the environment and countryside by supporting land management.
>
> Axis 3: Improving the quality of life in rural areas and encouraging diversification of economic activity. Axis 3 measures are implemented using the LEADER approach to rural development (Axis 4).

REFERENCES

Adshead, M. 2003. "Policy Networks and Sub-national Government in Ireland." In M. Adshead and M. Millar, eds., *Public Administration and Public Policy in Ireland*, 108–28. London: Routledge.

——— and J. Tonge. 2009. *Politics in Ireland — Convergence and Divergence in a Two-Polity Island*. Basingstoke: Palgrave Macmillan.

AEIDL (European LEADER Observatory). 2000. *Economic Competitiveness: Creating a Territorial Development Strategy in the Light of the LEADER Experience*, part 4. Brussels: LEADER European Observatory.

Barrington, R. 2012. *The Barrington Report: Time for Real Change?* Regional Studies Association, Irish Branch Conference Local Government Reform: Myth or Reality. NUI Maynooth, Mar.

Breathnach, P. 2013. "Regional Governance and Regional Development: Implications of the Action Programme for Local Government." Paper presented at the Regional Studies Association (Irish Branch) Conference, New Regional Governance in Ireland: Perspectives & Challenges. National University of Ireland, Maynooth, Jan.

Caldwell, W. 2010. "Planning and Management for Rural Development: The Role of Local Government." In D.J.A. Douglas, ed., *Rural Planning and Development in Canada*, 110–33. Toronto: Nelson.

Callanan, M., and J. Keoghan, eds. 2003. *Local Government in Ireland — Inside Out.* Dublin: Institute for Public Administration.

———, R. Murphy, and A. Quinlivan. 2013. "Economies of Scale in Local Government: An Irish Contribution to an International Debate." In E. Cherrier, ed., *Local Governance in the United Kingdom and in Ireland: So Far, So Near . . . .* Université de Lille II: Observatory on Local Autonomy.

Carnegie UK Trust. 2010. *A Common Rural Development Policy?* Dunfermline, Scotland: Carnegie UK Trust.

Cawley, M. 2009. "Local Governance and Sustainable Rural Development: Ireland's Experience in an EU Context." *Revija za geografijo/Journal for Geography* 4, 1: 53–64.

Creamer, C., N. Blair, K. Keaveney, B. O'Keeffe, and J. Driscoll. 2009. *Rural Restructuring: Local Sustainable Solutions to the Rural Challenge.* Armagh: International Centre for Local and Regional Development.

Cuddy, M. 1992. "Rural Development: The Broader Context." In M. Ó Cinnéide and M. Cuddy, eds., *Perspectives on Rural Development in Advanced Economies*, 65–78. Galway: Centre for Development Studies, Social Sciences Research Centre, University College Galway.

Department of Agriculture and Food. 1999. *A Strategy for Rural Development in Ireland — Government.* White Paper. Dublin: Stationery Office.

Department of Community, Rural and Gaeltacht Affairs. 2007. *Ireland CAP Rural Development Programme 2007–2013.* Dublin: CAP Rural Development Division, Department of Agriculture.

Department of Environment, Community and Local Government. 2012a. *Final Report of the Local Government/Local Development Alignment Steering Group.* Dublin: Department of Environment, Community and Local Government.

———. 2012b. *Putting People First: Action Programme for Effective Local Government.* Dublin: Department of Environment, Community and Local Government.

Department of Environment, Heritage and Local Government. 2008. *Green Paper* on Local Government — Stronger Local Democracy — Options for Change. Dublin: Department of Environment, Heritage and Local Government.

DeVries, M. 2013. "Perspectives on Recent Developments in Public Sector Reform in the Netherlands." Paper presented to Regional Studies Association (Irish Branch) Conference, New Regional Governance in Ireland: Perspectives and Challenges. National University of Ireland, Maynooth, Jan.

Dillon, Sara. 2010. "Anglo-Saxon/Celtic/Global: The Tax-driven Tale of Ireland in the European Union." *North Carolina Journal of International Law & Commercial Regulation* 36: 1–54.

Douglas, D.J.A. 2005. "The Restructuring of Local Government in Rural Regions: A Rural Development Perspective." *Journal of Rural Studies* 21: 231–46.

——— and B. Annis. 2010. "Community Development: A Cornerstone of Rural Development and Planning." In D.J.A. Douglas, ed., *Rural Planning and Development in Canada*, 281–328. Toronto: Nelson.

——— and B. O'Keeffe. 2009. "Rural Development and the Regional Construct: A Comparative Analysis of the Newfoundland and Labrador and Ireland Contexts." In G. Baldacchino, R. Greenwood, and L. Felt, eds., *Remote Control: Governance Lessons for and from Small, Insular, and Remote Regions*, 77–113. St. John's: ISER Books.

Esparcia, J., M. Moseley, and J. Noruega. 2000. *Exploring Rural Development Partnerships in Europe: An Analysis of 330 Local Partnerships across Eight EU Countries.* UDERVAL Uiversidad de Valencia and Countryside and Community Research Unit, Cheltenham and Gloucester College of Higher Education.

European Commission. 1988. *The Future of Rural Society.* Com(88)501 Final. Luxembourg.

———. 2011. *Community-led Local Development, Cohesion Policy 2014–2020.* Brussels: European Commission.

European Court of Auditors. 2010. *Implementation of the LEADER Approach for Rural Development — Special Report No. 5.* Luxembourg: European Union Publications.

European Social Fund Evaluation Unit. 1999. *ESF & Local Urban & Rural Development Operational Programme.* Dublin: ESF Evaluation Unit.

European Spatial Planning Observatory Network (ESPON). 2006. *Governance of Territorial and Urban Policies; project 2.3.2.* Luxembourg: ESPON.

Feehan, J., and D. O Connor. 2009. "Agriculture and Multifunctionality in Ireland." In J. McDonagh, T. Varley, and S. Shortall, eds., *A Living Countryside? The Politics of Sustainable Development in Ireland*, 123–38. Aldershot: Ashgate

Fine Gael and Labour. 2011. *Government for National Recovery 2011–2016* (Programme for Government).

Fitzgerald, G. 2005. *Ireland in the World: Further Reflections*. Dublin: Liberty Press.

Greenwood, R. 2010. "Policy, Power and Politics in Rural Planning and Development in the Canadian State." In D.J.A. Douglas, ed., *Rural Planning and Development in Canada*, 86–109. Toronto: Nelson.

Harvey, B. 1994. *Combatting Exclusion: Lessons from the Third EU Anti-Poverty Programme in Ireland*. Dublin: Combat Poverty Agency.

Hourigan, J. 2004. *Ireland and the European Union: The First Thirty Years, 1973–2002*. Dublin: Lilliput.

Humphreys, E. 2011. "Local Development in Ireland: From Innovation to Stagnation . . . But What Next in Times of Crisis?" Local Development Network. www.ldnet.eu.

Irish Local Development Network (ILDN). 2013. "Stronger Local Democracy Co-Ordination, Development, Delivery and Participation." www.ildn.ie/publications.

Kearney, B., E. Boyle, and J. Walsh. 1995. *EU LEADER I in Ireland; Evaluation and Recommendations*. Dublin: Stationery Office.

Lee, J.J. 1989. *Ireland 1912–1985*. Cambridge: Cambridge University Press.

Indecon International Economic Consultants. 2008. *Indecon Review of County/City Development Board Strategic Reviews and Proposals for Strengthening and Developing the Boards*. Dublin: Department of the Environment, Heritage and Local Government.

Mantino, F. 2011. *Developing a Territorial Approach for the CAP — A Discussion Paper*. Brussels: Institute for European Environmental Policy.

Marshall, A. 2007. "EU Structural Funding in Ireland's Capital City: Europeanization and Regeneration in Dublin." *Irish Geography* 40, 2: 168–83.

Maye, D., J. Kirwan, and R. Simpson. 2010. *New Modes of LEADER Governance in Ireland: Assessing the Impact of Rural Development Policies (RuDI)*. Cheltenham: Countryside & Community Research Institute.

McDonagh, J. 2001. *Renegotiating Rural Development in Ireland*. Aldershot: Ashgate.

———, T. Varley, and S. Shortall. 2009. *A Living Countryside? The Politics of Sustainable Development in Rural Ireland*. Surrey: Ashgate.

Metis GmbH with AEIDL and CEU. 2010. *Ex-Post Evaluation of LEADER+*. Vienna: Metis, presented to the European Commission.

Moore, B. 2013. "Stand Up and Fight Changes to Rural Services Says Campaigner." *Irish Examiner*, 22 May.

National Economic and Social Council (NESC). 1994. *New Approaches to Rural Development*. NESC No. 97. Dublin: NESC.

O'Hara, P., and P. Commins. 1998. "Rural Development: towards the New Century." In S. Healy and B. Reynolds, eds., *Social Policy in Ireland; Principles, practice and Problems*. Dublin: Oak Tree Press.

ÖIR Managementdienste GmbH. 2004. *Methods for and Success of Mainstreaming LEADER Innovations and Approaches into Rural Development Programmes*. Final Report executive summary. Commissioned by European Commission DG Agriculture, Unit G4. Vienna: Österreichisches Institut für Raumplanung GmbH.

———. 2012. *Synthesis of Mid-term Evaluations of Rural Development Programmes 2007-2013*. Vienna: Österreichisches Institut für Raumplanung GmbH.

O'Keeffe, B. 2009. "Regional and Local Development in Ireland: The Potential of LEADER Partnerships to Provide Municipal Government." *Lex Localis: Journal of Local Self-Government* 7, 3: 257-71.

———. 2012. "Local Government in Times of Austerity: Reflections on Ireland." In E. Cherrier, ed., *Local Governance in the United Kingdom and in Ireland: So Far, So Near . . .* Université de Lille II: Observatory on Local Autonomy.

——— and D.J.A. Douglas. 2009. "Rural Development in Newfoundland and Labrador and Ireland: Governance and Its Prospects and Potentials." In G. Baldacchino, R. Greenwood, and L. Felt, eds., *Remote Control: Governance Lessons for and from Small, Insular, and Remote Regions*, 237-58. St. John's: ISER Books.

Organization for Economic Co-operation and Development (OECD). 2001. *Local Partnerships for Better Governance*. Paris: OECD.

———. 2006. *The New Rural Paradigm: Policies and Governance*. Paris: OECD.

———. 2010. *Agricultural Policies and Rural Development: A Synthesis of Recent OECD Work*. Paris: OECD.

———. 2012. *Promoting Growth in All Regions*. Paris: OECD.

Ó Riordáin, S. 2010. "Assessing the Local–Centre Government Policy Relationship in Ireland." Doctoral dissertation, NUI Maynooth, Department of Geography.

Papadopoulos, A.G., and C. Liarikos. 2007. "Dissecting Changing Rural Development Policy Networks: The Case of Greece." *Environment and Planning C: Government and Policy* 25, 2: 291-313.

Parker, M. 2009. *Map Addict: A Tale of Obsession, Fudge and the Ordnance Survey*. London: HarperCollins.

Quinn, B. 2009. "Regional Policy and Politics." In N. Rees, B. Quinn, and B. Connaughton, eds., *Europeanisation and New Patterns of Governance in Ireland*,

103–21. Manchester: Manchester University Press.

Rees, N., and B. Connaughton. 2009. "Europeanisation: A Catalyst for Change." In N. Rees, B. Quinn, and B. Connaughton, eds., *Europeanisation and New Patterns of Governance in Ireland*, 12–33. Manchester: Manchester University Press.

RuDI. 2010. *Assessing the impacts of Rural Development Policies (including LEADER).* Extended Policy Brief. Frankfurt am Main: Institute for Rural Development Research at the Johann Wolfgang Goethe University.

Turok, I. 2000. *Local Partnership in Ireland: Report of the OECD.* Paris: OECD.

Walsh, J., and J. Meldon, eds. 2004. *Partnerships for Effective Local Development.* Charlerois: Université Libre de Bruxelles.

Ward, N., and P. Lowe. 2006. *The UK Government's Vision for the Common Agricultural Policy.* Memorandum to the House of Commons Environment, Food and Rural Affairs Committee Inquiry into the Government's Vision for the Common Agricultural Policy. Centre for Rural Economy, University of Newcastle upon Tyne.

CHAPTER 13

Mobilizing Place for Regional Collaboration and Development

Sarah-Patricia Breen, Sean Markey, Jen Daniels, and Kelly Vodden

INTRODUCTION

Place is both shaped by and a context for the world around us, at varying scales and geographies. Our assets (e.g., human and natural resources, social and cultural capital) occur in places, our services are delivered in places, our governance occurs in places, and our identities are formed and reinforced in places, which in turn help to further shape place. Within the study of development, place plays a key role, illustrating how factors such as culture, natural resources, human capacity, and others combine to create a unique environment that influences development opportunities and practices. Within the emergent theoretical perspective of new regionalism, place is a key theme. New regionalism is based on the reconceptualization and resurgence of the region as a result of political and economic restructuring that began in the 1980s. It has been researched at both a macro and micro scale and incorporates various themes in addition to place, including multi-level governance and integration (Hettne et al., 1999; Storper, 1999; MacLeod, 2001).

This chapter explores two case study regions, British Columbia's Kootenay region and the Kittiwake region of Newfoundland and Labrador, as presented by a team of researchers studying Canadian regional development as part of an ongoing exploration of new regionalism within the context of rural Canada. Both case studies illustrate differing ways place impacts development. Within this chapter, both case studies will discuss region and place identity and its role in the development process, as well as examples of place-based development initiatives.

THE PROJECT AND METHODS

"Canadian Regional Development: A Critical Review of Theory, Practice and Potentials" is a research initiative that has investigated how Canadian regional development has evolved since the 1990s and the degree to which Canadian regional development systems have incorporated new regionalism into their policy and practice. The study utilizes an analytical framework of new regionalism consisting of five key themes, including place-based development. The three goals of the project were: (1) to undertake a critical assessment of the application and relevance of new regionalism in the Canadian context; (2) to seek Canadian innovations in regional development; and (3) to understand how these innovations are evolving and if and how they are being shared across space in networks of regional development practice (Canadian Regional Development, 2011).

The project involves conducting an empirical assessment of Canadian regional development using a multi-level, mixed methods approach that includes case studies at federal, provincial, and regional levels and examines linkages both within and between these levels. In addition to interviews with officials of federal and provincial organizations (e.g., Western Diversification, Atlantic Canada Opportunities Agency), we identified case study regions to help assess regional development based on five key themes of new regionalism: place-based development, governance, knowledge flow and innovation, rural–urban interdependency, and integration. Methods used include a review of published literature and related government and non-government reports, and interviews with key respondents from government, non-government organizations, and academic and practitioner associations. Additionally, this chapter is informed by previous research by the authors in their respective regions (Vodden, 2009; Daniels et al., 2010; Markey et al., 2007, 2011).

Throughout 2011 and 2012, interviews were completed with key regional respondents. Web-based searches identified key individuals and agencies within each of the regions. Additional recommendations were made by interview respondents. Regional actors, local and regional governments, and established agencies in three selected development arenas (economic development, recreation, and water/watershed management) were given priority status for comparative purposes across the project. Seventy-four semi-structured interviews were completed based on the five themes of new regionalism. Various elements of place and place-based development were investigated through the interview process, including: regional definition, unique regional assets, collaboration, participation, identity, branding, and resource management.

NEW REGIONALISM AND REGIONAL DEVELOPMENT

Overview

New regionalism has emerged as both a reactive and proactive response to recent forces of political and economic restructuring. Reactively, regions are pursuing collaborative approaches to mitigating the loss of senior government and industrial interventionist roles in the development process. Proactively, integrated development, at a regional scale, offers opportunities to address the complexities of territorial planning and to mobilize the strategic competitive advantages of place-based assets within a globalized economy, a recurring objective in the development initiatives presented throughout this volume. As a result, new regionalism occupies an intermediating position between the abandonment of traditional patterns of top-down stewardship and the appeal of local control and place-sensitive intervention.

This "push" away from state stewardship is associated with negative impacts surrounding the limited capacity of select regions to adjust to the forces of restructuring and to compete with an expanded competitive field for the delivery of amenities, services, and infrastructure required to both retain and attract capital and labour. These changes have reshaped state relationships with communities and regions, resulting in a withdrawal of post-war patterns of (re)investment and responsibility for directing economic and social development and mitigating market cycles and failure. Polèse (1999) characterizes this shift as a movement away from a mandate of ensuring interprovincial and interspatial equity in favour of an enabling approach to facilitating development (i.e., steering, not rowing). Enabling development requires that a greater burden of responsibility be placed on local actors and institutions. As a result, government withdrawal may be viewed as abandonment to the vagaries of market forces and demographic trends, or as a progressive approach to fostering greater levels of community/regional capacity and resiliency (Kitson et al., 2004; MacLeod, 2001).

Despite the challenges posed by political and economic restructuring, researchers have revealed a variety of benefits associated with adopting a regionalist approach to development. These benefits are grounded in a more comprehensive understanding of the development process and the specific context (i.e., spatial, natural, social, political) in which the development is taking place. Economic benefits, social processes, and territorial development drive the "pull" towards new regionalism. Key within new regionalism is the potential to improve a region's economic, social, or environmental situation through intervention (Polèse, 1999). The economic benefits of regionalism serve as the main drivers of new regionalist efforts, with a focus on enabling communities to exert more control over the use of surrounding resources and to exploit niche markets and the diversification opportunities associated with improved transportation and communication infrastructure (Douglas, 1999).

The emphasis on social process in regional development holds significance to the economic development of regions and their governance. Regionalism fosters different institutional structures and relationships in an attempt to compensate for government withdrawal and to innovate to establish better local participation and regional collaboration (Storper, 1999; MacLeod, 2001; Scott, 2004). The literature is clear on both the advantages and pitfalls associated with the localization of power. The opportunity to include local knowledge in development decisions brings nuance and buy-in to development activities. This may address problems associated with top-down policies that seek to achieve inter-regional efficiency at the expense of local diversity. In addition, the co-location of decision-makers and the place of development impact may yield local and long-term sustainability advantages (Bradshaw, 2003).

The ascendancy of the territorial over the sectoral development model (discussed by O'Keeffe in Chapter 12) is also inherent within new regional-ist planning and offers a variety of benefits for addressing impacts associated with industrial restructuring. At a conceptual level, territorial planning al-lows regional decision-makers and planners to view resource operations as part of the regional economy rather than as isolated activities. The absence of direct or formal industry–town linkages may reduce interaction and any sense of mutual responsibility; but regional economic planning can pro-vide a foundation for re-linking resource activity in an integrated way to surrounding communities, recapturing the realities of functional spaces. In addition, a territorial approach provides a potential framework with which to actualize and monitor local outcomes. Regionalizing community benefits will better enable planners to construct and maximize intended or potential regional spread effects of various development initiatives (Kuyek and Coumans, 2003).

Canadian Regional Development

Canada is a country of regions in many respects and on a variety of scales. The diversity in geography and social and political history and the continu-ing diversity in political and economic evolution foster distinctiveness among the country's regions. The sheer scale of the Canadian geopolitical space — from the Arctic north to the wine, fruit, and tobacco regions of the south, and from the long-settled fishing communities of the Atlantic seaboard to the urban-industrial centre and the cattle, grain, and oil econ-omies of the more recently settled prairies — lends a degree of intensity to the country's regionalism not found in many other countries. Canada has been variously depicted in terms of its regions, using climatic, physio-graphic, and other physical features, political delineations (e.g., provinces, or groups of provinces, and territories), economic regions, and various other descriptors. Whatever the rationale, criteria, or measure used, this regional reality is central to the Canadian story and to the country's condi-tion today — and to its future.

Prior to the 1950s, Canada lacked a formal program for addressing the structural problems associated with rural and hinterland economies, al-though the issue of regional disparities had been recognized (Fairbairn,

1998). During the 1950s, the federal government began to adopt explicit regional development policies (Savoie, 1992). As Reed (1990) argues, staples theory — asserting that economic growth is defined by and dependent upon such staple products as lumber and minerals (Innis, 1930) — proved influential to the adoption of regional development strategies as official government policy; this provided governments with the theoretical justification for intervention in the economy to reduce regional disparities. Government intervention in creating the infrastructure and assigning the regulatory mandate for resource development was intended to set the stage for a modern, diversified economy. However, there was no real plan to facilitate or to improve development prospects beyond a "branch plant" economy (Reed, 1990). As a result, governments and communities have lacked a more comprehensive, holistic understanding of development, and a consistent regional development strategy for Canada has been lacking throughout the post-war period.

After 1945, regional disparities and attention to uneven development, along with a period of relative national prosperity, were key motivating forces in governments becoming more directly involved in promoting regional development. The focus on regional disparities influenced the policies and programs launched by successive governments to address underdevelopment. Governments tended to visualize communities and regions in terms of what they were lacking (i.e., needs or weaknesses) and measured comparative prosperity and regional health using limited economic indicators (Savoie, 1992). In effect, this program focused on poverty reduction, not on comprehensive development (Fairbairn, 1998). By addressing economic deficiencies through regional development programs, governments envisioned that regions would be propelled along a linear path to prosperity. In this interpretation of development, the region is simply a spatial unit, very much conducive to an empty-vessel approach to development: pour financial resources into an area and development opportunities will necessarily result.

There are five critical shortcomings of the regional development programs launched in the post-war period (Markey et al., 2005). (1) These programs are characterized by poor co-ordination of policies and policy objectives between levels of government. (2) The theories relied on to develop regional development were often either weak or misunderstood. (3) Policies largely ignored differences in place, treating diverse communities and regions uniformly simply because they were located in the same geographic region. (4) Regional development was defined by a deficiency-based approach intended to address perceived needs as opposed to addressing the underlying conditions and causes of underdevelopment. (5) Efforts by the state to address underdevelopment resulted in varying degrees of regional dependency. These critical shortcomings all highlight the overarching failure to consider the importance of place.

There is mounting evidence of a re-emergence of the regional perspective in planning in Canada, consistent with the patterns observed internationally in new regionalist literature. However, while it can be characterized as a re-emergence, the regional perspective has arguably evolved. What is happening at present is claimed to be different from the past and is occurring for different reasons, with different implications for planning and policymakers in terms of challenges and opportunities. Several characteristics of this regional re-emergence are worth noting. While new regionalist literature, often written from a European perspective, suggests that current forms of regional development tend to take a more integrated, territorial approach, in Canada economic development has been and continues to be a central and formative dimension of a re-emerging regional planning. Most area-wide or regional collaborations also continue to be primarily for a single purpose or issue-based (e.g., water, tourism, waste management, economic development). Those regional planning initiatives that have continued with little or few interruptions since the 1960s or 1970s are few in number and have been based on collaborative, consultative models of inter-municipal co-operation. Where local governments were restructured into regional municipalities regional planning has continued, albeit in conformity with the physical planning requirements of provincial planning legislation. In a small but important number of cases, bioregional and related perspectives have been a key underpinning to multi-community and inter-municipal collaborations.

THE ROLE OF PLACE IN DEVELOPMENT

Place-based development is a holistic and targeted intervention that seeks to reveal, utilize, and enhance the unique natural, physical, and/or human capacity endowments present within a particular location for the development of a community (or group of communities) and/or their biophysical environment. Place within the context of rural development is reflected in Massey's (1984) work, which recognizes that combinations of assets, populations, histories, and circumstances mean that general processes are always modified by the matrix of place. This contextual turn is found in a variety of ongoing rural research themes, including post-productivism, conceptualizations of the role of competitive (as opposed to comparative) advantage within the new economy, and the adoption of a territorial rather than sector-based orientation to rural policy development. Each of these themes provides insight into the role and meaning of place within the rural development process.

Post-productivism refers to the transformation, in values and economic activity, associated with a de-emphasis on primary resource production in favour of more diversified economic activities (Reed and Gill, 1997). Places function differently now than they did a decade or more ago. Mather et al. (2006) indicate that, in rural debates, the tendency is to present post-productivism in terms of dimensions rather than definitions. These dimensions include the nature and type of production (from commodity to non-commodity outputs), the multi-dimensionality of objectives associated with landscape and resources (including environmental, amenity, and ecosystem service values), and the importance of governance and representation (involving a greater diversity of actors and institutions) in land use and other areas of decision-making. In each of the characteristics, place exerts itself as a more dynamic factor in processes of social and economic development. Niche products that are more dependent on location and local capacity, such as the medicinal herbal products or native potato varieties of Chiloé (Chapter 7) or the Fair Isle patterns and wool of Shetland (Chapter 8), compete for attention with generic and "placeless" commodity products (Filion, 1998; Dawe, 2004). Natural resources remain important in post-productivist economies but in general are increasingly viewed as one set out of a repertoire of many local assets that may be used as vehicles for economic diversification.

Conceptualizations of competitiveness within the "new" economy are significant to place-based research. This work includes the resource orientation of post-productivism, but extends beyond. Turok (2004) identifies how the concept of competitiveness remains a poorly understood and deployed term. However, despite this, debates around economic restructuring and the transition from Fordism to post-Fordist production have paid considerable attention to the shift away from the importance of comparative advantage in favour of considerations of competitive advantage (Kitson et al., 2004). Comparative advantage is determined more narrowly by the fixed existence and quality of resources (Gunton, 2003). By comparison, competitive advantage is more complex. It depends on the inherent assets *and actions* (to capitalize on those assets) of a particular place to attract and retain capital and workers that have become much more mobile (Kitson et al., 2004). As a result, competitive advantage demands that places consider a wider variety of both quantitative (such as physical infrastructure, production, and location) and qualitative (such as social capital, innovation, and institutions) variables in economic development planning (MacLeod, 2001).

In response to the dynamics outlined by forces such as post-productivism in the new economy, increasing attention has been given to a territorial as opposed to sectoral approach to policy and planning. A territorial planning model allows for the integration of economic, environmental, social, cultural, and political dynamics in planning at a manageable scale. Additionally, a territorial approach recognizes the importance of contextual specificity to the process of development (Barnes et al., 2000; Markey, 2008). Rural development itself has struggled through and, for the most part, learned from the failures associated with top-down, uniform, non-participatory models of development (Halseth and Booth, 2003). Attention to territoriality is necessary to attain local buy-in and to benefit from local/regional knowledge, leadership, and other development assets. Finally, despite the seeming contradiction of scale inefficiency, territorial planning models can reduce duplication and lead to more lasting policy interventions (Pezzini, 2001; Bradford, 2005).

Collectively, these literatures provide a set of broader themes that help to inform and consolidate the understanding of the role of place in development and how development works in places, particularly when viewed through a new regionalist lens. While an economic focus remains, there is now greater consideration of culture, the environment, and community, as these are now sought-after assets in the new economy. The ascendancy of place brings a greater diversity of values (and a greater understanding of these values) to and for economic development. Through place, we gain an appreciation for a more comprehensive or "whole" economy, which is externalized and ignored in the narrow, space-based interpretation of resource exploitation in peripheral hinterlands. In addition, within the place economy, an appreciation for diversity means that difference matters. The question now is: if capital can locate anywhere, why would it locate here? This rethinking of "place" rather than "space" challenges homogeneous interpretations of "rural," uncovering the latent diversity noted in other rural research (Randall and Ironside, 1996).

REGION AND IDENTITY

An important aspect of place-based development is identity. As discussed in Chapters 1 and 2 and in the examples provided throughout this volume, place-based development draws on residents' sense of place and place identity. Identity, as argued by Escobar (2008), emerges from the articulation of difference and from everyday practices that occur at multiple levels. Identities and identity formation are relational and dialogic, a process involving the drawing of boundaries with the selective incorporation of some traits and exclusion of others (Escobar, 2008). Despite the complexity in defining regional identity, Paasi (2003) suggests that identity is often enacted through two intertwined processes: from above and from below. From above, regional identity is more about territorial control by government (aptly illustrated by O'Keeffe in Chapter 12); from below, it is a form of identification with, and representation of, a territory often associated with resistance.

Discussion of regional identity emerged within the literature parallel to the argument that the world, particularly in Western culture and politics, was increasingly moving towards the ideological triumph of total neo-liberalism (Paasi, 2004). With a long history of debate surrounding the definition and delineation of "regions," the question of regional identity is particularly vexing, as is the complexity of mobilizing regional identity for the purpose of regional and place-based development strategies. One reason for this challenge is the assumption that regional identity is an empirical phenomenon within a given area that can be analyzed using specific research materials and instruments, such as survey data or material artifacts that somehow capture or represent the region (Paasi, 2003; Escobar, 2008). With due diligence, we must ask what people mean when they speak of regional identity, because our understanding of what identity means in each case should be "a result of conceptualization and an actual research process, rather than a point of departure" (Paasi, 2003: 481). In other words, regions are not preordained units in which the Earth is divided; rather, they are geographically, culturally, politically, and historically contingent as well as socially relevant. Thus, in development research and practice, we must explore the connections of people to their environs, their life in various spaces, and their daily practices. From here, it is possible to consider how the notion of identity is at play, the spatial extent at which it operates, and, in turn, how region and identity are mobilized in place-based development. We explore these questions in two case study "regions" below. Regions, for the purposes of this study, were defined as groupings of multiple communities at the sub-provincial scale (versus multi-province regions in Canada, or macro regions made up of several countries, for example). Regional boundaries recognized in provincial development policy were selected as starting points for exploring the multitude of regions to which any given locale belongs.

CASE STUDIES

The Kootenay Development Region, British Columbia

British Columbia's Kootenay Development Region is found in southeastern British Columbia on the border of Alberta and the United States. The Kootenay Development Region is an aggregation of three regional districts: East Kootenay, Central Kootenay, and Kootenay Boundary (BC Stats, 2010).

These provincially recognized and legislated regional districts encompass rural municipalities and unincorporated areas for the purpose of delivering services and providing social, economic, and environmental initiatives.

The Kootenay region stretches over four mountain ranges (from east to west): the Rocky Mountains, the Purcell Mountains, the Selkirk Mountains, and the Monashee Mountains. A wide range of biodiversity exists in the region, as do many conservation areas and federal and provincial parks, including: Kootenay National Park, Kokanee Glacier Provincial Park, and Valhalla Provincial Park. Among the larger centres in the region are: Cranbrook, Nelson, Castlegar, Kimberley, and Grand Forks. As a result of its physical geography, the region is isolated, with an area of 57,787 km² (6.2 per cent of British Columbia) and a population of approximately 142,110 (BC Stats, 2010). The natural features of the region contribute to an economy strongly rooted in natural resources (e.g., forestry, mining), hydroelectric power generation, and tourism. Within the region are many of British Columbia's prominent resort communities, including Fairmont Hot Springs, Fernie, and Big White.

A review of completed interviews from across the region identified the following key themes:

- The importance of collaboration, partnerships, relationships in regional development
- The impact of demographic changes (e.g., age, out-migration, social capital)
- The importance of human and financial resources to the development process
- The role of external influences (e.g., the United States, Alberta), specifically pertaining to protectionism and localism
- The importance of (and concern for) infrastructure (e.g., communications, water treatment, housing), and its role in economic diversification
- A development focus on diversification — looking for natural fits, building on what exists
- The uniqueness of the Kootenays in terms of culture, quality of life, and physical geography

- The role of geography in shaping development: i.e., physical constraints, benefits, and regional identity.

These themes contain strong elements of place. The physical geography of the region was indicated to be a central factor not only within the local culture, but also in the economic development of the region. Identity and territorial definition are complex in a region with multiple overlapping social, cultural, economic, and political boundaries. Many interviewees clearly articulated differences in the defined political boundaries versus the boundaries of the region they identify with culturally. Other interviewees identified functional regions or corridors related to transportation routes and flows of economic activities. Questions around regional identity illustrated that within the larger Kootenay region, as well as within the regional districts, there are many distinct sub-regions. Just as identities are layered (Chapter 4), so too are regions — and regional identities. These regions ranged from being social-cultural (e.g., interviewees expressed feelings of separation or differences from other areas within the region) to political (groups of closely collaborating local governments), to development-focused (boundaries associated with development initiatives are industry). Some identified regions were official and defined by organizational boundaries; others were unofficial, with flexible borders. Identified regions, as shown in Figure 1, include, but are not limited to: (1) the Boundary, (2) the Tri-City Region (Nelson, Trail, Castlegar), (3) Lower Kootenay Lake, (4) Slocan Valley, (5) Upper Kootenay Lake, (6) Cranbrook–Kimberley, (7) the Columbia Valley, and (8) the Elkford Valley.

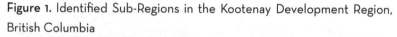

Figure 1. Identified Sub-Regions in the Kootenay Development Region, British Columbia

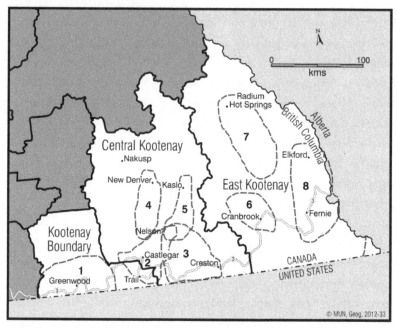

In terms of place and identity being used to mobilize development, interviewees provided many examples of place-based initiatives within the Kootenays. These development initiatives range in organization and purpose, but share the commonality of being specific to the assets of the Kootenay Region, where they are building on what they have, whether natural, physical, and/or human capacity. We have selected four examples to illustrate these processes.

The *Carbon Neutral Kootenays* is an initiative spearheaded by the Columbia Basin Trust, incorporating the whole of its territory (see Figure 2), which encompasses most of the Kootenay Development Region, excluding the Boundary area. This initiative is intended to tackle climate change in an appropriate and context-specific manner for local communities and municipalities. Additionally, the initiative is meant to address what climate change means for the region and what action can be taken locally. This initiative is a collaborative effort, not only between the Columbia

Basin Trust, an important regional development institution linked to hydroelectric development, and the regional and local governments, but also including outside academics and other local agencies. Elements of collaboration and a concern for long-term sustainability of the region are strong place-based indicators.

Figure 2. Columbia Basin Trust Catchment Region in the Kootenay Development Region, British Columbia

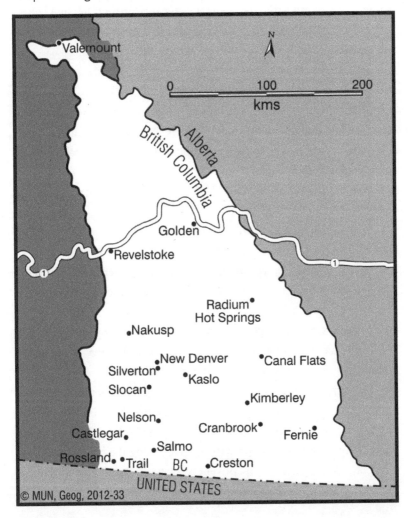

Branding the Boundary is a marketing initiative specific to the Boundary area within the Kootenay Boundary regional district. An economic development agency within the Boundary took the initiative to hire a company to study the local amenities (physical and cultural) within the Boundary in order to develop a place-specific marketing campaign. The Branding the Boundary initiative exhibits strong place-based indicators by tying competitive advantage directly to the region and the assets of the Boundary area and by seeking to define a specific regional identity.

In terms of industrial development, the area surrounding the *City of Trail* has a history of economic development tied to Teck-Cominco, a lead-zinc smelter. This sub-region has identified the existing industrial base, not as a negative, but as a positive asset. Through careful study multiple ways to develop new industries have been identified, based on the by-products and spinoffs tied to the current industry, some of which Teck itself has capitalized on and others that local entrepreneurs have picked up. This is also a good example of building on existing regional assets. Local economic development agencies are also seeking to foster local entrepreneurialism (rather than simply seeking external businesses) to contribute to economic diversification and are seeking to leverage their industrial identity.

Lastly is the example of niche marketing, attracting people to the region who want to be there for what the region has to offer in terms of amenities (e.g., lifestyle, recreation opportunities), either as local entrepreneurs or business owners, or those who have the ability to work remotely or who work from home offices. *Invest Kootenay* is one example of an initiative meant to entice people to the region, highlighting opportunities and lifestyle. This organization highlights not only available investment opportunities, but also showcases what the region has to offer. In addition to agencies such as this, communities are also recognizing natural assets and working to attract those people who can work anywhere, but wish to live there, such as filmmakers, athletes, consultants and other knowledge workers, etc. This development approach is again using the natural and built assets of place to foster competitiveness for both capital and workers. It also clearly defines a regional identity linked with amenities.

Kittiwake/Gander–New-Wes-Valley, NL

The Kittiwake/Gander–New-Wes-Valley region (see Figure 3) is located along the northeastern coast of insular Newfoundland. This region is delineated by the Regional Economic Development Zone (Kittiwake) and the provincial Rural Secretariat region (Gander–New-Wes-Valley), which have closely overlapping jurisdictions. The region is composed of 119 communities, 35 of which are incorporated municipalities (KEDC, 2012). The total population is 48,850 living within an area of 14,000 km² (Community Accounts, 2006 census). Six communities with more than 2,000 residents make up nearly half the region's population, including the service centre of Gander. The zone also includes three island municipalities accessible only by boat and two of Newfoundland's 10 Mi'kmaq bands.[1] The Kittiwake economic zone includes three distinct eco-regions: the interior central Newfoundland forest, coastal north shore forests, and eastern hyper-oceanic barrens (NL, 2012). Fishing, retail sales, clerical work, management, and fish processing are the region's most common occupations (Community Accounts, 2006). The region was one of those in Newfoundland targeted for resettlement of communities "with no great future" in the late 1950s and early 1960s in an era where government policy pursued a triple thrust of industrialization, modernization, and centralization (Maritime History Archive, 2004). Many communities located on the hundreds of small islands off the coast of Newfoundland and Labrador were relocated. However, the people of three occupied islands within the Kittiwake zone, accessible only by ferry, resisted relocation pressures, becoming part of a movement of resistance and community development that resulted in the formation of rural development associations across the province (including Change Islands and Fogo Island, discussed further by Fürst in Chapter 4).

In 2009 this region was involved in a community-based research project that sought to better understand regional and community planning, particularly issues around plan implementation. This project was a partnership between the provincial Rural Secretariat Executive Council and Memorial University together with Kittiwake Economic Development Corporation (KEDC), the then Department of Innovation Trade and Rural Development (since changed to Innovation, Business and Rural Development or

IBRD),and members of the communities involved. Kittiwake/Gander–New-Wes-Valley was selected as a part of the Canadian Regional Development project because evidence demonstrates there is considerable variability in sub-regional planning characteristics and capacities, as well as a keen interest among community leaders and regional government in regional development processes.

Figure 3. Kittiwake/Gander–New-Wes-Valley, Newfoundland and Labrador

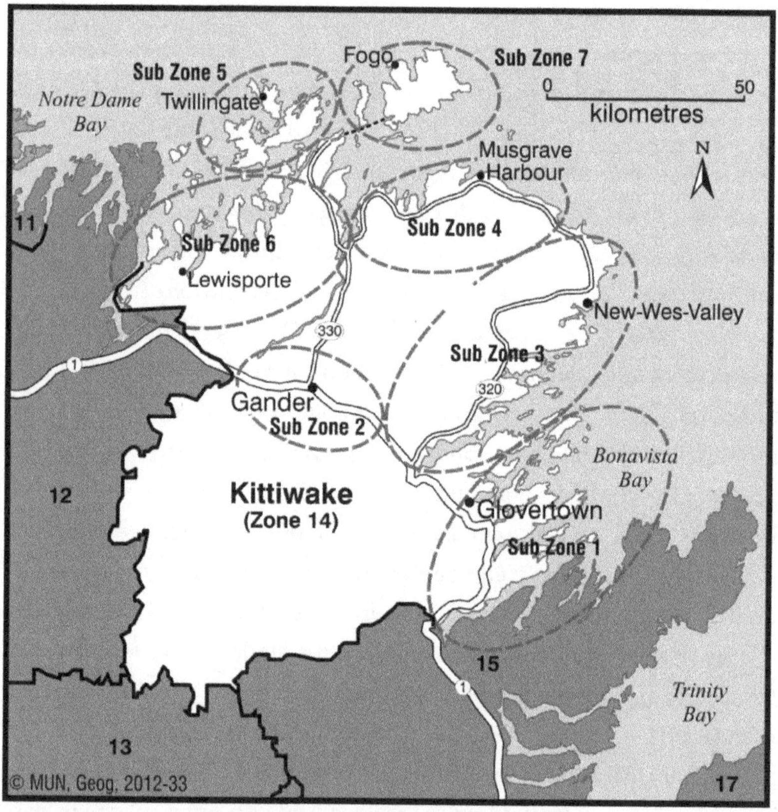

Notions of territory and identity strongly resonate with the concept of place: in the creation of individual and collective sense(s) of place as well as place-making. As discussed above, the process of "bounding" regions is noted to be incredibly complex and dynamic, and is largely contingent on

historical, social, political, and environmental contexts of a particular place (e.g., Allen et al., 1998; Paasi, 2003). Preliminary analysis of the interviews and past research experience in Kittiwake illustrate such complexity and dynamism. Yet, despite these challenges, there also notable examples of how sense(s) of place and networks of practice (largely grounded in place) have successfully fostered development initiatives.

Territorial definitions are highly varied across the "region" of Kittiwake/ Gander–New-Wes-Valley. Notions of what makes a territory differ across the area. Sub-territorial understandings of place and historical-cultural understandings are often stronger than the sentiments regarding the region as a whole. In terms of defining the region, the name "Kittiwake" was established with the advent of the Regional Economic Development Boards (REDBs) or zone boards in 1996. Under the administration KEDC, Kittiwake ("zone 14") is generally well recognized as a community partner by those involved in community and regional development. The name Gander–New-Wes-Valley was designated by the provincial Rural Secretariat, which was developed in 2004 and covers essentially the same area as Kittiwake. According to interview results, as a recognizable entity, the Gander–New-Wes-Valley region does not resonate as strongly with community players as the region in which they belong. Politically defined regions are generally treated as less personally meaningful and at times are perceived negatively when they are in conflict with culturally defined regions. This negative perception is exacerbated in cases where there is limited successful collaboration between government and community partners and between rural and urban players. Territorial definition is intimately linked with notions of home and belonging, which are in turn tied to identity. Those regions (i.e., sub-regions within Kittiwake) with the strongest resonance tend to be areas where there has been a long-standing (or at least strong) historical and cultural connection between communities or between people within a particular community and their involvement with the environment. Connections between residents and their surrounding environments are demonstrated through a largely resource-based economy, including both subsistence and cash-based activities.

The sub-regional areas defined by KEDC — which include the municipalities in question and their respective surrounding areas — are: Eastport

Peninsula, Gander, Gambo/New-Wes-Valley, Gander Bay North/Deadmans Bay, Twillingate/New World Island, Lewisporte, and Fogo Island/Change Islands (see Figure 3). However, interview respondents also indicated regions delineated by their respective watersheds, such as Gander River, Northwest River, Indian Bay River watersheds, and by bays (e.g., Bonavista and Notre Dame bays), as well as by emerging functional regions between smaller communities and regional centre(s) (e.g., Glovertown and Gander, Summerford, and Lewisporte).

Using Paasi's (2003) model of identity formation for the case of Kittiwake, territorial identity is often best characterized as being mobilized in development as a mode of resistance — to forces of centralization, globalization, and/or homogenization, for example. It is used as a means to encourage development that showcases pride, strength, and uniqueness of place. This can be illustrated in the region's past, as in the formation of rural development associations discussed above, but also in the following three recent development initiatives.

First, in 2007, the Kittiwake Economic Development Corporation initiated a buy-local campaign, which was branded as "Keep it in Kittiwake." This message is primarily directed to consumers as a way of encouraging awareness around local produce and the promotion of local food consumption in the region. While not without challenges, the campaign has achieved numerous successes to date, including: banding together local farmers and seafood harvesters to educate the public; launching awareness campaigns to grocers and restaurants in the area; and providing resource packages to vendors with producers' information. It has also received accolades from the Newfoundland and Labrador Regional Economic Development Association for excellence in best practices in community economic development (Skeard, 2012).

Second, regional branding is also very apparent through efforts to promote tourism in the area. Destination Gander's slogan, "One Destination, Three Vacations," is intended to promote the region as a whole, with Gander as the central hub. This slogan highlights the diversity of day trips (or multi-day trips) that one can make by using Gander as the central location, including: a trip up to Twillingate/New World Islands' "Iceberg Ally"; a ferry ride across to Fogo Island and Change Islands; and a drive down the Eastport Peninsula, known as "the road to the beaches." This also serves as an exemplar of the potential benefits that could be derived through integrated strategic planning between rural and urban communities. It also serves as one of many indications that the regional centre of Gander is also very much dependent on its rural peripheries, a theme that was apparent through interviewees' responses.

Third, local watershed management groups provide an example of place-based resource governance, which offers an alternative to centralized management options. Since the early 1990s, the Gander River, the Northwest River, and the Indian Bay River have each had formal community-based watershed groups involved in resource management-related activities. While the Gander River Management Association (GRMA) is no longer officially active, the group set the stage for other similar organizations by fostering initiatives still operating today on the Gander River and on other river systems. These include: local enforcement teams (which have remained active through the Aboriginal Fishery Guardian Program, with members from the Glenwood Mi'kmaq First Nation and the Gander Bay Indian Band Council); the development of salmon counting fences; and a river-specific management plan. Other place-based resource governance initiatives in the region include the Fogo Island Fishing Cooperative, which has been in operation since the early twentieth century, and the Eastport Marine Protected Area (MPA). The Eastport MPA was established in 2005, an initiative largely based on the interest and conservation concerns of the Eastport Peninsula Lobster Protection Committee, a locally based organization.

DISCUSSION: PROMOTING PLACE AND PLACE-RESPONSIVE POLICY

The two case studies illustrate two key points related to place-based development. First, given the success of the examples discussed, it can be said that there is merit to place-based development strategies — many opportunities are out there to be explored, and characteristics of and attachments to place can be mobilized in many ways. However, the second point relates to the complexity of regions and identity, which leads to challenges with place-based development in clearly identifying and agreeing upon a region in order to move forward with place-based development opportunities. Regional boundaries can shift, depending on the subject at hand and the agencies involved, and over time. True to the essence of place-based development, there is no one-size-fits-all approach. Rather, careful consideration, communication, collaboration, and an intense grounding in and understanding of the local assets and dynamics of place are required.

Well thought-out, appropriate place-based development approaches — from local involvement in environmental stewardship to effective local marketing and branding — can be expected to lead to positive and promising outcomes. Nevertheless, our case studies suggest that support for place-based local/regional development through upper-level policy is limited. Policies at provincial and federal levels, by necessity, are formulated in general terms to guide the organization and actions of large bureaucracies so they can effectively reach desirable outcomes in a complex environment. As such, they reflect the values and goals inherited from those who came before, and they provide a strong justification for maintaining the status quo within existing institutions. Changing the policy focus to be more place-responsive, therefore, not only means changes in the formulation of those policies, but also challenges the understandings and frameworks on which they are premised, and the institutional structures they reinforce. Understanding this lineage, therefore, is important to enacting transformations.

A variety of factors identified in the literature help us to understand current shifts in policy focus (or in some cases, resistance to shifts) and the overall challenges of adopting place-based approaches (Reimer and Markey, 2008). One major challenge in Canada is a long public policy tradition rooted in individualism. Our institutions reflect this in their focus on individual rights, commitment to private property, and individual freedom. Community or collective development efforts run counter to this tradition. The integrated, holistic nature of place-based approaches further challenges the institutional structures of most of our governments. Sectoral divisions based on natural resources such as agriculture, forestry, fishing, and mining, for example, have tended to keep policy-makers apart when inter-sectoral issues arise. This is matched by the institutional separation of social concerns (employment, welfare, health, education, justice), thereby making it difficult to recognize and act where they converge.

Overall patterns of economic restructuring, which include tendencies towards urbanization and centralization of power and wealth, also undermine and inhibit place-based approaches. One example involves the continued cuts to funding in rural regions and resulting losses in local capacity to pursue community and regional development.

An additional challenge for place-based development is the need to remain critical or careful about notions of the local and about local approaches as necessarily superior (DuPuis and Goodman, 2005). Community development researchers have long recognized the danger of local processes being captured or controlled by specific local interests, particularly the local elite, under the guise of community or place-based development. Where there is no succession planning, this could also be viewed as an imbalance of control within development processes by a particular generation: older people not willing to share benefits and/or responsibilities. Both are examples of undemocratic processes that are not necessarily representative of a community or region but often claim to be. Scholars and practitioners who laud the local without a critical view exacerbate the suspicion with which place-based policies are often treated (Blank, 2005). Definitional obscurity and diversity in the literature dealing with place-based approaches as well as the complexity of identities within place, as discussed above and in other chapters in this volume, further contribute to this suspicion and even skepticism.

Our research illustrates that the role of identity is critical for fostering both authentic regional development processes and policy to support such initiatives. First, our case studies inform us that regional identity is a strong motivating force and binding agent that underlies various development initiatives. People and organizations are very committed to their place — and are seeking to pursue development activities that capitalize on and protect the assets of those places. Much work is needed, through transparent and collaborative processes, to operate in the context of overlapping boundaries and development priorities. Dangers clearly exist in hijacking local processes or trivializing identity through inauthentic representations of place for purely economic reasons. However, people's pride in and desire to protect their communities and regions both define and continually reinforce their sense of identity. This identity can then be drawn upon as an asset and resource in the development process, capable of providing common ground upon which to explore varying development pathways and opportunities.

Second, understanding identity is critical for developing effective place-based policy. Generalized development policies are clearly most effective when they are contextualized to the conditions and priorities of place. This requires a top-down capacity and willingness to adapt policy instruments, and the bottom-up capacity and willingness to mobilize and define local assets and priorities. Our cases show evidence of this effective "co-construction" of regional development policies and programs. Clearly, however, there is more work to be done, and along the way many ongoing frustrations will need to be recognized and channelled into productive development processes.

While the Kootenays and Kittiwake/Gander–New-Wes-Valley regions are unique, the pressures and opportunities they face from a development perspective are common with other rural (and island) locales within Canada and across many developed countries. Truly understanding regional development requires both perspectives: the specific and the general. This fact provides hope for regional development processes to be successful and to learn from each other, and for policy-makers to craft generalized yet successful and durable processes and programs that can be effectively tailored to local conditions.

ACKNOWLEDGEMENTS

We thank the members of the Canadian Regional Development project team for their participation and guidance in this research. We also gratefully acknowledge funding support from the Social Sciences and Humanities Research Council of Canada and the Harris Centre Applied Research Fund, Memorial University of Newfoundland. Finally, our sincere thanks for the generous time commitments made by community and regional participants to support our research.

NOTE

1.   A 2011 Order-in-Council provided the legal basis for the establishment of Qalipu Mi'kmaq First Nation Band, which includes all Newfoundland Mi'kmaq outside of Miawpukek First Nation territory, which includes nine bands.

REFERENCES

Allen, J., D. Massey, A. Cochrane, J. Charlesworth, G. Court, N. Henry, and P. Sarre. 1998. *Rethinking the Region*. London: Routledge.

Barnes, T.J., J. Britton, W. Coffey, W. Edgington, M. Gertler, and G. Norcliffe. 2000. "Canadian Economic Geography at the Millennium." *Canadian Geographer* 44, 1: 4–24.

BC Stats. 2012. Development Region 4 Kootenay Statistical Profile (pp. 1–10). Vancouver: BC Stats.

Blank, R.M. 2005. "Poverty, Policy, and Place: How Poverty and Policies to Alleviate Poverty Are Shaped by Local Characteristics." *International Regional Science Review* 28, 4: 441–64.

Bradford, N. 2005. *Place-based Public Policy: Towards a New Urban and Community Agenda for Canada*. Ottawa: Canadian Policy Research Networks.

Bradshaw, B. 2003. "Questioning the Credibility and Capacity of Community-based Resource Management." *Canadian Geographer* 47, 1: 137–50.

Canadian Regional Development. 2011. "Canadian Regional Development: A Critical Review of Theory, Practice and Potential." http://cdnregdev.ruralresilience.ca.

Community Accounts. 2006. Census. Economic Zone 14—Kittiwake Economic Development Corporation. http://nl.communityaccounts.ca/tablesandcharts. asp?_=vb7En4WVgb2uzqVjWQ.

Dawe, S. 2004. "Placing Trust and Trusting Place: Creating Competitive Advantage in Peripheral Rural Areas." In G. Halseth and R. Halseth, eds., *Building for Success: Exploration of Rural Community and Rural Development*, 223–50. Brandon, Man.: Rural Development Institute.

Douglas, D. 1999. "The New Rural Region: Consciousness, Collaboration and New Challenges and Opportunities for Innovative Practice." In W. Ramp, J. Kulig, I. Townshend, and V. McGowan, eds., *Health in Rural Settings: Contexts for Action*, 39–60. Lethbridge, Alta.: University of Lethbridge.

DuPuis, E., and D. Goodman. 2005. "Should We Go 'Home' to Eat? Toward a Reflexive Politics of Localism." *Journal of Rural Studies* 21, 3: 359–71.

Escobar, A. 2008.*Territories of Difference: Place, Movements, Life, Redes*. Durham, NC: Duke University Press.

Fairbairn, B. 1998. *A Preliminary History of Rural Development Policy and Programmes in Canada, 1945–1995*. Saskatoon: University of Saskatchewan, NRE Program.

Filion, P. 1998. "Potential and Limitations of Community Economic Development: Individual Initiative and Collective Action in a Post-Fordist Context." *Environment and Planning A* 30, 6: 1101–23.

Gunton, T. 2003. "Natural Resources and Regional Development: An Assessment of Dependency and Comparative Advantage Paradigms." *Economic Geography* 79, 1: 67–94.

Halseth, G., and A. Booth. 2003. "What Works Well; What Needs Improvement: Lessons in Public Consultation from British Columbia's Resource Planning Processes." *Local Environment* 8, 4: 437–55.

Hettne, B., A. Inotai, and O. Sunkel, eds. 1999. *Globalism and the New Regionalism*. Basingstoke: Macmillan.

Kitson, M., R. Martin, and P. Tyler. 2004. "Regional Competitiveness: An Elusive Yet Key Concept." *Regional Studies* 38, 9: 991–99.

Kittiwake Economic Development Corporation (KEDC). 2012. *2012–2014 Strategic Economic Plan*. http://www.kittiwake.nf.ca/documents/SEP-2012-2014.pdf.

Kuyek, J., and K. Coumans. 2003. *No Rock Unturned: Revitalizing the Economies of Mining Dependent Communities*. Ottawa: Mining Watch Canada.

MacLeod, G. 2001. "New Regionalism Reconsidered: Globalization and the Remaking of Political Economic Space." *International Journal of Urban and Regional Research* 25, 4: 804–29.

Maritime History Archive. 2004. "'No Great Future': Government Sponsored Resettlement in Newfoundland and Labrador since Confederation." http://www.mun.ca/mha/resettlement/rs_intro.php.

Markey, Sean. 2010. "A Primer on Place-Based Development." Working Paper CRD-3. Memorial University of Newfoundland, Corner Brook.

———, G. Halseth, and D. Manson. 2007. "The (Dis)connected North: Persistent Regionalism in Northern British Columbia." *Canadian Journal of Regional Science* 30, 1: 57–78.

———, ———, and ———. 2008. "Challenging the Inevitability of Rural Decline: Advancing the Policy of Place in Northern British Columbia." *Journal of Rural Studies* 24, 4: 409–21.

——— and K. Heisler. 2011. "Getting a Fair Share: Regional Development in a Rapid Boom-Bust Rural Setting." *Canadian Journal of Regional Science* 33, 3: 49–62.

———, J.T. Pierce, K. Vodden, and M. Roseland. 2005. *Second Growth: Community Economic Development in Rural BC*. Vancouver: University of British Columbia Press.

Massey, D. 1984. "Introduction: Geography Matters." In D. Massey and J. Allen, eds., *Geography Matters! A Reader*, 1–11. Cambridge: Cambridge University Press.

Mather, A., G. Hill, and M. Nijnik. 2006. "Post-Productivism and Rural land Use: Cul de sac or Challenge for Theorization." *Journal of Rural Studies* 22, 4: 441–55.

Newfoundland and Labrador (NL). 2012. "Ecoregions of Newfoundland." http://www.nr.gov.nl.ca/nr/forestry/maps/eco_nf.html.

Paasi, A. 2003. "Region and place: Regional Identity in Question." *Progress in Human Geography* 27, 4: 475–85.

———. 2004. "Place and Region: Looking through the Prism of Scale." *Progress in Human Geography* 28, 4: 536–46.

Pezzini, M. 2001. "Rural Policy Lessons from OECD Countries." *International Regional Science Review* 24, 1: 134–45.

Polèse, M. 1999. "From Regional Development to Local Development: On the Life, Death, and Rebirth(?) of Regional Science as a Policy Relevant Science." *Canadian Journal of Regional Science* 22, 3: 299–314.

Reed, M. 1990. "Managing for Sustainable Development: A Case Study of a Hinterland Community, Ignace, Ontario, Canada." Ph.D. dissertation, Department of Geography, University of Waterloo.

——— and A. Gill. 1997. "Tourism, Recreational, and Amenity Values in Land Allocation: An Analysis of Institutional Arrangements in the Postproductivist Era." *Environment and Planning A* 29: 2019–40.

Reimer, B., and S. Markey. 2008. *Place-based Policy: A Rural Perspective*. Ottawa: Human Resources and Social Development Canada.

Savoie, D. 1992. *Regional Economic Development: Canada's Search for Solutions*. Toronto: University of Toronto Press.

Scott, M. 2004. "Building Institutional Capacity in Rural Northern Ireland: The Role of Partnership Governance in the LEADER II Programme." *Journal of Rural Studies* 20, 1: 49–59.

Storper, M. 1999. "The Resurgence of Regional Economics: Ten Years Later." In T.J. Barnes and M.S. Gertler, eds., *The New Industrial Geography: Regions, Regulation and Institutions*, 23–53. New York: Routledge.

POSTSCRIPT

Place Peripheral: Place-based Development in Rural, Island, and Remote Regions

Godfrey Baldacchino, Kelly Vodden, and Ryan Gibson

A QUITE DIFFERENT REALITY

Economic geographers, development scholars, local development practitioners, and policy analysts who deal with remote regions, in both islands and rural areas, can be expected at some point to come face to face with a fundamental challenge. How are communities safeguarded and livelihoods sustained in such areas, even as these spaces become regarded, and regraded, as increasingly peripheral to/in the global economy, their inhabitants written off as net losers; their businesses, organizations, and infrastructure unworthy of investment? Such a crippling and fatalist diagnosis is inevitable if these people and places find themselves part of a script governed by an ongoing and inexorable process of out-migration and urban agglomeration, fuelled by the dictates of late capitalism and the allures of neo-liberal ideology. In this book, we have dared to present a vision, and an expectation, of a quite different reality.

Place Peripheral offers, we hope, a compelling overview of rural, island, and remote regional practices the world over, though with a clear focus on the North Atlantic. In this grand sweep, we have sought to effectively counter the dominant paradigm and discourses of development with a re-articulation of place, location, leadership, and identity. We offer these as key assets or resources, and as the bases for timely strategies that reconceptualize the future of these places, and perhaps in this way assure them of *a* future. In unabashedly championing place-based development, *Place Peripheral* offers an opportune counterpoint to the narratives of marginalization, inferiority, victimization, and dependency that often dominate the study of rural and small island development in Canada, the North Atlantic, and beyond. There are other stories to be told.

We started this book by discussing "development in place": how place-based development approaches have garnered increasing attention and how governance and capacity-building, with a focus on enhanced agency, can facilitate their pursuit. We began by exploring the idea and semiotics of "place peripheral" and what this phrase means in contemporary scholarship. In this discussion, there is a re-articulation of peripheral regions as central to processes of place-based and identity-based development efforts. Places are both meaning makers and meaning markers: with and through those who inhabit them, they produce and articulate notions of locality and identity to expand horizons of aspiration, forge new economies, refresh livelihoods, and embolden communities in fundamentally distinct and transformative ways that are not subservient to larger, urban centres and are more respectful of human scales.

AN EXCITING RE-PIVOTING

The main part of the book has been organized in two sections. The first part addresses the "why" question, and has a more theoretical and conceptual flavour: we investigate the very idea of place as the bedrock upon which place-based development initiatives unfold. Here, we dismiss such rash statements as the "death of geography" or the "death of distance"; instead, we posit that the socio-physical and cultural aspects of place remain critical to its attractiveness. While modern information and communication technologies (ICTs) have revolutionized connectivities, they cannot replace the materiality of human settlement and the layers of emotional geography that such sites command and attract. Nor are they equally accessible or yielding of equivalent implications for rural and urban areas. Nevertheless, ICTs have extended unlikely lifelines to the erstwhile isolated, reconfiguring many peripheries as new and exciting centres in their own right and enabling particular, nuanced forms of production and consumption that enterprising peripheral communities can identify and exploit. Often, these forms commodify notions of the periphery itself — via place branding, cultural and natural assets, niche manufacturing, or boutique accommodation. It is this technology-supported re-pivoting that demands and deserves serious scholarship.

Through numerous examples and case studies, the chapters in Part I conceptualize and illustrate the role and sense of place in core–periphery dynamics; contrasting appreciations of place and landscape between newcomer and native, seasonal and permanent residents; the changing nature of place and place expression through music and film, in particular the story and lyrics of an indie-rock band; and the effect of characterizations and attachments to place on education, location, and employment decisions. It is clear that matters of place are matters of deep significance — to development and to individuals' lives. Part I introduces us to the difficult choices people make about place, whether the choice of a young person to leave a rural community for a post-secondary education in an urban setting, of a tourist to visit a remote North Atlantic island, of an urban refugee to relocate there, or of a policy-maker considering whether a small island community warrants attention and support. Such decisions bring questions of identity, meaning, and values to the fore and influence the dynamics that shape the places described in this volume. These dynamics include immigration, out-migration, and return migration, investment and disinvestment, artistic expression and cultural revitalization, volunteerism, the building of social networks, governance, local food production and consumption, and entrepreneurialism, to name a few.

By combining theoretical foundations with an empirical analysis of case study experiences, this first section contributes to a growing literature that unpacks how place works to sustain and renovate communities and economies in what might appear at first glance as unlikely locations for such renewal. The authors in Part I also introduce tensions associated with differing visions and representations of place, along with consequent changes in landscapes and relationships. They draw from and critically examine concepts such as authenticity (and inauthenticity) and identity re-engineering. Rather than seeing tradition and modernity as either/or scenarios, the certainty and necessity of change are acknowledged and the possibility of "renovated place associations" is presented. In other words, understandings of place can "put a new face to old constructions of cultural reference" (Walsh, Chapter 5).

NO SILVER BULLET

These renovated understandings and associations are important, but they are hardly enough. Understanding place in order to be better able to negotiate it is a complex undertaking. The rich interdisciplinarity that is one of this volume's strengths — ranging from geography to cultural studies, from ethnomusicology to planning, and from economic sociology to tourism marketing — is essential but hardly sufficient to secure a deep sense of the subject matter. Moreover, if place matters, how a sense of place informs policy may be possible to understand only through unique contexts, so that out-of-context extrapolations and translations are fraught with danger and slippage. And we must also be just as wary and suspicious of lofty rhetoric that speaks of small islands and remote rural regions manifesting "resilience," bravely "bouncing back" against the odds, when this exercise could be a case of misguided triumphalism, propagandistic wish-fulfillment, or the unfolding of a top-down technocratic branding exercise. Build it; but they will not necessarily come. Indeed, we need to be bold and investigate cases where place-driven developments have not just succeeded but also failed — something that, admittedly, we and our collaborating authors have largely neglected in this book. We also need to examine whether any registered successes — including those that feature in this collection — have been maintained in the medium term; and, last but certainly not least, we need to interview and give voice to those who leave the periphery, not just to those who stay.

We have sought to translate and flesh out these largely theoretical reflections into practical lessons in Part II of this book. Here is the "how" stuff: we showcase some of the many applications and designs, as well as dangers and pitfalls, resorted to for creating more sustainable, livable communities and regions. There are references to place-based local economy initiatives in Chiloé (Chile) and Prince Edward Island (Canada); the contributions of arts and culture-based programs to rural revitalization in Shetland (Scotland) and Gravelbourg (Canada); parallel cultural renaissances and efforts to network and share lessons island-to-island in Newfoundland (Canada) and Tasmania (Australia); a place-branding exercise for the Isle of Man; and reformulation of the "territorialization-regional identity" nexus in Newfoundland and British Columbia (Canada). The chapters of this section are more descriptive and oriented around the emergence and operationalization of specific development interventions; the policies, processes, and partnerships that have supported their implementation; and their socio-economic consequences, where these are identifiable.

Peripherality remains, at its heart, a social construction, though with vital material expressions. Yet, if it is a social construction, then it is important to unpack the (re)production of peripherality as much as its reconfiguration. Peripheries don't become centres overnight and, in fact, may never escape the material and economic characteristics that have been used to assign them this label. Moreover, as the authors in this volume have assiduously pointed out, regions considered peripheries by some may be considered quite differently by others. There is no magic bullet in the development of peripheral regions; nor is there any single meaning we can assign to place or to periphery: the core themes of this volume. In examining and/or engaging in place-based development, we are effectively dealing with processes of meaning-making; and, as such, the exploration of multiple meanings and their implications for development is critical to these processes, to the future of rural, remote, and island locales, and to the quality of life of their residents.

WHAT IS PAST IS PROLOGUE

We set out to investigate how island, rural, and remote communities can address the challenges presented by globalization through governance and capacity-building strategies predicated on a deep sense of place. This place, to most, may be described unambiguously as the periphery; but it is, for all intents and purposes, the centre for those that choose it as their home or base. Place peripheral can be, and is, place central. Such a paradigm switch is easier to identify after the event, and proper longitudinal studies of this transformation at work are hard to come by. It is our hope and intent that our work will inspire others to deploy other methodologies in pursuit of such a sorely needed critical scrutiny of development in, and for, place — and to start, or continue, to tell those other stories that need to be told.

Subject Index

Author Index